Musical Impressions

By Herbert A. Leibowitz
Hart Crane: An Introduction to the Poetry

Musical Impressions:

Selections from

Paul Rosenfeld's

Criticism ❧ Edited

and with an Introduction

by Herbert A. Leibowitz ❧

Hill and Wang ❧ New York

"Wagner," "Strauss," "Schoenberg," "Berlioz," "Moussorgsky," "Debussy," "Ravel," and "Stravinsky" are reprinted from *Musical Portraits* (New York: Harcourt, Brace & Howe, 1920) by permission of Harcourt, Brace & World.

"The Nazis and *Die Meistersinger*," "*Gurrelieder*," "*Wozzeck*," "The Evolution of Stravinsky," "Bartók (1936)," "Charles Ives," "George Gershwin," and "*Ionization*" are reprinted from *Discoveries of a Music Critic* (New York: Harcourt, Brace & Co., 1936) by permission of Harcourt, Brace & World.

"The Tragedy of Gustav Mahler," "Bruckner," "Bartók (1923)," "The Group of Six," and "Satie and Impressionism" are reprinted from *Musical Chronicle (1917–23)* (New York: Harcourt, Brace & Co., 1923) by permission of Edna Bryner Schwab.

"Schoenberg and Varèse," "Thanks to the International Guild: A Musical Chronicle," and "Carl Ruggles" are reprinted from *By Way of Art* (New York: Coward–McCann, Inc., 1928) by permission of Edna Bryner Schwab.

"Jazz and Music: Music in America," "Beginnings of American Music," "Aaron Copland," "Roger Sessions," and "Edgar Varèse" are reprinted from *An Hour with American Music* (Philadelphia: J. B. Lippincott Co., 1929) by permission of Edna Bryner Schwab.

Contents

Introduction

"Nothing worthwhile can be accomplished in art without enthusiasm."

—ROBERT SCHUMANN, *Aphorisms*

"When I note the harmony and correspondence of a man and his words—such a one I deem to be the true musician."

—PLATO, *Laches*

IN 1920 Paul Rosenfeld established his reputation with his first book, *Musical Portraits*. Some of his essays had already appeared in such journals as *The Dial, The New Republic,* and *Seven Arts,* but at a time when the public and most artists were preoccupied with World War I. Now these essays were noticed and talked about. That an American critic had spoken out so boldly and authoritatively on the subject of modern music was alone newsworthy, for intelligent music critics were even rarer in America than composers.

The reader coming upon *Musical Portraits* for the first time finds a young man's book—uneven but immensely engaging, flawed perhaps by a certain monotony of attack but exciting, allusive, and unconventional. Here was a critic, not only sensible but readable; a cultivated, witty, mature mind with a style that was passionate and joyously wise. The author's very excesses were proof of an unmistakably lively intellect, as the opening of the essay on Schoenberg shows:

> Arnold Schoenberg of Vienna is the great troubling presence of modern music. His vast, sallow skull lowers over it like a sort of North Cape. For with him, with the famous cruel five orchestral and nine piano pieces, we seem to be entering the arctic zone of musical art. None of the old beacons, none of the old stars, can guide us longer in these frozen wastes. Strange, menacing forms surround us, and the light is bleak and chill and faint. . . .

If we recall the tremendous furor, bewilderment, disgust, and shock which greeted Schoenberg's "subversive" music, we can appreciate Rosenfeld's cool mastery of a difficult new musical speech and, even more, his lucid guiding of the reader in the remainder of the essay through the "cruel" labyrinth of Schoenberg's counterpoint and harmonic combinations, those "strange, menacing forms." The arctic images in the above passage convey the sense of the fire and ice of Schoenberg's art, the remote polar regions this Admiral Byrd of composition was exploring. That "vast, sallow skull" sums up in a phrase not only the demiurge of musical and cosmic discord but also the blasted landscape of the modern psyche over which he presided. Writing in the heat of the moment, Rosenfeld followed Robert Schumann's injunction that the critic must "highly honor the old, but also meet the new with a warm heart." "It is not enough," Schumann goes on, "that a journal mirror the present. The critic must outstrip fleeing time, and from the future fight the present as if it were already the past."[1] Rosenfeld was just such an agile and prescient critic.

Music criticism is a dangerous art. Its practitioner, first of all, faces the sheer vexing task of describing a piece of music accurately, without making it sound like some fantastic confection of his own ego or some musical Linear B. He must serve the composer by providing stringent, sympathetic commentary and by mediating between him and the unadventurous musical public. He must serve the public by educating and elevating its tastes. Virgil Thomson offers three informal criteria for the "perfect" music critic: he must have real warmth in him; he must have truth in him; and he must stick his neck out. Needless to say, such an array of virtues is hard to come by in one man. Paul Rosenfeld possessed them all, avoiding the usual mayhem between creators and critics.

Yet from the outset of his career, Rosenfeld aroused much

---

1. Robert Schumann, *On Music and Musicians,* translated by Paul Rosenfeld and edited by Konrad Wolff (New York, 1946), pp. 35, 47.

controversy. His detractors among musicologists accused him of faulty, amateurish scholarship, of ignorance of such facts as manuscript revisions and canonic forms. This charge can be dismissed quickly. Rosenfeld may not have been trained as a professional musician, and he may have at times avoided dry, academic discussion of details of musical technique, yet his discussions were always grounded in a knowledge of the composer's score. He spent days at his piano playing through the score of a concert he was to review, a practice he repeated when a young composer like Aaron Copland or Elliott Carter visited him to solicit his opinion of their latest sonata or song. His essays were free of pedantry. He was alert to the claims of form and technique; he only denied that they were anterior to or independent of musical content. Like George Bernard Shaw, he ridiculed sterile talk about key changes and shunned the kind of erudition that resulted in a scared rather than an excited and enlightened audience.

Musical Portraits lacks the calm density of *Discoveries of a Music Critic* (1936) and the sparkling wit of *An Hour with American Music* (1929), but it epitomizes the romantic criticism Rosenfeld practiced during his entire career and the quirky, lyrical style that was its vehicle. Since some readers have found Rosenfeld's interpretations strained and illicitly subjective, his style uncomfortably rhapsodic—more serious objections than those imputing technical carelessness—it would be well to air these charges and dispose of them by putting them to the test of an unbiased rereading.

Schumann tells a charming story which shows how far a listener may go in attaching imaginary meanings, his own sentimental program, to "absolute" music:

> I have fancied, in certain *Moments musicaux* of Schubert's, to perceive a suggestion of unpaid tailors' bills, so much do these breathe the bad moods of a *bourgeois*. Eusebius even declares that in one of his marches he sees the whole Austrian national guard pass by, preceded by

the bagpipers, and carrying sausages and hams on the points of their bayonets. But this interpretation is an excessively subjective one![2]

There is apparently a certain class of literal-minded people who cannot listen to the opening bars of Beethoven's Fifth Symphony without hearing fate knocking at the door. (Their opposite number only hear an insistent rhythm.) Such impressionism is quite harmless though not very helpful. Eusebius' whimsical vision nevertheless contains a valuable truth: although there is a danger one may conjure up musical interpretations out of one's own fantasy life, the need to translate meanings out of music is an extremely deep one. To deny the critic any right to describe the emotions, the expressive content, of a Mozart symphony, a Beethoven quartet, or an opera by Wagner would be an impoverishing puritanism. Music is not simply a structure of sound, explainable by the laws of physics; it is also a structure of feeling, but one, Susanne Langer reminds us, that has no "assigned connotations":

> It is a form that is capable of connotation and the meanings to which it is amenable are articulations of emotive, vital, sentient experiences. But its import is never fixed. In music we work essentially with free forms, following inherent psychological laws of "rightness," and take interest in possible articulations suggested entirely by the musical material.[3]

Rosenfeld was foremost a psychological critic, attentive to the proof in a piece of music of an ample or meager spiritual consciousness. Art was for him a hazardous discipline, "the battle for the sake of the central self—the adventure of the difficult way of truthful living," as he put it in *Port of New York*. To chronicle and interpret ·this adventure the critic needed vision and brazen assurance that his set of hierarchical

2. *Ibid.*, pp. 57–58.
3. Susanne Langer, *Philosophy in a New Key* (New York, 1962), p. 203.

values could measure truthfully "the inherent psychological laws of 'rightness.' " The music critic, like the composer, had to balance the subjective and the objective, otherwise he would be guilty of falsifying reality. Rosenfeld did not impose his own reveries on a Debussy nocturne or a Copland ballet. He understood that a composer's work cannot be seen solely as an episode in his spiritual autobiography; that it depends also on cultural and economic processes, the stresses, restrictions, and satisfactions of life in Vienna, New York, or Munich, and that it is conditioned by the music of past epochs. That is why Rosenfeld's procedure in essay after essay is dialectical, comparative, historical. When analyzing Schoenberg's music, for example, he relates the purely musical structures—wide intervals, contrapuntal distribution, musical pitches half sung, half spoken, and static rhythm—to the composer's specific "emotive, vital, sentient experiences": modern man's feeling of brokenness, stifled emotion, agony, and erotic disquiet. By demonstrating the internal consistency of shifts in style, how the atonality of *Pierrot Lunaire* and *Three Pieces for Piano* evolves from the sumptuous Wagnerism of *Verklärte Nacht*, Rosenfeld gives the reader a clear grasp of the conflict in Schoenberg between the romantic lyricist and the musical systematizer, between the logic of expression and the expression of logic.

It is precisely his copious literary style, enlisted on behalf of the composer, that is Rosenfeld's great strength. He is one of a handful of music critics who have found a way of talking about music that is both profound as criticism and eloquent as rhetoric. The analogies and metaphors that abound in Rosenfeld's writings are not ornamental substitutes for analysis and fact, but exacting ways into a composer's work, rich expansions of criticism that define for the listener the diverse tonalities and permutations of the modern musical sensibility. Not only did he explain the most baffling modern music without vulgarity and preciosity, but he judged this music of extreme difficulty on the spot with uncanny accuracy. This is a matter of public record and unchallengeable.

Consider two passages about radically different composers chosen from *Musical Portraits*. The first is a description of Debussy's impressionism:

> Structurally, the music of Debussy is a fabric of exquisite and poignant moments, each full and complete in itself. His wholes exist entirely in their parts, in their atoms. If his phrases, rhythms, lyric impulses, do contribute to the formation of a single thing, they yet are extraordinarily independent and significant in themselves. No chord, no theme, is subordinate. Each one exists for the sake of its own beauty, occupies the universe for an instant, then merges and disappears. The harmonies are not, as in other compositions, preparations. They are apparently an end in themselves, flow in space, and then change hue, as a shimmering stuff changes. For all its golden earthiness, the style of Debussy is the most liquid and impalpable of musical styles. . . . It is well-nigh edgeless. It seems to flow through our perceptions as water flows through fingers. . . . It is forever suggesting water—fountains and pools, the glistening spray and heaving bosom of the sea. . . .
>
> Yet there is no uncertainty, no mistiness in his form, as there is in that of some of the other impressionists. His music is classically firm, classically precise and knit. . . . The line never hesitates, never becomes lost nor involved. It proceeds directly, clearly, passing through jewels and clots of color, and fusing them into the mass. The trajectory never breaks. The music is always full of its proper weight and timbre. . . . His little pieces occupy a space as completely as the most massive and grand of compositions.

What strikes one about this passage is Rosenfeld's success in evoking the paradoxical nature of Debussy's art, that its texture is evanescent and "edgeless," like water, yet maintains an unwavering, almost mathematical precision of line, which water cannot do; that its atomic particles yet fuse into the mass. Apart from some stale poeticism—the "heaving bosom of the sea"—the style is a precise, undulating instrument capable of defining in sensuous images and discursive exposition, not the effects of, say, *Nuages, La Mer,* or *Pelléas et Mélisande,* so much as their color, weight, harmonic structure, rhythm, and immediacy. Rosenfeld does not embark on a foolish quest for verbal equivalents of Debussy's musical material, but rather, as Lewis Mumford has pointed out, translates abstract ideas into the language of feeling and sense experience, careful, however, not to sacrifice structure. Most important, the reader has gained access to Debussy's unprecedented world of "free forms" and incandescent feelings.

The second excerpt comes from the essay on Stravinsky:

> But through Stravinsky, there has come to be a music stylistically well-nigh the reverse of that of the impressionists. Through him, music has become again cubical, lapidary, massive, mechanistic. Scintillation is gone out of it. The delicate, sinuous melodic line, the glamorous sheeny harmonies, are gone out of it. The elegance of Debussy, the golden sensuality, the quiet, classic touch, are flown. Instead, there come to be great, weighty, metallic masses, molten piles and sheets of steel and iron, shining adamantine bulks. Contours are become grim, severe, angular. Melodies are sharp, rigid, asymmetrical. Chords are uncouth, square clusters of notes, stout and solid as the pillars that support roofs, heavy as the thuds of triphammers. Above all, there is rhythm, rhythm rectangular and sheer and emphatic, rhythm that lunges and beats and reiterates and dances with all the steely perfect tirelessness of the machine, shoots out and draws back, shoots upward and shoots down, with the inhuman motion of titanic arms of steel. Indeed, the change is as radical, as complete, as though in the midst of moonlit noble gardens a giant machine had arisen swiftly from

the ground and inundated the night with electrical glare and set its metal thews and organs and joints relentlessly whirring, relentlessly functioning.

Without bar lines or notes, Rosenfeld has managed to convey the characteristic architecture of Stravinsky's early music, especially of *Petrouchka* and *Le Sacre du Printemps,* its novel placing of rhythm in the forefront, and its stark mood, at once primitive and mechanistic, of relentless power. The chords *are* uncouth. The melodies *are* asymmetrical. The rhythms *do* lunge and repeat with an "inhuman motion." The final extended image of the giant machine in the moonlit garden grows logically out of the abstract adjectives which precede it, with the eerie effect of a futurist or Léger painting come to life.

There is nothing parochial about Rosenfeld's prose; it is a form of civilized discourse which enlarges the sense of the occasion—a performance of *Rosenkavalier,* say, or a recital at which a Copland sonata or Schoenberg quartet is premièred—to articulate principles of form and aesthetic theory. The style is the man-intense, probing, playing with ideas as a painter with a varied palette, yet without pose or swagger. His literary manners are the opposite of Shaw's. Where Shaw delighted in the role of controversialist, a sort of impudent master of revels who confessed that "justice is not the critic's business," Rosenfeld sought a stern impartiality and exposed his enthusiasms, biases, and judgments to disinterested scrutiny. Shaw, the moralist disguised as entertainer, is primarily a witty debunker of "spoof opera," the shabby performances of his favorite composers, and the Philistinism that dominated English musical life: poor orchestral execution, slipshod diction and acting, fat sopranos, incompetent stage directors who cheapened *Don Giovanni.* His prose in the newspaper pieces is so pithy, full of verve, and always on the attack that the reader fails to notice, or tacitly agrees to overlook, its thin musical substance. Shaw is not indispensable for understanding the music history of his time.

Rosenfeld, on the other hand, was at the nerve center of

modern music. While he could caustically denounce pandering to an audience's bad taste or any deviation from the composer's intentions, he concentrated his energies on the composer, not the performer. He was the enemy of priggish and mediocre art. His rigorous standards were supported by an erudition and a familiarity with the finest works European culture had to offer; his judgment was incorruptible; he was independent of all vested interests; his virtuosity was without personal abuse or self-regard; and he was impelled by empathy and an almost religious zeal for art. The typical Rosenfeld essay moves from praise to censure. Consequently the critical act with him was that rare thing, "a deed of life."

It was no accident that Rosenfeld was the one who quietly found a patron for Aaron Copland so that he would have the liberty to compose, unencumbered by financial worries; or that Hart Crane should have first read "Faustus and Helen" before a puzzled but moved gathering at one of Rosenfeld's casual *soirées* in Irving Place. Moreover, almost singlehandedly Rosenfeld five times took on the tiresome editorial duties of shaping *The American Caravan,* perhaps the most distinguished anthology of American artistic talent in our literary history. By the testimony of countless artists these selfless acts were routine.

It is ironic and alarming that a man of Rosenfeld's "myriad chivalries, drudgeries, and masteries,"[4] a gentle, civil, patriarchal man who concerned himself so passionately with the artist's needs and his culture's health, a critic moreover of great historical importance, should have fallen into almost total eclipse. There is no entry under Rosenfeld's name in Grove's *Dictionary of Music and Musicians,* and Wilfrid Mellers, in his recent exhaustive study of American music, *Music in a New Found Land,* does not so much as mention Rosenfeld in a footnote, even though for many years Rosenfeld was the only one who talked about the subject with salutary understanding.

4. Marianne Moore, "A Son of Imagination," *Paul Rosenfeld, Voyager in the Arts,* edited by Jerome Mellquist and Lucie Wiese (New York, 1948), p. 39.

How can we account for this neglect? Partly of course by the seemingly inescapable reversals of fashion. But mainly because Rosenfeld's virtues—responsibility, generosity, nobility—are not much in favor these days. They suggest a stiff and sedate mind, too reverent of art, preaching of spirituality and ignoring the pleasures of pathology as a requisite for insight. Perhaps in our cynicism we cannot trust such an ardent devotion to art. But whatever the reason, the loss to American letters is too great to tolerate. A review of Rosenfeld's career may therefore be of use in reconstructing his critical reputation.

> "Music comes to reveal itself as a form of communion with our fellow man—and with the Supreme Being."
> —IGOR STRAVINSKY, *Poetics of Music*

PAUL ROSENFELD was born in 1890 into a respectable middle-class Jewish family with a strong love of the arts. His father, a business man, read avidly—the works of Dickens, Gibbon, Macaulay, and Taine were among his favorites. His mother was a talented pianist. "I grew up amid an amount of spontaneous music-making," Rosenfeld reports in *By Way of Art*. As a boy he was sent to military school in Poughkeepsie, New York, where he came under the benign influence of a Mr. Hickok, the town music dealer, and of Arthur Moore Williamson, the school music master to whom *Musical Portraits* is dedicated. "Little men, making a creative effort, taking art seriously in an unresponding environment,"[5] they awakened his interest in such different composers as Bach, Schumann, and Wagner.

After graduating in 1912 from Yale, where his pursuits were more literary than musical, and attending the Columbia School of Journalism for a year, Rosenfeld took a trip to Europe that was to be crucial to his choice of vocation. While leisurely

5. Paul Rosenfeld, "All the World's Poughkeepsie," *Musical Quarterly*, XXIX (October, 1943), p. 473. This is a splendid autobiographical essay.

exploring the treasures of European museums, listening to all kinds of music, and steeping himself in tradition-laden pleasures, he repudiated the idea of expatriation as tempting but self-defeating. Unlike the scores of Americans who were soon to flock to Paris in search of artistic fulfillment, Rosenfeld believed that the effort to foster and create a complex, aesthetically rounded American art, unbeholden to European models, could only be made in America itself. His vague ambitions to write now found a focus. By good fortune, when he returned to New York in 1916, he was able to join an exciting community of cultural reformers that included Van Wyck Brooks, Waldo Frank, and Randolph Bourne.[6] World War I had injected an unpleasant political rancor into New York's cultural life, but it could only interrupt, not end, the creative ferment in music, literature, and painting.

Very quickly Rosenfeld became a "voyager in the arts" and an important member of all the concentric circles of artistic activity. Nobody seemed bothered that he refused to take sides in the bitter disputes that periodically broke out. His sensitivity and cheerful dependability had a steadying effect on all. (It is wholly in keeping with his character that Rosenfeld took care of Randolph Bourne on his deathbed.)

Waldo Frank assisted him in getting writing assignments for *The New Republic* and *Seven Arts*. His integrity, gusto, flow of genial analysis, and identification with the modernist movements in all the arts soon to mark his long, prolific career began prophetically with essays in *Seven Arts* concerning the new American composers and "291," Alfred Stieglitz' gallery and art temple on Fifth Avenue. Two experiences stand out as shaping Rosenfeld's future conception of what the critic (and society) might wish of its art: his friendship with Alfred Stieglitz and the people who gathered for talk and bonhomie at "291," and his first exposure to the music of Leo Ornstein.

6. For a full and excellent survey of this important cultural movement, see Sherman Paul's introduction to Rosenfeld's *Port of New York* (Urbana, Ill., 1961), pp. vii–lvi.

In many ways, "291" gave Rosenfeld a better education than Yale, or perhaps it would be more accurate to say he was in a better position to benefit from its unique atmosphere. In a brilliant essay on Stieglitz in *Port of New York* Rosenfeld recalls the spirit of the place that made it the unofficial sanctuary for new and experimental art from 1907 to 1917:

> If ever institution in America came to bring the challenge of the truth of life to the land of the free, and to show the face of expressivity to a trading society living by middle-class conventions, it was the little gallery, "291." "291" was an art gallery that was itself a work of art. Exhibitions of baffling work were hung . . . like scientific presentations of facts. . . . The many separate shows contributed to a single demonstration that grew like a tree—the demonstration of the world hour. It was a place where the work of the heart was let be, set clear of commercial entanglements, and allowed to do its work; and where the spirit of life came alive. . . . It was a place where people got very hot and explanatory and argumentative about rectangles of color and lumps of bronze and revealed themselves; and a place where quiet unobtrusive people suddenly said luminous things in personal language about paintings and drawings scornfully, authoritatively excluded by others, and revealed life. It was like a play. Nevertheless "291" was a laboratory.[7]

At "291" Rosenfeld experienced that enhancement, wisdom, and *revelation* which contact with artists always gave him. In Stieglitz' genius with the camera, conversation, and unprejudiced sponsorship of different artistic styles, Rosenfeld confirmed his sense that the imagination, risking, seeking, invading all of life, and wedded to "clear logic and technical skill," could thrive in America, even in the midst of a commercial spirit that

7. *Port of New York*, p. 257.

was "universally cheap and irreverent and indifferent." On "291's" walls, crowded with paintings and sculpture and photography, was visibly embodied art's revelatory power, a power at which Rosenfeld never ceased to wonder and which he undertook in his criticism to help the artist achieve. It was the artist's, and to a lesser degree, the critic's sacred calling to bring men closer to completing themselves by illuminating life in its multiple appearances and inner reality. In his faith that American art could combine an aristocratic excellence and refined taste with a robust democratic love of pluralism and sacramentalizing of the ordinary, Rosenfeld was in the mainstream of the Emerson-Whitman tradition. And this further meant that his criticism like theirs would avoid academic talk about art or a grasping ethical intention.

The second pivotal experience was brief but equally lasting in its effects. By chance Rosenfeld attended an *avant-garde* concert at which he heard for the first time the music of Leo Ornstein. The shock from the dissonant style of the young Russian-Jewish immigrant was immense, stirring in Rosenfeld a consciousness of the "age of steel, the feeling of today." It made the music of Wagner and Debussy seem stale and of the distant past. Here was a music which, if rough and fragmentary—and Rosenfeld later changed his mind about its intrinsic merits— sprang from a dynamic contact with the world of machines and electric power which was transforming the face and spirit of America.

All Rosenfeld's writings are henceforth governed by one overriding principle rather than by any uniform methodology. Rosenfeld believed that any self-betrayal of talent was due to the artist's withholding of himself from full contact with the "object" world around him and to his negligence of the resources of craft at his disposal. "Giving alone builds culture and cities for men," he said in *Port of New York,* and this conviction is the common root of his ethic and aesthetic. But some secret spiritual destitution seemed to lie at the heart of American culture, keeping its artists infantile, always yearning for some state of past primal innocence or else dreaming of a paradisiac future. The hard lesson of American art was that the artist could indulge this childishness, could evade the world as it existed in its richly contradictory realities, only at the exorbitant price of self-emasculation and incompleteness.

If a feeble art is a sure symptom of a sick society, and a dull, slack, and joyless one, too, what remedies might the critic prescribe to insure that health which alone interests? First of all, he could incite that awareness in the artist which would release within his art "the power of self-fulfillment" and "marry him to his own individuality." In practice this meant not permitting the artist to "play safe with life"; it meant scrutinizing the art of his age, as Rosenfeld himself did, whether in the first fumbling efforts of young composers like Copland and Roger Sessions or the lazy journeyman work of established figures like Richard Strauss, for formal weakness and failure of vision. With pertinacity and wit he would ask the composer, What satisfactions does your work provide for man? What does it say about you and your culture? What "form of communion with your fellow man" does your music disclose? Thus Rosenfeld championed the modern, not as a faddist who takes up the latest sleek fashion in the arts, but as a lucid and strict-minded humanist who compared the works of his contemporaries with the high achievements of the art of the past.

The remarkable unity and vitality of Rosenfeld's music criticism derives from his intuitive understanding that, as Virgil Thomson remarked in *Music Reviewed,* "you cannot set yourself against the creative forces of your age and be first-rate." Though a reflective and retiring person by temperament, Rosenfeld thoroughly enjoyed the contentions of the public forum. From his post as critic for *The Dial, The Nation,* and *The New Republic,* he reached an audience which, if not large, consisted of the influential intellectual and artistic elite, which was knowledgeable in painting and literature but relatively untutored in music, for whom he served as mentor. (He was of course also widely read by the musical world.) In retrospect what aided him most was his responsiveness to the literary-poetic, or experiential, content of music. As Charles Ives has said, he "had that gift of an almost immediate insight into the larger side of music, even if it brought technical processes to which he was unaccustomed—a penetrative discernment into its fundamental and innermost meanings."[8]

The basic themes of Rosenfeld's work are present in *Musical Portraits* and deepened in subsequent books. The artist cannot hide in or from his work; it is a portrait of his innermost being. He cannot escape his culture either, for he is also the inheritor of traditions, is acted upon by social forces that bind or liberate him. Musical conventions, too, are intimately linked to the character of the composer. The many passages of bombast and high-toned fakery that debilitate Liszt's work, the self-parody and grossness of Richard Strauss, the religiosity of Mahler raise the problem of why these composers squandered their musical gifts. Why did something meretricious creep into their music, making it a series of gestures and effects? Mainly because they lacked self-discipline, the uttermost devotion to the object.

More than personal failure, Rosenfeld argued, can corrupt a composer. The cooperation of society is required, too. For while a work of art emerges from the genius of the composer, sometimes independently of the tastes and forms of the age, as in late Beethoven, it also grows in a particular soil. Wagner's music is as much an expression of the nineteenth century's absorption with materialism, its "sense of outward power and inner unfulfillment," as Marx's *Das Kapital*. An ecological balance between the composer and his culture exists that can easily be tampered with, to the detriment of his art. The "crippled power" of Mahler's symphonies exemplifies most graphically the baleful consequences of a composer unfaithful to the "racial [or national] spirit of his people." The artist who is rootless turns impersonator. As an assimilated Jew who had denied the racial

8. Charles Ives, "Spokesman for an American Tradition," *Paul Rosenfeld, Voyager in the Arts*, p. 165.

heritage planted deep in his consciousness and was living on the sufferance of a hostile Viennese society, Mahler was set at war with himself. He "was never himself. He was everybody and nobody." Inevitably he wrote music that, imitating the externals of Beethoven and Wagner, was banal and self-pitying—overgrown ruins of incomplete emotion.

Rosenfeld finds the ideal in Moussorgsky's *Boris Godunov*: "The virtue of a thing that satisfies the very needs of life and brings to a race release and formulation of its speech." And in Debussy: "A thousand years of culture live in Debussy's fineness," that intangible aristocratic life style which is the flavorful essence of the French genius: clarity, restraint, poise, delicacy; the sensuous *galante* style of Rameau in a modern idiom.

Rosenfeld, however, is no simple-minded exponent of nationalism. He also stresses those historical continuities that cross national frontiers. He draws lifelines between composers of different eras, traces family trees from generation to generation: the rhythmical vivacity and plenitude that bind Berlioz and Stravinsky; the instrumental colors and timbres of Berlioz that reappear in Debussy, Ravel, Stravinsky, Strauss, and Bloch; the folk motifs and tavern songs of Moussorgsky and Stravinsky; the gigantic symphonic forms of Beethoven and Wagner, Mahler, and Bruckner; and so on.

Musical Chronicle (1923), a more miscellaneous book than *Musical Portraits,* records Rosenfeld's response to the growing pains of musical culture in America, in particular: the attempts of the Kneisel Quartet for over thirty-five years to gain an audience for chamber music; the introduction of amateur choruses, like that of the People's Music League, to investigate the polyphonic vocal literature of Palestrina and other fifteenth- and sixteenth-century composers, which failed to take hold; and the deleterious impact of World War I on musical life, especially the hysterical attack on all German music in the name of patriotism. For Rosenfeld it is a depressing tale of mediocre performances, poor programs, and the old American fear of "the completely developed human being"—the tyranny

of the lowest common denominator, the certifying of the public's complacent tastes. Describing the public's reaction to Stravinsky's *Concertino,* he draws this melancholy conclusion:

> The living artist comes to the folk with the offer of a
> contact with the present. He comes to them with the
> truth of an experience, with the fact of what his life is,
> of what their own lives are. He comes to tell them what
> is at work in the world today, what the tenure of his own
> existence is, what is happening or about to happen to
> them. And that is precisely what our musical and artistic
> public does not wish to know.[9]

But Rosenfeld refused to be disheartened by this mute conformity, and the following year published *Port of New York,* a
collection of fourteen extraordinary essays on such figures as
Randolph Bourne, William Carlos Williams, Marsden Hartley,
Van Wyck Brooks, and Alfred Stieglitz, who either succumbed
to the peculiarly American psychological deformity of unre-
latedness or who overcame it by "giving [themselves] completely to the American environment and the medium of [their]
art."[10]

The other essays in *Musical Chronicle* worth noting are the
early appreciation of Bruckner's music, the clumsy innocence,
good nature, and religious grandeur of which was marred by his
"unevolved sense of form"; a restatement of the reasons for
Mahler's poignant failure, "the cry of a great ruptured heart for
health"; and essays on Erik Satie and The Six that show
Rosenfeld's catholicity and perception about the sly, under-
stated French music as well as the heroic metaphysical music of
the Viennese tradition.

Rosenfeld's ability to present a coherent overview of the
complicated, unfolding history of modern music as it emerged
from romanticism, the period from Wagner to Bloch, makes the

9. Paul Rosenfeld, *Musical Chronicle* (New York, 1923) , p. 101.
10. Sherman Paul, in *Port of New York,* p. liii.

slim volume *Modern Tendencies in Music* (1927), written for
a popular series, a useful summary. It is one of Rosenfeld's lesser
works because he is forced to cover too many composers, but he
skillfully averts a mechanical classification of composers by
epochs. The radical changes and experiments in tone, harmony, instrumental use, and rhythm, or the decay of symphonic
form, for example, are seen as part of larger disturbances in the
intellectual and spiritual life of the West. Rosenfeld's flexible
conceptual framework, his habit of cultural comparison, allows
him to show how influences move between countries, how a
single powerful musical personality like Wagner obstructs those
who follow him, engenders revolts, how his influence wanes,
surfaces, is denied and acknowledged again.

Wagner is the logical starting point of Rosenfeld's survey
because although his descriptive music comes ultimately from
Beethoven's Ninth Symphony, he developed the romantic's
heroic sense of ecstatic individuality and the allure of self-
annihilation to its extreme. The forcefulness of his storm and
fire music echoes in many pages of Strauss, Varèse, and Stravinsky; the "ethereal delicacy" of parts of *Lohengrin, Tristan,* and
Parsifal is imprinted on the "eerie, fantastic, and gossamer-like
compositions of Debussy, Scriabin, and Schoenberg." Wagner's
music dramas stood massively in the way of the post-Wagnerian
composers. Strauss could forge a musical identity only when his
orchestral virtuosity combined with burlesque irony and pure
sensationalism, as in *Till Eulenspiegel* and *Don Juan.* When he
aped Wagner's grandiosity, he lapsed into the trivial sentimentality of *Ein Heldenleben.* Mahler's nine symphonies, "intended to continue the great religious, believing spirit of Wagner's art, actually evidence the impotence of the tradition about
the beginning of this century."[11]

But a contrary feeling about life and an art to clothe it
existed in Russia. What Stravinsky later sarcastically called "the

11. Paul Rosenfeld, *Modern Tendencies in Music* (New York, 1927),
p. 20.

murky inanities of the Art-Religion, with its heroic hardware, its arsenal of warrior mysticism, and its vocabulary seasoned with an adulterated religiosity"[12] was entirely missing in Moussorgsky. Wagner's heroes assert the value of their ego against the vast impersonal forces in the universe. Moussorgsky's, believing in the futility of revolt and an unfree will, passively yield to them. This difference of feeling is reflected in basic differences of style, melodic form, and rhythm. To Wagner's huge sheets of opulent sound Moussorgsky opposes a style drawn from the liturgy of the Russian Orthodox Church and Slavic folk music, "predominantly humble, stark, homely, popular, and altogether modest." Where Wagner's melodic line soars upward encompassing space, Moussorgsky's is prone to "sudden apathetic falls." And where Wagner's rhythm is emphatic, regular, and oceanic, Moussorgsky's has a nervous irregularity. Though he wrote little, "a whole world was to change its aesthetic views and recast its techniques of expression because of it."[13]

More refined and classical in form, Debussy's music is the legatee of Moussorgsky's world view. In him too we find a "will-and-directionlessness," a mistrust of the "testimony of the senses." The luminous color of our own mutability gliding by as in a dream, "the sinuous melodies" and "jewel-like instrumentation"—these permeate Ravel, Stravinsky's *Petrouchka* and *Le Rossignol,* Bloch's orchestration, De Falla, Strauss, and even Schoenberg's D-minor Quartet.

But the wheel turns again and the revolt is directed against Debussy. Stravinsky, "easily the greatest of personal forces in the contemporary musical world,"[14] is its leader and mover. Fascinated by the evolution of this "brilliant, daring, suggestive

12. Igor Stravinsky, *Poetics of Music* (New York, 1947) , p. 62.

13. *Modern Tendencies in Music,* pp. 14, 150.

14. My discussion of Stravinsky incorporates Rosenfeld's analysis from *Modern Tendencies in Music, By Way of Art* (New York, 1928) , and *Discoveries of a Music Critic* (New York, 1936). The quotations are taken from "The Evolution of Stravinsky," pp. 155–179.

musician," Rosenfeld kept returning to the music, rethinking settled opinions, admitting errors of judgment, praising its iconoclasm. One of the pleasures in reading Rosenfeld's criticism is to follow this continual reassessment of Stravinsky's work, which is also a tribute to his critical conscience.

Stravinsky's early compositions through *Les Noces,* especially *Petrouchka* and *Le Sacre,* were a strongly masculine reaction against the softness of much late-romantic music. In their nervous, percussive, plebeian drive they seemed to express a sense of the human being as automaton. Their affinity was to the "family characteristics" of nationalistic movement: the Russian brilliance of instrumental color, conciseness of expression, pantomimic spirit, animal vitality, and episodic structure; multirhythmicality, partiality to humble material, and relentless polytonalism. There were also likenesses to Debussy's impressionistic harmonies, the irony of *Till Eulenspiegel,* and the musical primitivism of *Elektra.*

As Stravinsky moves into his second period, his most perfect, Rosenfeld thought, he shifts from a "modified homophonic-harmonic principle of composition" to a "melodic-contrapuntal one." After flirting in his early works with "a certain passivity of feeling and negation of the individual's power of choice," he turns in *Les Noces, Renard, L'Histoire du Soldat,* and the *Symphonies for Wind Instruments* to a more "human scale." This marks a decisive break with nineteenth-century romanticism, music dependent on a literary or balletic program, and a rebirth of the humanist spirit that deals with "what men share in common." The forms of these works "are complete, their rhythms subtle; and certain in their effects, they completely and sustainedly express intense and deep feeling."

It was Stravinsky's neoclassical period that troubled Rosenfeld most. Its dry, archaizing spirit he deemed "progressive in the form of a reaction." He astutely recognized the severe orderliness and grandeur of the style of *Oedipus Rex* and Stravinsky's own avowed interest in the architecture of music, but it seemed to him willed. There was nothing intrinsically wrong in reviving old styles; it was a common feature of all cultures. "The business of reviving old forms, at least that of imposing their limits upon new creations, is a kind of criticism in the medium of music, a manner of assimilating the ideas of former men and epochs." Such rationalism was a rebuke to the "rhetorical heirs to the Beethoven tradition" and stood for "a world-idea that has long haunted and continues to haunt the race of men." But Rosenfeld suspected correctly that the restless Stravinsky would continue to search for new modes.

Rosenfeld's animus toward neoclassical elegance can be seen clearly in his analysis of Erik Satie, who initiates an era of formalism in French music, an "idea of music as a play of sonorities" in which the clown's jest coexists with the exquisite. Though valuing Satie's witty use of jazz and popular music—later on used more raucously by The Six—and appreciating its deliberate avoidance of the monumental, Rosenfeld was put off by some of the very traits Virgil Thomson esteemed in the Frenchman. Where Thomson, always something of a Parnassian, heard "inconsequence, quietude, precision, acuteness of auditory observation, gentleness, sincerity and directness of statement,"[15] Rosenfeld heard a "delight in pure movement" and the "replacement of feeling by surface emotions": a music that dwells exclusively on "the refined superficial sense." This was in contrast to Schoenberg's music, which in spite of a misguided leaning toward the analytical—paper music, Rosenfeld called it—uses "every musical resource at his disposal to body forth what is going on in his feelings"; passion is never far from the surface. But Rosenfeld's mixed feelings about Schoenberg's revamping of the musical vocabulary of the Viennese tradition never changed.

From the start of his career Rosenfeld dedicated himself to solving the problems of American music. As patron, propagandist, historian, and critic, he sought to help the American composer throw off the influence of German romanticism and to foster an environment that would be propitious to the creation

15. Virgil Thomson, *Music Reviewed* (New York, 1967), p. 33.

of a powerful and serious native music. James Huneker (1860–1921) had crusaded against the genteel alliance of musical establishment and reactionary audience. In advocating the "advanced" music of Wagner and popularizing the ideas of Nietzsche and Zola, he helped loosen the servile ties of American art to English models, thereby making it less parochial. But Huneker's intellectual coarseness and his excessive worship at the shrines of German culture made him uninterested in the plight of American music. He was content being the colorful dilettante and Bohemian.

Not so Rosenfeld. The history of American music, as he saw it in *An Hour with American Music* (1929), perhaps his sunniest book, was principally one of derivative composers like Edward MacDowell and Charles Martin Loeffler who, by virtue of "weak personalities" and a "chronic aversion to reality," succumbed to a sterile eclecticism. American music lagged behind the other arts in achieving independence and vigor because American composers refused to subject themselves in any "steady relation" to American life. Their work was thin-blooded, deficient in feeling other than nostalgia and childlike naïveté; consequently their musical structures lacked individuality.

The situation however was neither hopeless nor beyond change. Charles Ives entered the scene as Promethean life-giver to American music. And if Ives toiled in solitude, sometimes thinking he had "his ears on wrong," and if his music occasionally hearkened back to a state of idyllic innocence, it illustrated not just the promise but the fulfillment of maturity: a complex, fearless, and commanding musical mind thoroughly grounded in the American environment, conscious of his own and his nation's essences. As Wilfrid Mellers has pointed out, two qualities lie at the core of Ives's work: an "acceptance of life-as-it-is, in all its apparent chaos and contradiction," and an effort to reach a transcendental unity.[16] Rosenfeld was one of

16. Wilfrid Mellers, *Music in a New Found Land* (New York, 1964), pp. 44–45.

the very first to see in Ives a composer of genius and originality, whose experiments in atonality, polytonality, quarter tones, serial forms, and polyrhythm antedated their development in Europe by many years. (The American conception of rhythm, Rosenfeld noted, differed from the European pulse in being less intellectual and more unpredictable and "motory.") What buoyed Rosenfeld was that "there was nothing merely theoretical in these experiments. One senses a unity of feeling under all of them, under the unsuccessful no less than the successful, and a constant integration of vision and experience with the personality."[17] By moving out of the narrow zones of the self into the larger domain of the object, Ives had hit upon a unique style and aesthetic structure that organized peculiarly American impulses and attitudes, as in the *Concord Sonata* and the *Three Places in New England:*

> The forces conveyed by his music are deeply, typically American. They are the essences of a practical people, abrupt and nervous and ecstatic in their movements and manifestations—brought into play with a certain reluctance and difficulty, but when finally loosed, jaggedly, abruptly, almost painfully released, with something of an hysteric urgency; manifested sometimes in a bucolic irony and burlesque and sometimes in a religious and mystical elevation, but almost invariably in patterns that have a paroxysmal suddenness and abruptness and violence.

Ives was no isolated phenomenon. He inaugurated a strong and vital tradition, as the "coltish" music of Aaron Copland testified. Though his art was of a narrower scope than Ives's, its "motoriness and leanness and shape," its "taste for hot colors and garish jazziness," and its blend of rueful lyricism and brash humor speaks in a distinctly American voice.

The final proof of America's musical coming of age, however,

17. Paul Rosenfeld, "The Advent of American Music," *Kenyon Review,* I (Winter, 1939), p. 51.

was the work of Edgar Varèse. An emigré from France and originally a disciple of Debussy's impressionism, Varèse flourished in the New World. His frugal structures of sound made a deep impact on Rosenfeld, communicating "the massive feeling of American life, with its crowds, city piles, colossal organizations, mass production, forces and interests intricately welded; sounds that for a moment revealed them throbbing, moving, swinging, glowing with clean, daring, audacious life." Early works like *Octandre* and *Amériques* might still intersect at points with *Petrouchka* and *Le Sacre* in their primitivism and in the pungent clarity of each instrument, but *Arcana, Hyperprisms, Intégrales,* and *Ionization,* with their dominance of percussion and their almost classical symmetries, bring one closer to the twentieth century's sense of "the non-human universe" and "correspond with the science's newest sensations about matter." But while Varèse's art shuns all religious connotations and the *frissons* of cheap apocalypse, it admits a lyrical purity, a passionate geometry of the spirit. It is minimal art of cosmic dimension. Instrumentally Varèse is the Berlioz of the twentieth century, although his scores look sparse and empty on the page. Like moving rigid sculptures, by their abbreviated style and uncompromising lucidity, they suggest at times a defoliated soul, both physical and metaphysical desolation. Above all, Varèse meets Rosenfeld's most severe requirement: "The impulse is one of unity, or perfection, born of a wholeness in the psyche and moving toward a condition satisfactory to the entire man."

Discoveries of a Music Critic, Rosenfeld's last and in many ways best collection of essays, appeared in 1936. Though the Depression had wiped out most of Rosenfeld's private income and he found it hard at times to get journalistic assignments in an epoch almost doctrinally committed to seeing the artist's social consciousness uncontaminated by aesthetics, Rosenfeld's intellectual curiosity and his fervor for art remained unabated. In fact, the book showed a ripening of his gifts and a broadening of his commentary. Essays on the court masque, Monteverdi,

Bach, Mozart, Cimarosa, and Beethoven take up the first third of the book and serve as a preface to what becomes an informal comprehensive view of musical history from the romantic Mozart to Stravinsky, Bartók, and George Gershwin. Rosenfeld exposes his major themes to mature and leisurely analysis. A remark by E. T. A. Hoffman on Beethoven in 1807 crystallizes Rosenfeld's philosophy of art and music criticism: "Music, in particular Beethoven's and Mozart's, could make a man a *Geisterseher*, a percipient of the realm of the inner truth of life, the metaphysical realm of essences and ideas. This conception was one of the lights of the whole romantic movement."[18] In Beethoven's late quartets, the struggle between freedom and necessity is transcended by an art ultimately rational in its inner organization and mysterious in its union of private self with mankind.

That the artist was a healer to his people and that "the work of art is one of the great potential agents of relationship among a democratic people" is the cornerstone of Rosenfeld's musical faith. But the rise of Nazism, with its usurpation of Wagner's music for its own monstrous political ends, forced Rosenfeld to re-examine the whole question of nationalism in music. "The Nazis and *Die Meistersinger*" is a moving paean to the artist's power to embody spontaneously in his art the uncoerced union of individuals in a social order. The historical Hans Sachs and Wagner's operatic hero were the "asserters of the inviolacy of the private conscience and the personality, the prophets of symbiosis"—ideas anathema to the Nazi regime and its ideology of the superior race. The artist cannot be held responsible for such a perverse misuse of his pure motive:

> For all artists are fundamentally "anarchists." Their in-
> tuitions reveal to them a continually changing order, and
> their embodiment of the symbols of this continually
> changing order adjusts them spontaneously to it. They
> touch material selflessly and shape it in accordance with

18. Quoted in *Discoveries of a Music Critic*, p. 8.

> its own nature and the idea to which it conforms; and
> work is a joy to them, an end in itself. And the social
> order to which they are natively directed could easily be
> an order . . . in which labor got its just reward, and so-
> cial, political, and intellectual advantages were shared
> by all.

Despite years of listening to bad music, reading mediocre
books, and looking at academic paintings, Rosenfeld never
renounced his faith in the artist as the guardian, lover, and
interpreter of the spirit. He never lost his hunger for, or sense of
awe at, the full consciousness that only a great work of art can
open to us. Many critics have had Rosenfeld's clear intelligence,
but not many, as the essays in *Discoveries of a Music Critic*
prove, have had in addition—vision.

In the forties Rosenfeld was planning two books—a historical
study of genres and a critical biography of Ives to be written
with Elliott Carter. To judge by the high quality of Rosenfeld's
journalism during the war years we have lost immeasurably by
his premature death in 1946 of a heart attack. A new generation
of music lovers and critics has grown up unaware of their debt
to Rosenfeld for their ability to accept the varieties of modern
music that are now a natural part of our common musical
culture. But we cannot afford to let Rosenfeld remain a dim
figure in the pages of a textbook, not even that poignant figure
Albert Goldman has evoked: the good man in an age of brilliant neurotics who created an interest in the modern and
passed by. There is alive in his essays a compassion and a
wisdom we seem to have let slip out of our criticism and, even
worse, out of our national life. The recovery of such a sane
mind might well signal a return to that cultural health Rosenfeld spent his life in promoting.

HERBERT A. LEIBOWITZ

A Note on the Text

IN SELECTING ESSAYS for this volume, I have been guided by Paul Rosenfeld's long and important association with the history of modern music. For the sake of coherence, I have omitted essays on such classic composers as Mozart—with regret, for Rosenfeld displays the same skill and acumen in these discussions as he does when explaining Schoenberg or the modern American composers. The essays are arranged dialectically rather than chronologically in conformity to Rosenfeld's own habitual practice.

I have left Rosenfeld's punctuation virtually untouched. It is highly idiosyncratic, especially in the use of semicolons, but tampering with it would have meant destroying the integrity and rhythm of his thinking. I have, however, slightly altered the spelling of some proper names, bringing them up to date with modern conventions—for example, Strawinsky has been changed to Stravinsky.

Since Rosenfeld refers to musical compositions by both foreign and English titles, the reader will find these cross-referenced in the Index. Unless otherwise noted, all footnotes are mine.

Acknowledgments

I WISH TO THANK the following people for their help in preparing this book. The deep knowledge of my friend Albert Goldman of Columbia University about all kinds and aspects of music and his conversations about Rosenfeld's musical aesthetics taught me a great deal. My friend Professor Nathan Lyons of The City University of New York never flagged in his belief that Rosenfeld's "old-fashioned" critical virtues needed to be set before and learned by today's reading public. Professor Hannah Charney of The City University of New York graciously translated many passages from German to English, and my friend and colleague Professor Paul Zweig of Columbia University performed the same task with many French passages.

I would like to thank Professor Stavros Deligiorgis of The Center for Advanced Study, University of Illinois, for reading the introduction and for supplying the epigraph from Plato. I would also like to thank Miss Sheila Keats for helping me with much musical information. Most of all, however, I wish to pay tribute to Mr. Arthur Wang, president of Hill and Wang, for undertaking a project ritualistically endorsed and declined by almost every "big" publisher in the country. His courage has made it possible to end the scandalous neglect of Rosenfeld's music criticism.

I

The Viennese Tradition

I

The Viennese Tradition

Wagner

WAGNER'S MUSIC, more than any other, is the sign and symbol of the nineteenth century. The men to whom it was disclosed, and who first sought to refuse, and then accepted it, passionately, without reservations, found in it their truth. It came to their ears as the sound of their own voices. It was the common, the universal tongue. Not alone on Germany, not alone on Europe, but on every quarter of the globe that had developed coal-power civilization, the music of Wagner descended with the formative might of the perfect image. Men of every race and continent knew it to be of themselves as much as was their hereditary and racial music, and went out to it as to their own adventure. And wherever music reappeared, whether under the hand of the Japanese or the semi-African or the Yankee, it seemed to be growing from Wagner as the bright shoots of the fir sprout from the dark ones grown the previous year. A whole world, for a period, came to use his idiom. His dream was recognized during his very lifetime as an integral portion of the consciousness of the entire race.

For Wagner's music is the century's paean of material triumph. It is its cry of pride in its possessions, its aspiration toward greater and ever greater objective power. Wagner's style is stiff and diapered and emblazoned with the sense of material increase. It is brave, superb, haughty with consciousness of the gigantic new body acquired by man. The tonal pomp and ceremony, the pride of the trumpets, the arrogant stride, the magnificent address, the broad, vehement, grandiloquent pronouncements, the sumptuous texture of his music seem forever proclaiming the victory of man over the energies of fire and sea and earth, the lordship of creation, the suddenly begotten railways and shipping and mines, the cataclysm of wealth and comfort. His work seems forever seeking to form images of grandeur and empire, flashing with Siegfried's sword, commanding the planet with Wotan's spear, upbuilding above the heads of men the castle of the gods. It dares measure itself with

the terrestrial forces, exults in the fire, soughs through the forest
with the thunderstorm, glitters and surges with the river, spans
mountains with the rainbow bridge. It is full of the gestures of
giants and heroes and gods, of the large proud movements of
which men have ever dreamed in days of affluent power. Even
Tristan und Isolde, the high song of love, and *Parsifal,* the
mystery, spread richness and splendor about them, are set in an
atmosphere of heavy gorgeous stuffs, amid objects of gold and
silver, and thick clouding incense, while the protagonists, the
lovers and saviors, seem to be celebrating a worldly triumph,
and crowning themselves kings. And over the entire body of
Wagner's music, there float, a massive diadem, the towers and
parapets and banners of Nuremberg the imperial free city,
monument of a victorious burgherdom, of civic virtue that on
the ruins of feudalism constructed its own world, and demonstrated to all times its dignity and sobriety and industry, its
solid worth.

For life itself made the Wagnerian gesture. The vortex of
steel and glass and gold, the black express-packets plowing the
seven seas, the smoking trains piercing the bowels of the mountains and connecting cities vibrant with hordes of business men,
the telegraph wires setting the world aquiver with their incessant reports, the whole sinister glittering faëry of gain and
industry and dominion, seemed to tread and soar and sound
and blare and swell with just such rhythm, such grandeur, such
intoxication. Mountains that had been sealed thousands of
years had split open again and let emerge a race of laboring,
fuming giants. The dense primeval forests, the dragon-haunted
German forests, were sprung up again, fresh and cool and
unexplored, nurturing a mighty and fantastic animality. Wherever one gazed, the horned Siegfried, the man born of the earth,
seemed near once more, ready to clear and rejuvenate the globe
with his healthy instinct, to shatter the old false barriers and
pierce upward to fulfilment and power. Mankind, waking from
immemorial sleep, thought for the first time to perceive the sun
in heaven, to greet the creating light. And where was this music

more immanent than in the New World, in America, that essentialization of the entire age? By what environment was it more justly appreciated, Saxon though the accents of its recitative might be? Germany had borne Wagner because Germany had an uninterrupted flow of musical expression. But had the North American continent been able to produce musical art, it could have produced none more indigenous, more really autochthonous, than that of Richard Wagner. Whitman was right when he termed these scores "the music of the 'Leaves.'" For nowhere did the forest of the Niebelungen flourish more lushly, more darkly, than upon the American coasts and mountains and plains. From the towers and walls of New York there fell a breath, a grandiloquent language, a stridency and a glory, that were Wagner's indeed. His regal commanding blasts, his upsweeping marching violins, his pompous and majestic orchestra, existed in the American scene. The very masonry and riverspans, the bursting towns, the fury and expansiveness of existence shed his idiom, shadowed forth his proud processionals, his resonant gold, his tumultuous syncopations and blazing brass and cymbals and volcanically inundating melody; appeared to be struggling to achieve the thing that was his art. American life seemed to be calling for this music in order that its vastness, its madly affluent wealth and multiform power and transcontinental span, its loud, grandiose promise might attain something like eternal being.

And just as in Wagner's music there sounds the age's cry of material triumph, so, too, there sounds in it its terrible cry of homesickness. The energy produced and hurled out over the globe was sucked back again with no less a force. The time that saw the victory of industrialism saw as well the revival or the attempted revival of medieval modes of feeling. Cardinal Newman was as typical a figure of nineteenth-century life as was Balzac. The men who had created the new world felt within themselves a passionate desire to escape out of the present into the past once more. They felt themselves victors and vanquished, powerful and yet bereft and forlorn. And Wagner's music expresses with equal veracity both tides. Just as his music is brave with a sense of outward power, so, too, it is sick with a sense of inner unfulfilment. There is no longing more consuming, no homesickness more terrible, no straining after the laving, immersing floods of unconsciousness more burning than that which utters itself through this music. There are passages, whole hours of his, that are like the straining of a man to return into the darkness of the mothering night out of which he came. There is music of Wagner that makes us feel as though he had been seeking to create great warm clouds, great scented cloths, wide curtains, as though he had come to his art to find something in which he could envelop himself completely, and blot out sun and moon and stars, and sink into oblivion. For such a healer Tristan, lying dying on the desolate, rockbound coast, cries through the immortal longing of the music. For such a divine messenger the wound of Amfortas gapes; for such a redeemer Kundry, driven through the world by scorching winds, yearns. His lovers come toward each other, seeking in each other the night, the descent into the fathomless dark. For them sex is the return, the complete forgetfulness. Through each of them there sounds the insistent cry:

> "Frau Minne will
> Es werde Nacht!"*

There is no tenderness, no awareness of each other, in these men and women. There is only the fierce, impersonal longing for utter consumption, the extinction of the flaming torch, complete merging in the Absolute, the weaving All. In each of them, desire for the void mounts into a gigantic, monstrous flower, into the shimmering thing that enchants King Mark's garden and the rippling stream and the distant horns while Isolde waits for Tristan, or into the devastating fever that chains the sick Tristan to his bed of pain.

* " 'Mistress Love wants
   It to be night!' "

For all these beings, and behind them Wagner, and behind him his time, yearn for the past, the prenatal, the original sleep, and find in such a return their great fulfilment. Siegmund finds in the traits of his beloved his own childhood. Siegfried awakes on the flame-engirdled hill a woman who watched over him before he was born, and waited unchanged for his ripening. It is with the kiss of Herzeleide that Kundry enmeshes Parsifal. Brünnhilde struggles for the forgiving embrace of Wotan, sinks on the breast of the god in submission, reconciliation, immolation. And it is toward an engulfing consummation, some extinction that is both love and death and deeper than both, that the music of his operas aspires. The fire that licks the rock of the Valkyrie, the Rhine that rises in the finale of *Götterdämmerung* and inundates the scene and sweeps the world with its silent, laving tides, the gigantic blossom that opens its corolla in the Liebestod and buries the lovers in a rain of scent and petals, the tranquil ruby glow of the chalice that suffuses the close of *Parsifal,* are the moments toward which the dramas themselves labor, and in which they attain their legitimate conclusion, completion, and end. But not only his finales are full of that entrancement. His melodic line, the lyrical passages throughout his operas, seem to seek to attain it, if not conclusively, at least in preparation. Those silken excessively sweet periods, the moment of reconciliation and embrace of Wotan and Brünnhilde, the "Ach, Isolde" passage in the third act of *Tristan,* those innumerable lyrical flights with their beginnings and subsidings, their sudden advances and regressions, their passionate surges that finally and after all their exquisite hesitations mount and flare and unroll themselves in fullness—they, too, seem to be seeking to distill some of the same brew, the same magic drugging potion, to conjure up out of the orchestral depths some Venusberg, some Klingsor's garden full of subtle scent and soft delight and eternal forgetfulness.

And with Wagner, the new period of music begins. He stands midway between the feudal and the modern worlds. In him, the old and classical period is accomplished. Indeed, so much of his

music is sum, is termination, that there are times when it seems
nothing else. There are times when his art appears entirely
bowed over the past; the confluence of a dozen different tendencies alive during the last century and a half; the capping of
the labor of a dozen great musicians; the fulfilment of the
system regnant in Europe since the introduction of the principle of the equal temperament. For the last time, the old
conceptions of tonality obtain in his music dramas. One feels
throughout *Tristan und Isolde* the key of D-flat, throughout
Die Meistersinger the key of C major, throughout *Parsifal* the
key of A-flat and its relative minor. Rhythms that had been
used all through the classical period are worked by him into
new patterns, and do service a last time. Motifs which had been
utilized by others are taken by him and brought to something
like an ultimate conclusion. The ending, the conclusion, the
completion, are sensible throughout his art. Few musicians have
had their power and method placed more directly in their
hands, and benefited so hugely by the experiments of their
immediate predecessors, have fallen heir to such immense musical legacies. Indeed, Wagner was never loath to acknowledge his
indebtedness, and there are on record several instances when he
paraphrased Walther's song to his masters, and signaled the
composers who had aided him most in his development. Today,
the debt is very plain. At every turn, one sees him benefiting,
and benefiting very beautifully, by the work of Beethoven. The
structure of his great and characteristic works is based on the
symphonic form. The development of the themes of *Tristan*
and *Die Meistersinger* and *Parsifal* out of single kernels; the
fine logical sequence, the expositions of the thematic material of
Parsifal in the prelude and in Gurnemanz' narrative, and its
subsequent reappearance and adventures and developments,
are something like a summit of symphonic art as Beethoven
made it to be understood. And his orchestra is scarcely more
than the orchestra of Beethoven. He did not require the band
of independent instrumental families demanded by Berlioz and
realized by the modern men. He was content with the old,

classical orchestra in which certain groups are strengthened and to which the harp, the English horn, the bass tuba, the bass clarinet have been added.

And his conception of an "unending melody," an unbroken flow of music intended to give cohesion and homogeneity to his music dramas, was a direct consequence of the efforts of Mozart and Weber to give unity to their operatic works. For although these composers retained the old convention of an opera composed of separate numbers, they nevertheless managed to unify their operas by creating a distinct style in each of them, and by securing an emotional development in the various arias and concerted numbers. The step from *Don Giovanni* and *Euryanthe* to *Tannhäuser* and *Lohengrin* does not seem quite as long a one today as once it did. Indeed, there are moments when one wonders whether *Lohengrin* is really a step beyond *Euryanthe,* and whether the increase of power and vividness and imagination has not been made at the expense of style. Moreover, in much of what is actually progress in Wagner the influence of Weber is clearly discernible. The sinister passages seem but developments of moments in *Der Freischütz;* the grand melodic style, the romantic orchestra with its sighing horns and chivalry and flourishes, seem to come directly out of *Euryanthe;* the orchestral scene painting from the sunrise and other original effects in *Oberon.*

Even Meyerbeer taught Wagner something more than the use of certain instruments, the bass clarinet, for instance. The old operatic speculator indubitably was responsible for Wagner's grand demands upon the scene painter and the stage carpenter. His pompous spectacles fired the younger man not only with *Rienzi.* They indubitably gave him the courage to create an operatic art that celebrated the new gold and power and magnificence, and was Grand Opera indeed. If the works of the one were sham, and those of the other poetry, it was only that Wagner realized what the other sought vainly all his life to attain, and was prevented by the stockbroker within.

And Chopin's harmonic feeling as well as Berlioz' orchestral

wizardry played a role in Wagner's artistic education. But for all
his incalculable indebtednesses, Wagner is the great initiator,
the compeller of the modern period. It is not only because he
summarized the old. It is because he began with force a revolution. In expressing the man of the nineteenth century, he
discarded the old major-minor system that had dominated
Europe so long. That system was the outcome of a conception of
the universe which set man apart from the remainder of nature,
placed him in a category of his own, and pretended that he was
both the center and the object of creation. For it called man the
consonance and nature the dissonance. The octave and the
fifth, the bases of the system, are of course, to be found only in
the human voice. They are, roughly, the difference between the
average male and the average female voice, and the difference
between the average soprano and alto. It is upon those intervals
that the C-major scale and its twenty-three dependents are
based. But with the coming of a conception that no longer
separated man from the rest of creation, and placed him in it as
a small part of it, brother to the animals and plants, to everything that breathes, the old scale could no longer completely
express him. The modulations of the noises of wind and water,
the infinite gradations and complexes of sound to be heard on
the planisphere, seemed to ask him to include them, to become
conscious of them and reproduce them. He required other more
subtle scales. And with Wagner the monarchy of the C-major
scale is at an end. *Tristan und Isolde* and *Parsifal* are constructed upon a chromatic scale. The old one has had to lose its
privilege, to resign itself to becoming simply one of a constantly
growing many. If this step is not a colossal one, it is still of
immense importance. The musical worthies who ran about
wringing their hands after the first performance of each of
Wagner's works, and lamented laws monstrously broken, and
traditions shattered, were, for once, right. They gauged correctly
from which direction the wind was blowing. They probably
heard, faintly piping in the distance, the pentatonic scales of
Moussorgsky and Debussy, the scales of Scriabin and Stravinsky

and Ornstein,* the barbarous, exotic, and African scales of the future, the one hundred and thirteen scales of which Busoni speaks. And today there are no longer musical rules, forbidden harmonies, dissonances. Siegfried has broken them along with Wotan's spear. East and West are near to merging once again. No doubt, had there been no Wagner, the change would have arrived nevertheless. However, it would have arrived more slowly. For what he did accomplish was the rapid emptying of the old wine that still remained in the wineskin, the preparation of the receptacle for the new vintage. He forced the new to put in immediate appearance.

The full impact of these reforms, the full might of Wagner, we of our generation doubtlessly never felt. They could have been felt only by the generation to whom Wagner first disclosed himself, the generation that attained maturity between 1850 and 1880. It was upon the men of those days that he did his full work of destruction and revival. It was in them he battered down walls. It was them he made to hear afresh, to stretch and grow in the effort to comprehend him. At the moment we encountered Wagner, his work was already something of a closed experience, something we were able to accept readily and with a certain ease because it had been accepted and assimilated by an entire world, and become part of the human organism. Its power was already slightly diminished. For instance, Wagner the musician was no longer able to make either Wagner the poet or Wagner the philosopher exist for us as they existed for the men of the earlier generation. Only Houston Stewart Chamberlain† still persisted in trying to stand upon the burning deck whence all the rest had fled. For us, it was obvious that if Wagner's work throned mightily it was because

* Leo Ornstein (1895–   ), American composer whose extremely dissonant music was championed by Rosenfeld in the 1910's and 1920's.

† Houston Stewart Chamberlain (1885–1927), son-in-law of Richard Wagner. Born in England, Chamberlain became a highly nationalistic student of German culture and wrote two books on Wagner.

of his music, and oftentimes in spite of his verse and his doctrine. For us, it was a commonplace that dramatic movement
and the filling up of scenes by the introduction of characters
who propose pointless riddles to one another and explain at
length what their names are not, are incompatible; that poetry
does not consist in disguising commonplace expressions in
archaic and alliterative and extravagant dress; that Wotan
displays no grasp of the essentials of Schopenhauer's philosophy
when he insists on dubbing Brünnhilde his Will.

And yet, whatever the difference, most of Wagner's might was
still in him when first we came to know his music. The spell in
which he had bound the generation that preceded ours was still
powerful. For us, too, there occurred the moments when Siegfried's cavernous forest depths first breathed on us, when for the
first time *Die Meistersinger* flaunted above the heads of all the
world the gonfalon of art, when for the first time we embarked
upon the shoreless golden sea of *Tristan und Isolde*. For us, too,
the name of Richard Wagner rang and sounded above all other
musical names. For us, too, he was a sort of sovereign lord of
music. His work appeared the climax toward which music had
aspired through centuries, and from which it must of necessity
descend again. Other, and perhaps purer work than his, existed,
we knew. But it seemed remote and less compelling, for all its
perfection. New music would arrive, we surmised. Yet we found
ourselves convinced that it would prove minor and unsatisfactory. For Wagner's music had for us an incandescence which
no other possessed. It was the magnetic spot of music. Its colors
blazed and glowed with a depth and ardor that seemed to set it
apart from other music as in an enchanted circle. It unlocked us
as did no other. We demanded just such orchestral movement,
just such superb gestures, just such warm, immersing floods, and
were fulfilled by them. That there would come a day when the
magnetism which it exerted on us would pass from it, and be
seen to have passed, seemed the remotest of possibilities.

For we accepted him with the world of our minority. For each
individual there is a period, varying largely in extent, during

which his existence is chiefly a process of imitation. In the
sphere of expression, that submission to authority extends well
over the entire period of gestation, well into the time of
physical maturity. There are few men, few great artists, even,
who do not, before attaining their proper idiom and gesture,
adopt those of their teachers and predecessors. Shakespeare
writes first in the style of Kyd and Marlowe, Beethoven in that
of Haydn and Mozart; Leonardo at first imitates Verrocchio.
And what the utilization of the manner of their predecessors is
to the artist, that the single devotion to Wagner was to us. For
he was not only in the atmosphere, not only immanent in the
lives led about us. His figure was vivid before us. Scarcely
another artistic personality was as largely upon us. There were
pictures, on the walls of music rooms, of graybearded, helmeted
warriors holding mailed blonde women in their arms, of queens
with golden ornaments on their arms leaning over parapets and
agitating their scarves, of women throwing themselves into the
sea upon which ghastly barks were dwindling, of oldish men
and young girls conversing teasingly through a window by a
lilac bush, that were Wagner. There were books with stories of
magical swans and hordes of gold and baleful curses, of phan-
tasmal storm ships and hollow hills and swords lodged in tree
trunks awaiting their wielders, of races of gods and giants and
grimy dwarfs, of guardian fires and potions of forgetfulness and
prophetic dreams and voices, that were Wagner. There were
adults who went to assist at these things of which one read, who
departed in state and excitement of an evening to attend
performances of *Die Walküre* and *Tristan und Isolde,* and who
spoke of these experiences in voices and manners different from
those in which they spoke, say, of the theater or the concert.
And there were magnificent and stately and passionate pieces
that drew their way across the pianoforte, that seized upon one
and made one insatiable for them. Long before we had actually
entered the opera house and heard one of Wagner's works in its
entirety, we belonged to him and knew his art our own. We
were born Wagnerians.

But of late a great adventure has befallen us. What once seemed the remotest of possibilities has actually taken place. We who were born and grew under the sign of Wagner have witnessed the twilight of the god. He has receded from us. He has departed from us into the relative distance into which during his hour of omnipotence he banished all other composers.

He has been displaced. A new music has come into being, and drawn near. Forms as solid and wondrous and compelling as his are about us. Little by little, during the last years, so gradually that it has been almost unbeknown to us, our relationship to him has been changing. Something within us has moved. Other musicians have been working their way in upon our attention. Other works have come to seem as vivid and deep of hue, as wondrous and compelling as his once did. Gradually the musical firmament has been reconstellating itself. For long, we were unaware of the change, thought ourselves still opposite Wagner, thought the rays of his genius still as direct upon us as ever they were. But of late so wide has the distance become that we have awakened sharply to the change. Of a sudden, we seem to ourselves like travelers who, having boarded by night a liner fast to her pier and fallen asleep amid familiar objects, beneath the well-known beacons and towers of the port, waken suddenly in broadest daylight scarcely aware the vessel has been gotten under way, and find the scene completely transformed, find themselves out on ocean and glimpse, dwindling behind them, the harbor and the city in which apparently but a moment since they had lain enclosed.

It is the maturing of a generation that has produced the change. For each generation the works of art produced by its members have a distinct importance. Out of them, during their time, there sparks the creative impulse. For every generation is something of a unit.

> *Chaque génération d'hommes*
> *Germant du champs maternel en sa saison,*

Garde en elle un secret commun, un certain noeud
*dans la profonde contexture de son bois . . .**

Claudel assures us through the mask of *Tête d'Or*. And the
resemblances between works produced independently of each
other within the space of a few years, generally so much greater
than those that exist between any one work of one age and any
of another, bears him out. The styles of Palestrina and Vittoria,
which are obviously dissimilar, are nevertheless more alike than
those of Palestrina and Bach, Vittoria and Handel; just as
those of Bach and Handel, dissimilar as they are, have a greater
similarity than that which exists between those of Bach and
Mozart, of Handel and Haydn. And so, for the men of a single
period the work produced during their time is a powerful
encouragement to self-realization, to the espousal of their destiny, to the fulfilment of their life. For the motion of one part
of a machine stirs all the others. And there is a part of every
man of a generation in the work done by the other members of
it. The men who fashion the art of one's own time make one's
proper experiment, start from one's own point of departure,
dare to be themselves and oneself in the face of the gainsaying
of the other epochs. They are so belittling, so condescending, so
nay-saying and deterring, the other times and their masterpieces! They are so unsympathetic, so strange and grand and
remote! They seem to say, "Thus must it be; this is form; this is
beauty; all else is superfluous." Who goes to them for help and
understanding is like one who goes to men much older, men of
different habits and sympathies, in order to explain himself,
and finds himself disconcerted and diminished instead, glimpses
a secret jealousy and resentment beneath the mask. But the
adventure of encountering the artist of one's own time is that of

* Paul Claudel, *The Head of Gold:*
  "Every generation of men
   Budding in its season from the maternal field
   Keeps a common secret, a kind of knot
    in the deepest texture of its wood . . ."

finding the most marvelous of aids, corroboration. It is to meet one who has been living one's life, and thinking one's thoughts, and facing one's problems. It is to get reassurance, to accept oneself, to beget courage to express one's self in one's own manner.

And we of our generation have finally found the music that is so creatively infecting for us. We have found the music of the post-Wagnerian epoch. It is our music. For we are the offspring of the generation that assimilated Wagner. We, too, are the reaction from Wagner. Through the discovery we have come to learn that music can give us sensations different than those given us by Wagner's. We have learned what it is to have music say to us, "It is thus, after all, that you feel." We have finally come to recognize that we require of music forms, proportions, accents different from Wagner's; orchestral movement, color, rhythms, not in his. We have learned that we want an altogether different stirring of the musical caldron. A song of Moussorgsky's or Ravel's, a few measures of *Pelléas* or *Le Sacre du Printemps*, a single fine moment in a sonata of Scriabin's, or a quartet or suite of Bloch's, give us a joy, an illumination, a satisfaction that little of the older music can equal. For our own moment of action is finally at hand.

So Wagner has retreated and joined the company of composers who express another day than our own. The sovereignty that was in him has passed to other men. We regard him at present as the men of his own time might have regarded Beethoven and Weber. Still, he will always remain the one of all the company of the masters closest to us. No doubt he is not the greatest of the artists who have made music. Colossal as were his forces, colossal as were the struggles he made for the assumption of his art, his musical powers were not always able to cope with the tasks he set himself. The unflagging inventive power of a Bach or a Haydn, the robustness of a Handel or a Beethoven, the harmonious personality of a Mozart, were things he could not rival. He is even inferior, in the matter of style, to men like Weber and Debussy. There are many moments, one finds, when his scores show that there was nothing in his mind, and that he simply went through the routine of composition. Too often he permitted the system of leading-motifs to relieve him of the necessity of creating. Too often, he made of his art a purely mental game. His emotion, his creative genius were far more intermittent, his breath far less long than one once imagined. Some of the earlier works have commenced to fade rapidly, irretrievably. At present one wonders how it is possible that one once sat entranced through performances of *The Flying Dutchman* and *Tannhäuser*. *Lohengrin* begins to seem a little brutal, strangely Prussian lieutenant with its militaristic trumpets, its abuse of the brass. One finds oneself choosing even among the acts of *Tristan und Isolde,* finding the first far inferior to the poignant, magnificent third. Sometimes, one glimpses a little too long behind his work not the heroic agonist, but the man who loved to languish in mournful salons, attired in furred dressing gowns.

Indeed, if Wagner seems great it is chiefly as one of the most delicate of musicians. It is the lightness of his brush stroke that makes us marvel at the third act of *Tristan,* the first scene of the *Walküre.* It is the delicacy of his fancy, the lilac fragrance pervading his inventions, that enchants us in the second act of *Die Meistersinger.* Through the score of *Parsifal* there seem to pass angelic forms and wings dainty and fragile and silver-shod as those of Beardsley's *Morte d'Arthur.*

But the debt we owe him will always give him a vast importance in our eyes. The men of today, all of them, stand directly on his shoulders. It is doubtful whether any of us, the passive public, would be here today as we are, were it not for his music.

The Nazis and *Die Meistersinger*

DIRECTLY AFTER THE NEWS that the Nazis had captured the government of Germany reached us, we learned that on the day of their *coup d'état* they had commanded the Berlin Opera to perform *Die Meistersinger von Nürnberg*. To those of us eager to see American artists, by musical or poetic means, project a symbol of the national idea as magnificent as the symbol of the German superindividual entity constituted by Wagner's comic masterpiece, this latter revelation brought an additional shock.

Various phenomena indicate that such an American expression is within the bounds of possibility and may actually appear during the next few years. And the image of an audience of Nazi porkers self-righteously taking in the concluding scene of the music drama, identifying their sinister Fascist state with the bright democratic order figured there, adopting the composer as their prophet and justifying their ways to men with his vision, made us wonder whether the comparable American expression would be the boon to civilization we had hoped it might prove, and might not turn out as susceptible of brutal perversion as this fragrant German work.

That the Nazis' identification of their national idea with the one *Die Meistersinger* symbolizes is false and perversive, is not to be doubted. Of course, the music drama is definitely German in idea and in expression, the most traditionally German of all Wagner's compositions. And still where the gods are, there surely is merriment today over Hitler and his followers' attempt to gild their Fascist order by identifying it with the relationship, the bond, the inner coherence and order among the German forces which Wagner felt and expressed, and which, after hovering coronally over the work, seems actually to descend into the matter at the close and display itself through the massed exultant figures on the stage, and in the music. And it meant no tyranny, no dictatorship whether of a monarch, a class, a faction, or the collectivity. *Die Meistersinger,* true, is a nationalistic work, like its predecessor, Weber's *Der Freischütz,* and its Russian coeval, Moussorgsky's *Boris Godunov*—certainly the greatest of the pieces that express the sheerly German life. But the social bond and order it embodies and displays is a spontaneous one, that of a free society of men with their soil sacred in their midst, in this instance the order latent among and adumbrated by Germans at their perihelion of freedom and power in the 1860's. The prelude outlines the idea. Stiff, ponderous, bourgeois, militaristic, pedantic, idealistic, the essences are full of malice and sentiment and strength. They conflict with each other, they quarrel and snarl: suddenly, at the signal of some marshaling power that seems to rise from among them out the depths, their conflict ends, and they unite in an orderly, mighty, aspiring, polyphonic progress. The drama but expands that idea, augmenting and extending the expression of the chivalric, bourgeois, plebeian, massive, pedantic, and idealistic Germany and its potential concordance in a free fellowship of spirited and aspiring knights and burghers, artists and people, against the background of the Free City of Nuremberg at its highest.

All nationalistic art, that of other musicians and poets as well as that of Wagner, is the product of individualizing, democratic times and movements and of individuals. All nationalistic art is expressive of the national superindividual entity at the moment that entity offers to form itself freely in the union of individuals —a formation inevitably flowing from the inner liberty of the individual. In itself this sort of art constitutes an emergent individual's fraternal embrace of those freemen, present and future, a circumstance that in part accounts for the peculiarity of the form of nationalistic pieces of music. This is frequently a variation or an expansion of some traditional musical form or musical forms of the folk it expresses, or one inclusive of variations and expansions and even citations of such a form or forms; and a result of the sometimes unconscious, sometimes deliberate, but natural tendency of the composer to express his national essences, sometimes humorously, sometimes ironically, always affectionately, through molds related to the musical ones that have helped reveal these forces to himself, and which he has unconsciously absorbed. Thus, while the libretto of *Die Meistersinger* contains the figure of the old German poet Hans Sachs and echoes the rules of the Guild of Mastersingers and includes a poem of the historical Sachs, the score reflects "three hundred years of German music," from the chorales of the Reformation through the polyphony of Bach, the shakes of Handel, and Beethoven—the first of the *Diabelli Variations*—and Weberesque flourishes for the violins, up to Wagner's own *Tristan*.

And just as every nationalistic work of art constitutes an emergent individual's fraternal embrace of the past and present and future freemen of his nation, so too it constitutes his embrace of the superindividual entity emergent among them all. Spengler indicates as much. At least, he assures us that nationalistic ideas appear among a people at the period of its life when, in consequence of a growing individualism, it is removing its allegiance from the person of the monarch and transferring it to an idea which symbolizes the relationships of its members, and to the superindividual entity born of and inclusive of them all; nationalistic art but expressing that national idea and unity through form. Thus it is republican art: and various instances of it, instances other than Wagner's, too, lend substance to this thesis of the historian. A great literary nationalistic expression, the chronicle plays of Shakespeare, with their apotheosis of the "island set in silver," significantly date from a period of English life where, after the defeat of the great Armada, only the personal popularity of the reigning monarch, Elizabeth, checked the arrogation on the part of the Commons of the supreme rule to itself. With her death, the struggle with the Crown began; and not forty years after the composition of *Richard II* and the rest of the chronicles, the English had decapitated their king and proclaimed a commonwealth. If thereafter they returned to constitutional monarchical rule, the doctrine of the "divine right of kings" was nonetheless dead among them forever, and by 1688 with it the last vestiges of absolute monarchy. Toward this English republicanism—at least that of the Commonwealth, elder brother of the American with its general principle of the equality of all men—the chronicles may even be thought contributory, since the playwright who brings the figures of kings on to the stage, letting them confess their inmost thoughts to the audience and making one of them declare, "Uneasy lies the head that wears a crown," puts every one of his spectators in the way of conceiving, and thus potentially becoming, a king, and feeling himself in some respects superior to him. Wyndham Lewis has called Shakespeare probably most justly, "the king-killer."—The date of another great nationalistic drama, *Wilhelm Tell* by Schiller, coincides for its part with the collapse of feudalism in western Germany during the revolutionary years. Its author, incidentally, was an honorary citizen of the first French republic. Still another great literary expression of nationalistic ideas, the writings of Maurice Barrès, dates mainly from the 1880's and 1890's, the decades during which the French as a whole were definitely withdrawing their allegiance from the houses both of Bourbon and of Bonaparte and affirming their republic for the third and final time.

This connection is indicated also by the circumstances surrounding the production of nationalistic music from Weber to De Falla. The first nationalistic opera, by virtue of its definitely German feeling, its German forest feeling, and its expression of this experience in a form inclusive of German-Bohemian folk songs and arias and choruses in the folk-song style, was Weber's *Der Freischütz:* the whole nationalistic movement in music being originally German and impelled to a degree by Herder's critical work. Now *Der Freischütz* dates from the years when, disappointed by their sovereigns' repudiation of the liberal pledges made them during the wars of liberation against Napoleon, the German peoples were traversed by republican tendencies. The work's first performance took place on the fifth anniversary of the battle of Waterloo, probably by no means fortuitously, and the coincidence was remarked. The piece in itself was an expression of the dawning feeling of self-reliance: it is significant that the *deus ex machina* of the finale is not the prince but a venerable anchorite "who dwells in the woods." A subsequent body of nationalistic art, in this instance Polish, the work of Chopin, was also synchronous with a liberal and republican movement, that of Polish intolerance of Russian despotism: and its idealized national dance rhythms have conveyed revolutionary-republican ideas to many of its audiences. The nationalistic music of the Russian Five* also dates from the liberal decades of Russian life when, in consequence of the reforms of Alexander II—themselves to a degree inspired by the broad human revelations of such Russian artists as Gogol and Turgenev—the Russian people for the first time began to feel its fatherland its own. It is significant that while originally patronized by the court, the music of the Five fell from grace as the reaction triumphed: Rimsky complains that *Mlada,* the first of his operas produced during the extremely reactionary reign of Alexander III, was snubbed by the powers, the Czarina and her children alone assisting at one of the matinee performances of the new piece. And De Falla's nationalistic Spanish music but anticipated by a few years the proclamation of the second Spanish republic and the initiation of democracy.

Wagner himself, at least the Wagner of the first three parts of the *Ring,* with their recapitulations of the old Teutonic pantheism, and of *Tristan* and the consciously Germanic *Meistersinger,* was, of course, a liberal, a revolutionary, and an anarchist. All five of these works of his date from the period before the patronage of Ludwig II of Bavaria, the successes of Bismarck in unifying most of the German peoples under their thirty-odd monarchs, and the influence of Cosima had recon-

---

* Balakirev, Moussorgsky, Borodin, Rimsky-Korsakov, and Cui, a group of Russian composers who drew much of their material from Russian life, folk motifs, and history.

ciled him with monarchism. It is well known that the tetralogy
was conceived by him during his revolutionary days in Dresden
prior to 1848, that the figure of Siegfried was partially inspired
by his friend the anarchist Bakunin, that the Brünnhilde of the
"second day" was the New Woman, and thus, since Woman was
always somewhat the Race for Wagner, and the race feminine—
das menschlich-weibliche—the free new people. The idea of *Die
Meistersinger* had come to him in its first vague form while he
was reading Gervinus' extremely nationalistic-democratic *History of German Literature* in 1845. As late as 1859, while he was
completing *Tristan* and when the idea of the *Meistersinger*
must have been in process of final clarification, he wrote to
Mathilde Wesendonck that he was for France and Sardinia in
the current war (Napoleon III's for the liberation of Italy),
since Austria and Germany were the contemporaneously regres-
sive and reactionary powers. It is noteworthy also that while he
was composing the prelude of the *Meistersinger* at Biebrich on
the Rhine, his eyes were drawn continually to the distant
prospect of Mayence. He does not tell us what he felt as he
gazed out, and perhaps he did not clearly know; but for us the
reference is significant: like Nuremberg, *das goldene Mainz* had
been a free city.

And evidence internal to his musical comedy, the action
itself, impresses on us the relation of its idea not only to that of
the liberal and democratic state but to a state the very opposite
of the Nazis' totalitarian one and its brutal tyranny of a class, a
faction, and its domination of the individual by the collectivity.
Let us briefly glance at the action. It exhibits a knight, Walther, who comes to Nuremberg of his own will to become the
citizen of the free city. It repudiates the authority of the past,
the "rules" of the mastersingers' guild, and glorifies experiment; if there is any authority, it says, it resides in the spirit,
alike in the poet and in the people. An individual emergent
from the people, Hans Sachs, represents that spirit, indeed
"includes the whole" within himself; and, generously enacting
it, induces the final union of all its representatives in the light

of the great day before the walls. The grand chorus in the third
act is set to the words in which the historical Sachs hailed
Martin Luther, the asserter of the inviolacy of the private
conscience and the personality, the prophet of symbiosis. At the
conclusion of the drama, Sachs bids the people look for a unity,
no longer recoverable in a royalty deluded by false and foreign
ideas of majesty, but in the honor of the German masters, the
German artists, and German art—we have said that the work of
art is one of the great potential agents of relationship among a
democratic people. The Holy Roman Empire, symbol of auto-
cratic rule and authority external to the human being, might, if
it would, fall to dust. The good spirits would nonetheless favor
the nation. The curtain falls on a scene of triumphant concord
among spirited individuals and a people that situates the
national idea at the inevitably single goal of the aspirations of
free Germans.

Indeed, if any national idea is different from the Nazis', it is
this: and with it all the national ideas that are the content of
nationalistic art. If when rightly seen they make for the establishment of any political state, it is ultimately toward (dreadful
name) the "anarchist commune," the commune of individuals
who neither rule others nor are ruled by them, and, freely
active—aware of their embodiments of the whole in which they
live and move and have their being—are the state and enact it.
Intrinsic symbols of the superindividual entity which exists
among and over individuals, like Wagner's Sachs they bring
other individuals into harmony with that entity and thus give
life to all. And the individual ultimately is the man who wants
neither to rule nor to be ruled, and for whom work and
workmanlike quality and the perfect function of the whole of
which he is an organic part are ends in themselves; and who, no
matter what mental and physical distinctions nature has raised
between him and other individuals and whatever his job, freely
enacts the whole in continual consciousness of the whole within
and without himself. His city, his land, alone are free.

For all artists are fundamentally "anarchists." Their intuitions reveal to them a continually changing order, and their embodiment of the symbols of this continually changing order adjusts them spontaneously to it. They touch material selflessly and shape it in accordance with its own nature and the idea to which it conforms; and work is a joy to them, an end in itself. And the social order to which they are natively directed could easily be an order based on the private ownership of the means of production, and the operation of those means for profit, in which labor got its just reward, and social, political, and intellectual advantages were shared by all.

Such, then, is the social order adumbrated by *Die Meistersinger* and other great nationalistic pieces. And into our faces there stares the truth that these liberating symbols of the free community can be misunderstood and made, like *Die Meistersinger,* to appear to gild a state the very contrary of the one related to the idea they body forth. There is the incident of the Nazis and that very piece—a sinister one, for what was involved was not only the attempt to make a great and representative German composer appear the prophet of a state which, the tyranny of a faction, of the collectivity over the individual, seeks to turn society into a mass of mechanical parts moved by a superior power—in Fascism, the rule, the organization, is all, the individual nothing; there is "regimentation in the place of initiative, authority in place of self-government, dogma in the place of experiments, obedience in the place of responsibility, submission in the place of conscience." (This is the sort of state which Wagner could not but have scorned, for both in art and life he was one of the most self-reliant, experimental of men: and nicknamed himself *Freidank*.) What was also involved was an attempt to turn Wagner into an academy, to make of his work a sort of musical dogma, a new set of rules and prescriptions which would serve to forbid musical experiment and in this way, too, suppress the self-regulating individual by depriving him of his power to express himself. Thus those of us in America who had been cheered by the signs that great American nationalistic works of art, projecting the national idea

through musical or poetic means or both, and providing us with
the basis for a superior unity, were within the bounds of
possibility and might actually prove the event of the next few
years, have been compelled to ask ourselves whether the possibility that these expressions might not serve even viler perver-
sions of their ideas than that contrived by the Nazis with
Wagner's comic opera, does not provide a good reason for
urging the artists to desist from their attempts. But the reply
has always been negative. In the first place, the motive making
for nationalistic art is a good and an irrepressible one. In the
second, it seems possible that intelligence and perspicuity might
make the ideas and symbols of this kind of art unpervertible.
What has been the trouble with many of the nationalistic works
produced in the past has been the carelessness and trustfulness
with which they have been given to the world by their authors.
In expressing the national idea, the authors have failed to
envisage the chances for misunderstanding lying in their paths,
and thus failed to guard against such misunderstanding by
making their ideas so plain, so definite, that none can mistake
them and use their works as weapons against their own objec-
tives. They were thus a little less than highly intelligent:
Wagner himself, for all his genius, was a very naïve man: one of
the greatest of musical poets, chock-full of powerful and delicate musical feeling, but relatively simple-minded. One has but
to read his writings and to compare the prolixity and slowness
and looseness of his form with the far terser, quicker forms of
such moderns as Debussy, Schoenberg, Berg, and for that matter
the later Beethoven, to become aware of it. Hence, like his
fellows, he doubtless imagined that the ideas he was communicating in his music, and the symbols with which he communicated them, were intelligible to the least of men: and that blind
confidence has proved, at least from the viewpoint of the
present hour, to have been fatal.

Precisely how the new poets and dramatists and musicians,
those of present America in particular, are to go about making
their expressions of the national idea unmistakable, we unfor-

tunately cannot say. They alone can discover how, if a way is indeed discoverable. We can merely fervently warn them that, in engaging in conveying to the nation the national idea as moments of energy and freedom constitute it, they must be with caution bold and speak with greatest clearness—in consciousness of the immensity of the profit to life that might flow from utmost clarity, and the immensity of the mischief to it that failure of the strongest lucidity might potentiate.

The Tragedy of Gustav Mahler

SOMEWHAT as Dante and his guide stood before certain damned in Hell do we stand before the failed endeavors of Gustav Mahler. We cannot pass these hulking haggard symphonies and songs as we pass by other failures offered us by the concert seasons. Stale and tired and scarce living as these musics are, they nevertheless, each time we encounter any one of them, make us to stop still in pity and turn distressedly about them. For they are monuments of anguished aborted life, like indeed to torture-masses devised by the imagination of a ferocious medieval god for the punishment of transgressors against him. They call before the vision the blocks of ice in the circle of traitors in the Inferno that contain each its wretched congealed soul. They, too, these dusty and feeble instrumental piles, are in some strange terrible way part living. Underneath the heaped banalities, beneath false Beethoven and conscious naïvetés and unfresh lyricism, there writhes a vein of living green, and struggles piteously for release. We sense a caked and buried face; hear parched lips and cracked laryngeal chords straining to frame speech. The hoarse and infinitely fatigued voice is seeking to sob, to pray, to bless, but its tone breaks and rasps and faints in the dust. It seems to be begging something of us, entreating us to do something. But what it is it demands of us we do not know, or, if we guess, do not know at all how to meet and gratify it.

The fact that the composer of Mahler's nine symphonies and many songs was a Prospero among conductors, a profound and magical interpreter of Beethoven and of Wagner, a poet who made other orchestral leaders seem pedestrian, is not what makes his efforts at creation appear torture-blocks in our eyes. It is not pity that stirs us. We are neither stirred nor wrung by the scores of Weingartner, also a great conductor and an unsuccessful composer. What hurts us when Mahler's works are performed is, that his miscarriages refer always to a living impulse behind them, to an inventive power not unrelated to his interpretative; that each gargantuan symphony and song cycle bears evidence to the failure of a creative surge to realize itself in any solid form. Something did go down in battle in Mahler's compositions that was noble and high, and that we would gladly have seen triumphant. Even in the pompous *Kapellmeistermusik* of his Fifth, Sixth, and Seventh Symphonies, sharp vestiges of originality pierce through the billowing rubble. Sometimes, it is nothing more than his miraculous gift of instrumentation that is green among the charred ruins; and all that reconciles us in all the world to the man, are some moments when the music permits us to observe his usage of the modern orchestra, so much more simple and reserved and sharp than Strauss's; grants us the pleasure of hearing the cutting razor edge of a band in which brass and reeds predominate, of feeling the nasal, astringent, brilliant quality of his favorite daring combinations of wood and trumps.

Sometimes, to this salvaged joy another adds itself. Mahler manages at times, despite secondhandedness, suspiciousness of thematic material, to establish well a definite mood. Even if we blush a little at his themes, we feel, say, the excitement of the nightly, death-haunted bacchanal, in the first section of *Das Lied von der Erde*. At intervals, the atmosphere of a landscape is fixed; the world darkens visibly as a solitary oboe executes its repeated quaver; and for a brief while, we taste something of the food the composer intended setting before us, know his sick yearning for life, his loneliness, the bitter savor of ashes on his lips as he waits alone for death. Or, a shimmer of the living world is caught in a splinter of mirror, and we feel in Mahler's music the nerve-weariness of men in our time, or get a naturalistic picture of shrilling workpeople on holiday parade to the parks, or whiff old-world wholeheartedness while a horn sings as sings the posthorn in German forests. Or, a passage of sustained music suddenly makes its appearance; the interlude of the last section of *Das Lied von der Erde,* with its harshly croaking clarinets and horns, its groaning, mordant polyphony; or one of the gallows-humorous scherzi, half scurrilous, half fantastic, so original with Mahler. And for an instant we are half-reconciled with the legend that the man was a great composer.

But the living stuff is lost in the great unfilled voids of the canvases. A small power is wrecked in the attempt to develop a space entirely too great for the reach of the undertaker. As forms, things, these symphonies crumble and do not live. The living breath does not run through the instrumental masses and make them with each tone they give, sculpt some great reality that was in the heart of the composer, and that he had to discover to the world. The great embracing feeling that descended from the head of a Beethoven or a Wagner into their fingertips and through these into the cohorts of instruments, we know, did not succeed in leaving Mahler's cranium. We guess his intentions from his programs and his reported conversations. We guess them from certain associations revealed by the themes and instruments themselves.

But while there is always in Mahler something present for the eye; there is most often nothing for the ear. His works are like vast spineless ships that look majestical enough while they lie high on the beach, but that break in two or capsize or sink as soon as one attempts to float them on the sea. Mahler is helpless on nearly every page. With all his prodigious orchestral technique he cannot touch. There is always the beginning of something in his scores. His vast and Bruckner-like themes heave on with terrific stride, then break down suddenly, and there is a void, while the band makes certain developments or roundings-out that have no existence for the sense. A song begins; a few notes are sweet; then, suddenly, there is a banal, stale note, from which one turns as from a sour breath. Such are the turns in the "Chorus Mysticus" of the Eighth Symphony, on the words "Das unbeschreibliche, hier wird es getan"; in the twelfth and thirteenth bars of the last movement of the Third, where Mahler attempts to round out his pseudo-Beethovenish adagio theme; in the second section of *Das Lied von der Erde*, where the singer gives "Ich hab' Erquickung Not"; in innumerable other spots of the score.

Or, he begins a broad flowing movement as in the finale of the Third Symphony, and loses momentum. He begins endless recapitulations. He repeats over and over again sweet cadences or harmonies on which he has happened; lingers over them, fond and narcissistic as a mother over the antics of a spoiled child. When he has to conclude, under pain of becoming a bore even to his own patient self, his ending is quite arbitrary, a suddenly stitched-on close, with much brilliant brass and percussion. And, so, the positive achievements of his talent are counterbalanced and made naught overwhelmingly by his banalities. The gallows-humorous scherzi are followed by the sort of trumpet tunes which are very nice for the servant girl when she goes out Sunday afternoons. A fine bit of scene painting, a passage of poignant music right off the wheel of modern life, is suddenly dragged down by a "consoling" theme of organ-grinder beauty. Whole movements palpably "faked," written without sincere feeling, as the third, fourth, and fifth of *Das Lied*, spoil what pleasure one can extract from those sincerely felt. And even where there is some success in representation, the testimony of haggard senses and tired pulses which exists in everything Mahler brought forth, leaves one with a painful sense of failed life. Not even the energy and affection lavished by conductor Mengelberg on every one of Mahler's scores he essays; nor even the unflagging effort to relieve the intention and make the hollow music communicate what Mahler wanted to say, can lift these sinking bulks.

It went to parch in the wilderness, Mahler's vine of life, because, whether or not he was aware fully of his motive, his work was built about his own person. Mahler's center was not in his composition, much as he thought it there. It remained always within himself; and although a vivid impulse drove him to selfless expression, a far stronger wrenched the impulse into service to an arid egoism. The man was slave, more than ever he guessed, to a desire of setting his own figure amid the symbols and panoply of greatness. He needed the public to feel certain glorious things about him, toward him; to take him and place him by its reverence and love and admiration among the immortals, among the serene figures grouped in the Valhalla of musicians about Beethoven. It was, in spite of his belief, Beethoven that he wanted to be more than Gustav Mahler; for he needed bitterly that the public perceive in him the benign symphonist, the great heart-whole lover of men; he wanted the love of men to come out to him, he wanted to give them something that would force from them toward himself a glowing stream of affection. And this motive was always uppermost in his breast when he approached his worktable.

For Mahler was, there cannot be question, one of those unfortunate persons who cannot center their interest in another human breast, and give themselves completely in love. He was, certainly, one of those unfortunates for whom life inevitably must represent a struggle toward an ambitiously conceived goal, must have a definite egocentric purpose: because the living of life itself is so devoid of deep satisfactoriness to them. It was easy enough for Goethe to declare, "Es kommt offenbar im Leben aufs Leben, und nicht auf ein Resultat desselben an."* For things in themselves were nourishing to him. But for poor Gustav Mahler, life was a waste, a procession of disappointments, a garden whose smoldering fruits turned ashen in his mouth. Precisely what it was that kept him from properly slaking his thirst at the brook that runs right through the front

* " 'It often happens in life that nothing reaches a final form.' "

dooryard of all the world, we cannot more than guess about. The man's confession that of the impressions which he tried to realize in his music the greater portion was received during the first five years of his existence, turns one's guesses in the direction of a hurt done him in infancy.

It is not to be entertained, that he, any more than any other normally intelligent child, entered the world incapacitated to fulfill himself toward his fellows. His yearning, so perpetually green in him, for the days when he was a nursling on the Bohemian plain; the hearkening back to the impressions of infancy that might have come to the bright little boy of the poor tavernkeepers; his visions of death, all his hours, as a return homeward, an entrance into the secret inner life of the universe, are not, we suspect, merely the fantastic thinking of a man who, having never possessed a capacity for living, consoles himself by glorifying the state closest to prenatal existence. In their sincerity, their earnestness, they seem rather more indications of the fact that the bliss of this time had been so very intense, so inordinately sensitizing that the attachment to his own infantile nature became overstrong in the man; that it displaced zest for adventure, and made the pain of maturity too unbearable for hearty acceptation. It seems strange to consider that the man whom one knew as a harried, bitterly compressed-mouthed conductor, a tortured head cut loose from the body, should once have been an infant clutched too hard to the breast of a woman. But such we are forced to see him; it is only in this fashion that we are able to explain his crippledness. All children meet the world, death, and the devil as they grow. Only, in certain, some inherent, unbroken toughness which nature gave them at birth asserts itself, and closes the wounds inflicted by the grisly companions. But in Mahler, the ability to find the way to men had been enfeebled by oversensitization; and the wounds inflicted on him become fatal.

And it would, indeed, have required, that he might meet and repel the enemies in wait for him, an almost inordinately stalky toughness in the inner column of young Mahler's spirit. For

Mahler was born a Jew. And to be born a Jew, particularly in the Austria of the 1860's, was not intensely conducive to the sustainment of that fresh faith in life, that relaxed love of men, from which great song springs. It was, on the contrary, a circumstance full of baleful encouragement to those who had been hurt, to button tighter and hug ever closer to themselves the ancient gray overcoat of fear. The quick was menaced by the sharp swords of the repressed but very living hostility of the surrounding population; and to expose it was to invite almost inevitable pain; to have more rocks thrown on the wavering column of confidence in self, satisfaction in self, faith in the greenness of life; to have ever heavier chains hung on the arms when they moved of instinct in the great embracing rhythms. For whatever in the growing lad wanted cause for not projecting his interest, his love into the objective world, and fulfilling himself, there waited (as it waits in every land on every child of Jews) the distrust, the antagonism, the exclusiveness, of alien peoples, with its gift of the sentiment of inner unworth, of tribal inferiority. And this fact must have helped arrest the already inhibited spontaneity of the heart, with unresting counsel of niggardliness.

And then, the atmosphere of the Jewish community itself does not make free, healthy living, easy. Generation had bequeathed to generation, in a sort of convulsive laying on of hands, a nervous tension, a sort of clamp and suspension, in the entrails, a strain all over the body, legacy of centuries of uncertain, difficult existence. Even in the Austria of the sixties, as in the America of the new century, where fear of physical persecution does not always press, the necessities of life still forced and do force a sort of unhealthful wakefulness in the Jew, a fear of the sense, a distrust of relaxation, a lurid sort of consciousness. The Germans and Czechs about Mahler's home, for example, could let go their wakefulness; could let themselves down into the landscape as cattle let themselves down upon the sward to munch. They, the farmpeople, could accept the moment, drain it fearlessly and irresponsibly as they drained their steins.

Mahler, the unrooted, the inheritor of trading-wits, could never do so.

Besides, the world into which Mahler issued in career, had little power to make good the wrong. The sudden industrialization of Germany and of Austria, the strongly "Americanizing" tendency of society, had taken the accent from the quality of things and placed them on the quantity of them. The artist has to do with the preservation of the quality of life; and the artist was not invited by a time that had no spiritual values. Or, if he was, he was invited only to stimulate nerves wearied by a harried, empty existence, to give sensations to folk incapable of procuring them for themselves. Had Mahler been strong, it is possible he might have resisted the world, as other men have done. But he was weak, and so he could not help being weakened further by the vulgar atmosphere in which he had to share. Publicity was the mother of the Muses. All the world was a stage; never might one forget the presence of an audience. All about him was a frenzied Bismarckianization of music; a St. Vitus dance of concerts, operas, festivals, premières, nether-Rhenish music debauches, Napoleonic careers modeled on misconceptions of the life of Wagner and of Nietzsche, newspaper logrolling by music publishers, Richard Strauss, a great externalized music life. Poison must have come into the man with every breath, much as he would have avoided it.

And thus the writing of "great" music became the end of Mahler's days. Since he had not within him the power to satisfy himself in living; since he could never quite be a man in the street; he turned to composition, turned to it more and more to indemnify himself as he aged. Since he had the rudiments of creativity in him, and could feel the immensity of the emotional release which Beethoven and which Wagner had gotten from their art; since he himself got an enormous release in presenting their works; he commenced, with logical illogicality, aping the external attributes of their art in hopes of gaining the power of self-expression that had been theirs. He set out to become "great." For being sterile, he supposed that their ability to love, to create, had come to them through a power over musical means; and supposed that if he made the gesture of grandeur, and if the public responded to that gesture as it responded to the music of the masters, he would achieve what a kinder nature had given them and not given him. So he took his talent, and began forcing it to flesh arbitrarily conceived schemes. Perceiving the philosophical weight of Beethoven and Wagner, he began searching for an aprioristic metaphysical orientation. It was a literary composer, in the bad sense, that he became. His ideas were not permitted to come to him as musical shapes and lines. It was rather more as autobiographical material, as philosophic theory, as haunting and vaguely outlined emotion, that work seems first to have entered his consciousness. The process of music-making seems to have been a secondary one; a turning of concepts *into* music with the assistance of a prodigious musical technique and a virtuosic orchestral sense. That, the strange unfreshness of his idiom demonstrates. Beethoven, Schubert, Mendelssohn, Wagner, Bruckner, Brahms, haunt his pages. For, feeling nothing so much as the desire to feel, to be creative, to be musicful; he perforce thought the thoughts that had already come into the world. He was the sentimentalist, searching out emotion for its own sake, and luxuriating in it. And one feels always that, whenever he did manage to achieve emotions, he never let them do anything to him, really; and that there was something unhealthily wakeful in him watching himself under the influence of feeling; prodding him on to register an idea which might be of use to him in composition; pouncing on him at every quiver of his nerves with the cry, "Now, at last, you are giving me something which I can use in creating!" Never does he seem entirely lost. Even his naïveté, his *Glockenbimbamblümchen* vein, wants a complete ingenuousness. The childlike tones are hollow; there is something haggard and worn in the pretended overflow of spirits. He is putting on clothes, we see; he is trying to feel so that something will happen to him and make him like the strapping and heart-fresh and solid Germans who made the style of the folk songs.

He had all the nonartist's obsession with technical processes. His scores seem written with a view to the work of the pedantic analyzer; he was asking the pedants to crown him magister. His symphonies are stiff-jointed with a sort of formal classicism. They have not so much the spirit as the mannerism of the great classic form-givers. On the engraved page, the writing looks like Haydn's, like Beethoven's. But it wants indeed the necessity, the athleticism, of theirs. And, since he could not feel, he took to making music by brute force; drove his orchestra to climaxes with sadistic vehemence, as though he would ravish an aesthetic emotion from the hearers. He called for immense apparatus, reaching a ridiculous apotheosis in the *Symphonie der Tausend* in the effort to achieve greatness through enormity of means. He dragged by the hair into his works poems of Goethe and Nietzsche, of Klopstock and Rhabanus Maurus, as well as lyrics from *Das Knaben Wunderhorn,* in the hope of making these giants labor for him. One of his commentators marvels at the daring with which Mahler, in his Third Symphony, goes from a setting of Nietzsche's "Drunken Song" to a setting of a folk lyric. *Sancta Simplicitas!* Poor Mahler would have gone from a setting of St. Francis' *Hymn to the Sun* to a setting of the Pennsylvania timetable, had he thought the deed enormous and revolutionary and creative. He would have written a solo for the Saint Esprit, had he thought it possible to persuade that potentate to participate in the performance of one of his symphonies. His was indeed a piling of many suffering Pelions on many indignant Ossas.

And still, we cannot dismiss the man with a wave of the hand. Sentimentalist though he was, there was too much intensity, too much heartfelt yearning in him to make his case a ludicrous one. There is something not unnoble in the longing for the power to know the human lot, when it is passionately felt. And Mahler's cry for life was the cry of a great ruptured heart for health. There are too many genial moments in his compositions; there is too much marvelously piercing color in his instrumentation, to let us forget how great a potentiality lay in him awaiting redemption. It is with a profound sympathy that we watch this poor sick Jew, years since his decease, still wring his hands in the sere mounds of his music, and call to the universe to give unto him a thing which the universe cannot give, and that is found either in the human heart itself, or nowhere at all.

Bruckner

THE FIRE in Bruckner had free channel. Logs were not felled across its road. No neuro-watchman sprang alert as to an alarm when it began its stirring and coilings preparatory to motion, and promptly set to beating it from its course and driving it in alien directions. No haggard fear commenced running about, hissing, "Take care, this is not modern; this is not the symphony of the future; this is not what is wanted by our time; this will not free the Austrian youth and let floods of life over the sands; this is not greater than Brahms; this is not the most important form of music; this is not carrying Beethoven further than Beethoven could go." Something did not shrill, "Yonder is a man, your contemporary, who has done revolutionary work; make this modern, make it new and important; you must give just this nuance, you must give just that tone!" There was no floating baseless mind to interfere, to wrench the bud from its root, to commence kneading and forcing and trimming, to look into the world and get ideas and then give the musician back his substance wrapped in tight neat packages. There was the fire, only; rising, towering, finding its path; and the road before it was clear of obstructions.

What came out of Bruckner and became song of instruments is unmarred by the choking fingers of the floating mind; witness of the easiness of the passage it had into the world. Symphonies and religious services composed by him have the innocency and the largeness of such stuffs as are dredged deep where life has no weakness. The music is the speech of the heart, simple and direct and unaffected, and reverent and strong in mood. There is no room for jewelry, for the facile, for the pretty, where these grave and lofty tones are found. Bruckner's symphonies have scarce commenced heaving their mighty volumes through time, before we know we are come into the world of deep breaths and far vistas and profound experience. We hear some one singing; singing as though none were near to hear the song, and as though it issued forth for its own good sake; singing out of great ecstasies and great solitudes. The tones have their own distinct accent, strong and uncouth and soft-colored. A horn commences its dreamful speech over *pianissimo* strings; and what comes is old, something which must have been in every *allemande*, something which must have been in Allemanic forests long since, and that was again in Weber; and which is new nevertheless, freighted with new solemnity and melancholy and pain.

And Bruckner's works are large in form as in conception. They bring us into contact with an elemental and taurian strength. The lung capacity of the man, the vast span and breadth of his themes and thematic groups make the majority of composers seem asthmatic. The rhythmic hurl, curve, and freshness of his rude, lumbering, and troll-like scherzi subjects; the Homeric delight shown by him in ruddy sonorities, in the exuberant blasts of the reinforced brass; the cubical bulk of so many of his opening and final movements, make it appear to the fancy as though an elemental spirit had broken forth. Once the slow, oxlike power is gotten in motion; once the Bruckner orchestra begins squaring its great monoliths of tone, then, mountainous things commence to happen. The great gradual climaxes of the adagios of the symphonies; the long powerfully sustained ecstasies with their wildly and solemnly chanting trumpets, have something almost terrible in their vehemence and amount. The great battering-rams are slowly gotten in action. But, once heaved forward, they crash walls down.

The man was an innocent, seeing only his own idea. Modern music has no greater example of perfect unsophistication and oneness. Bruckner must have lived in complete obliviousness of his surroundings. A sort of rudimentary consciousness of things was there, perhaps, sufficient to steer him through a few duties; but the greater part of this man was walking always in the high cathedral of his vision. Waltz-blooded Vienna could scarce have existed for him. What rumbled and flowed beneath his windows; what he passed through in his courses through the streets, was vapor merely. Where a world felt lightness of life and the decay of a state and modern commercial tempi, there the little organist found the walls and windows and vaulting of a cathedral nave; and the high experiences that transformed themselves imperceptibly into the solemn trumpetings and ecstatic gamuts of his unworldly musics. No brother in blank Carthusian aisles could have paced sunken further in prayerfulness, God-passionateness, and Lenten mood, than Bruckner through the city roads. There was the Father in heaven. There was the Father in heaven, and not the houses and the people. There was the Father in heaven who could open his robes and hang them about his child in the cold as the walls of a woolen tent. There was no realness in the world except the sovereign moments when he lifted his child out of the lonely gray air into his bosom, and held him tight with his hand till the good minute went and the clouds of beatitude dwindled in the sad color of the world.

Here was the paradox: the medieval God-lover, God-embracer, in contemporary Vienna! Bruckner not only was an innocent; he was a mystic, too. On the back of this subject of Francis Joseph's, there sat the robe of the world-estranged seer. The German mystics are his kinsmen more than are the musicians; more than is the religio-philosophical Beethoven of the Ninth Symphony and the *Missa Solemnis,* from whom he stems; more than is the pietistic Bach, whose God-love he shared. To be sure, Bruckner remains an Austrian composer in his idiom, if not in his thought. His love for soft orchestral effects, for rich full color, links him with Schubert. Like Schubert, he speaks major in the minor keys. Indeed, there are pages of his that make him seem the most Austrian of all composers; the one least affected by Italian sweetness, and imbued most strongly with the uncontaminated racial traits. The contemporary of Wagner and Brahms and Franck, Bruckner brings to mind not so much the refinements of his own century as the uncouthness of the Allemanic tribesmen, his ancestors, who smeared their long hair with butter and brewed thick black beers. For all the magnificences of his orchestration, he remains the Upper Austrian peasant, uncultivated, clumsy, naïve. One of his works, a *Te Deum*, is qualified with the adjective "peasant"; all his work, so heavy-limbed and slow-blooded, deserves the title. The spirit of lightness, of the graceful dance, of the delicate jest, of the subtle half-statement, present in so many Austrian musicians, in Mozart, for example, is absent almost entirely from his work. Absent, too, is the gaiety and charm and sweetness of Schubert. Bruckner's dance is all hoofs, all heavy springs, and drunken fury. Even the trios of his scherzi, tender, dreamy, and intermezzo-like, have a certain predominant homeliness and humbleness. The good-natured, sluggish South German farmer dreams across his sunny land.

And yet, of course, one finds oneself setting him by the side of the religious mystics. One feels in Bruckner a complete removal from the world of objective reality, a completer tendency to consider all events purely from a psychological viewpoint, a completer habit of perceiving in the outer world merely the image of his own inner, than one finds either in the later Beethoven or in the most Mennonite pages of Bach's cantatas. It is in the company of a seer like Jacob Boehme, say, that one finds oneself instinctively placing him. In the square massive symphonies of the modern, as in the confessions of the seventeenth-century imaginer of the *centrum naturae*, the "virgin Sophia," one glimpses the workings of a similar excessive transformation of the lust of the eye and the other senses into the power of mystical and almost hallucinatory vision. There are pages in the adagios of Bruckner that appear strangely akin to the records of his inner experiences left by the cobbler of Görlitz; to the experiences of the mystic marriages, the perception of fiery symbols, the progression from lugubrious depressed states through ecstasy to tranquillity. How it comes that in listening to the performances of ninety instrumentalists on their fiddles, pipes, and horns, one should enter through such forbidden doors: that, it is not easy to explain. Perhaps the cause of the strange communication lies in Bruckner's predilection for themes of a chorale or hymnlike character. It is possible that it results from the general austere and yet strangely soft and tender character of his style. His harmony is rich, solemn, stately. He delighted in the use of full, grandiose progressions of chords in the brass, through which harp music sweeps. His climaxes are slow, distended, piercing; it is possible that the solemn tones of the trombones, the sobbing of horns through pulsating chords of shrilling wind and strings, are in some measure the origin of the sensations communicated. It may be that the general character of the work, merely, predisposes one to interpret so the ecstasies. We cannot say for sure. It is doubtful whether any analysis of form, no matter how keen and scientific it may be, can arrive at elucidating these mysteries of art. And yet, we know full well that just as, in some mysterious manner, the Bruckner scherzi bring one the sensations of being in the open air, of seeing the green earth and gray sky, so, too, the Bruckner adagios give us the sensations of an inner hallucinatory vision. The light that goes up in us from the chanting of the clear, high, loud orchestra in those movements, is not, we are somehow positive, the light that comes from the sun. It is not the light irradiated into an hundred tints by the orchestra of Debussy and the other impressionists. It is the dazzling shine that some dreaming men have suddenly seen piercing at them from out an opaque wall, or seen flooding upward at night from earth strewn thick with leaves.

A universal genius, of course, the man scarcely was. Immense though his breath, his oxlike power of sustainment, the power of his rhythmical impulse were; clear though the channel through which he gave himself to the world was; something, something important, was wanting in his mentality. One feels composers dwarf in stature beside him. His muscle is greater than theirs. Yet, they are shapelier, nimbler, livelier than this lumbering man. He seems one of the Titans who sought to storm Olympus; never one of the calm gods who vanquished the frenzied Ossapilers.

The balance, the round development, the many-sidedness which were Beethoven's, for example, never were in Bruckner, it seems. The maturity upon which solid musical culture can erect itself did not come to him. Had Bruckner grown to the point where condensation, close interpretation, rigorous selection of material would have become a necessity to him, it is possible he might have accomplished loftier things. His rhythmical sense, his feeling for color, particularly the color of horns, was superior to the master of Bonn's. And still, his achievement is really vaguer than Beethoven's; for the reason that his sense of form remained unevolved. The corner movements of the symphonies, in particular, for in the organization of scherzi and adagios Bruckner was far more able, suffer from brokenness. They are not really organic. They heave directly into life, it is true; Bruckner's attacks are exciting and daring; he begins right in the middle of things. But when, in accord with the demands of sonata form, he introduces his second subject, or, more exactly, his second group of subjects, one finds that apparently the trajectory has been broken and another one is commenced. It is as though the composer were commencing his work over again. Beethoven made sure that a musical logic demanded, at a certain place, the entrance of the lyrical theme. But Bruckner appears to have trusted to another logic; one perhaps not musical, for the justification of the entrance of the balancing principle. He merely sets a second piece beside the first; and leaves us to reconcile them in our minds as best we may. Not before the arrival of the development section does he commence his own "composition" of the two warring principles.

With all his faults, Bruckner remains the most neglected of symphonic composers. To be sure, there is no major symphonist, Brahms, Schubert, and Tchaikovsky excepted, whose work is not neglected by the conductors of the American orchestras. Even here in New York, where two resident and two visiting orchestras play regularly,* Beethoven himself is known to the concert public principally through five or six of his nine symphonies. Mozart is even more shabbily treated. Once, or, at the utmost, twice a year, a program holds the *Jupiter,* or the G-minor Symphony. The rest—is silence. But, when compared with Haydn, Mozart is as one being rushed. Ever since the departure of the terrible Dr. Muck,† Haydn the symphonist remains very much in the abodes where the eternal are, and returns but seldom to the earth. The lions of the podium now rampant are very insensitive to the beauties of the adorable Haydn. They are too busy savoring to the full the subtleties of the C-major Symphony of Schubert, the *From the New World* of Dvořák, to penetrate the scores of one of the most perennially fresh and delicate of composers. Smaller, though scarcely less brilliant, men fare quite as illy at their hands. Scarce ever are to be heard the symphonies of the generous and colorful Borodin. Sibelius is miserably neglected. So, too, are the modern Frenchmen. The hard, scintillant B-flat Symphony of d'Indy is the rarest of visitors. That of Dukas is entirely unknown. Unknown are the works of Magnard.‡ Meanwhile the program-makers invariably find opportunities galore for bringing before their audience the indecent exposures of Tchaikovsky.

But of all symphonists, it is Anton Bruckner who is most severely mistreated. For he wrote little besides symphonies. As

* The two resident orchestras were The Philharmonic Society of New York and The Symphony Society of New York, which were merged in 1928; the two visiting orchestras were the Boston and Philadelphia Symphonies.

† Karl Muck (1859–1940), German conductor who conducted the Boston Symphony first in 1906 and was made permanent conductor in 1912. His pro-German sentiments during World War I led to his internment until the end of the war and his dismissal from his post.

‡ Albéric Magnard (1865–1914), French composer and student of Vincent d'Indy's. Magnard was interested in "musical architecture, not poetic expression."

composer, he is principally the composer of nine massive compositions of the sort. The body of his chamber music is a very slight one. The chief of his compositions other than his symphonies are a few church works, the *Peasant Te Deum,* and three instrumental masses. In performing him with great infrequency, the orchestral leaders are consequently effectively depriving the man of the life rightfully his, and us, the public, of the music of a weighty artist. For he lives either in the symphony concert, or no place at all.

It is not difficult to guess why a spirit as mighty as Bruckner's should be kept, like a genie of the *Arabian Nights,* corked in a jar by the confraternity of musicians. The musicians, for their part, harp on Bruckner's grotesqueries. There are two composers on whom musicians are most stupid, Moussorgsky, and the Austrian mystic. Every day one meets some solemn performing person who informs one that Moussorgsky could not compose; and one has but to mention the name of Bruckner to him, too, to hear remarks equally inane. Bruckner "was a madman"; did he not most childishly dedicate his Ninth Symphony *Zum lieben Gott?** To be sure, the dedication makes one smile. But then, Bruckner had presented his Eighth to His Imperial and Royal Apostolic Majesty Francis Joseph I, Emperor of Austria and Apostolic King of Hungary, etc., etc.; and for a devout Austrian there was only one person to whom one might fittingly present a ninth, the Francis Joseph beyond the clouds. Moreover, the "madman" had taken the opening phrase of Isolde's Liebestod and fugued it! And though tomes have been written to prove that several centuries before Bruckner other composers lifted the same theme from Wagner and fugued it, the musicians must have their little joke.

No, it is the confraternity that is grotesque. If *Boris* is withdrawn from the repertory of the Metropolitan Opera House, to the applause of all the Henry T. Fincks;† if the

* "For the love of God."

† Henry T. Finck (1854–1926), music critic for *The Nation* and prolific author. He wrote books on Chopin, Wagner, Grieg, and Richard Strauss.

conductors of the metropolitan orchestras neglect above all others the symphonies of Anton Bruckner, it is not for the reason the Russian and the Upper Austrian could not make music. It is for the reason that the rarefied air that blows through the works of both demands lungs stouter and hearts higher than the musical unions and the company of the conductors can plentifully supply. One can scarcely be a practicing musician and do the little jobs the public demands musicians do, and still feel life with the altitude and the solemnity and reverence with which these men felt it. The world would first have to be lost to one.

Strauss

STRAUSS was never the fine, the perfect artist. Even in the first flare of youth, even at the time when he was the meteoric, dazzling figure flaunting over all the baldpates of the universe the standard of the musical future, it was apparent that there were serious flaws in his spirit. Despite the audacity with which he realized his amazing and poignant and ironic visions, despite his youthful fire and exuberance—and it was as something of a golden youth of music that Strauss burst upon the world—one sensed in him the not quite beautifully deepened man, heard at moments a callow accent in his eloquence, felt that an unmistakable alloy was fused with the generous gold. The purity, the inwardness, the searchings of the heart, the religious sentiment of beauty, present so unmistakably in the art of the great men who had developed music, were wanting in his work. He had neither the unswerving sense of style, nor the weightiness of touch, that mark the perfect craftsman. He was not sufficiently a scrupulous and exacting artist. It was apparent that he was careless, too easily contented with some of his material, not always happy in his detail. Mixed with his fire there was a sort of laziness and indifference. But, in those days, Strauss was unmistakably the genius, the original and bitingly expressive musician, the engineer of proud orchestral flights, the outrider and bannerman of his art, and one forgave his shortcomings because of the radiance of his figure, or remained only half-conscious of them.

For, once his period of apprenticeship passed, and all desire to write symphonies and chamber music in the styles of Schumann and Mendelssohn and Brahms, to construct operas after the pattern of *Tannhäuser* and *Parsifal* gone out of him, this slender, sleepy young Bavarian with the pale curly hair and mustaches had commenced to develop the expressive power of music amazingly, to make the orchestra speak wonderfully as it had never spoken before. Under his touch the symphony, that most rigid and abstract and venerable of forms, was actually displaying some of the novel's narrative and analytical power, its literalness and concreteness of detail. It was describing the developments of a character, was psychologizing as it had hitherto done only in conjunction with poetry or the theater. Strauss made it represent the inflammations of the sex illusion, comment upon Nietzsche and Cervantes, recount the adventures, somersaults, and end of a legendary rascal, portray a hero of our time. He made all these intellectual concepts plastic in a music of a brilliance and a sprightliness and mordancy that not overmany classic symphonies can rival. Other and former composers, no doubt, had dreamt of making the orchestra more concretely expressive, more precisely narrative and descriptive. The *Pastoral Symphony* is by no means the first piece of deliberately, confessedly programmatic music. And before Strauss, both Berlioz and Liszt had experimented with the narrative, descriptive, analytical symphony. But it was only with Strauss that the symphonic novel was finally realized.

Neither Berlioz nor Liszt had really embodied their programs in living music. Liszt invariably sacrificed program to sanctioned musical form. For all his radicalism, he was too trammeled by the classical concepts, the traditional musical schemes and patterns to quite realize the symphony based on an extra-musical scheme. His symphonic poems reveal how difficult it was for him to make his music follow the curve of his ideas. In *Die Ideale,* for instance, for the sake of a conventional close, he departed entirely from the curve of the poem of Schiller which he was pretending to transmute. The variations in which he reproduced Lamartine's verse are stereotyped enough. When was there a time when composers did not deform their themes in amorous, rustic, and warlike variations? The relation between the pompous and somewhat empty *Lament and Triumph* and the unique, the distinct thing that was the life of Torquato Tasso is outward enough. And even *Mazeppa,* in which Liszt's virtuosic genius stood him in good stead, makes one feel as though Liszt could never quite keep his eye on the fact, and finally became engrossed in the weaving of a musical pattern fairly extraneous to his idea. The *Faust Symphony* is, after all, an exception. Berlioz, too, failed on the whole to achieve the musical novel. Whenever he did attain musical form, it was generally at the expense of his program. Are the somewhat picturesque episodes of *Harold in Italy,* whatever their virtues, and they are many, more than vaguely related to the Byronism that ostensibly elemented them? The surprisingly conventional overture to *King Lear* makes one feel as though Berlioz had sat through a performance of one of Shakespeare's comedies under the impression that he was assisting at the tragedy, so unrelated to its subject is the music. And where, on the other hand, Berlioz did succeed in being regardful of his program, as in the *Symphonie Fantastique,* or in *Lélio,* there resulted a somewhat thin and formless music.

But Strauss, benefiting by the experiments of his two predecessors, realized the new form better than anyone before him had done. For he possessed the special gifts necessary to the performance of the task. He possessed, in the first place, a miraculous power of musical characterization. Through the representative nicety of his themes, through his inordinate capacity for thematic variation and transformation, his playful and witty and colorful instrumentation, Strauss was able to impart to his music a concreteness and descriptiveness and realism hitherto unknown to symphonic art, to characterize briefly, sparingly, justly, a personage, a situation, an event. He could be pathetic, ironic, playful, mordant, musing, at will. He was sure in his tone, was Low German in *Till Eulenspiegel,* courtly and brilliant in *Don Juan,* noble and bitterly sarcastic in *Don Quixote,* childlike in *Tod und Verklärung.* His orchestra was able to accommodate itself to all the folds and curves of his elaborate programs, to find equivalents for individual traits. It is not simply "a man," or even "an amatory hero" that is portrayed in *Don Juan.* It is no vague symbol for the poet of the sort created by *Orpheus* or *Tasso* or *Mazeppa.* It is Lenau's hero himself, the particular being Don Juan Tenorio. The vibrant, brilliant music of the upsurging, light-treading strings, of the resonant, palpitating brass, springs forth in virile march, reveals the man himself, his physical glamour, his intoxication that caused him to see in every woman the Venus, and that in the end made him the victim as well as the hero of the sexual life. It is Till Eulenspiegel himself, the scurvy, comic rascal, the eternal dirty little boy with his witty and obscene gestures, who leers out of every measure of the tone poem named for him, and twirls his fingers at his nose's end at all the decorous and respectable world. Here, for once, orchestral music is really wonderfully rascally and impudent, horns gleeful and windy and insolent, woodwinds puckish and obscene. Here a musical form reels hilariously and cuts capers and dances on bald heads. The variation of *Don Quixote* that describes with woodwinds and tambourine Dulcinea del Toboso is plump and plebeian and good-natured with her very person, is all the more trenchantly vulgar and flat for the preceding suave variation that describes the knight's fair, sonorous dream of her. There is no music more plaintively stupid than that which in the same work figures the "sheep" against which Don Quixote battles so valiantly. Nor is there any music more maliciously, malevolently petty than that which represents the adversaries in *Ein Heldenleben.* So exceedingly definite is the portrait of the Hero's Consort, for which Frau Richard Strauss, without doubt, sat, that without even having seen a photograph of the lady, one can aver that she is graced with a diatonic figure. And, certainly the most amusing passage of *Sinfonia Domestica* is that complex of Bavarian lustihood, Bavarian grossness, Bavarian dreaminess, and Bavarian good nature, the thematic group that serves as autoportrait of the composer.

And just as there seemed few characters that Strauss could not paint, in those days, so, too, there seemed few situations, few atmospheres, to which he could not do justice. A couple of measures, the sinister palpitation of the timpani and the violas, the brooding of the woodwinds, the dull flickering of the flutes, the laboring breath of the strings, and we are lying on the deathbed, exhausted and gasping for air, weighed by the wrecks of hopes, awaiting the cruel blows on the heart that will end everything. Horns and violins quaver and snarl, flutes shrill, a brief figure descends in the oboes and clarinets, and Till has shed his rascal-sweat and danced on the air. The orchestra reveals us Don Juan's love affairs in all their individuality: first the passionate, fiery relation with the Countess, quickly begun and quickly ended; then the gentler and more inward communion with Anna, with the boredom resulting from the lady's continual demand for sentiment and romantic posturing; then the great night of love and roses, with its intoxicated golden winding horns, its ecstatically singing violins; and finally the crushing disappointment, the shudder of disgust. The battle in *Ein Heldenleben* pictures war really; the whistling, ironical wind machine in *Don Quixote* satirizes dreams bitingly as no music has done; the orchestra describes the enthusiastic Don recovering from his madness, and smiles a conclusion; in *Also Sprach Zarathustra* it piles high the tomes of science, and waltzes with the superman in distant worlds.

And then, though less fecund an inventor than Liszt, less rich and large a temperament than Berlioz, Strauss was better able than either of his masters to organize his material on difficult and original lines, and find musical forms representative of his programs. Because of their labors, he was born freer of the classical traditions than they had been, and was able to make music plot more exactly the curves of his concepts, to submit the older forms, such as the rondo and the theme and variations, more perfectly to his purpose. Compositions of the sort of *Till Eulenspiegel, Tod und Verklärung,* and *Ein Heldenleben,* solidly made and yet both narrative and dramatic, place the symphonic poem in the category of legitimate musical forms. The themes of *Till* grow out of each other quite as do the themes of a Beethoven symphony or of *Tristan* or of *Parsifal.* Indeed, Strauss has done for the symphonic poem something of what Wagner did for the opera. And not an overwhelming number of classical symphonies contain music more eloquent than, say, the "Sunrise" in *Also Sprach Zarathustra,* or the final variation of *Don Quixote* with its piercing, shattering trumpets of defeat, or the terrifying opening passage of *Tod und Verklärung.* For Strauss was able to unloose his verve and fantasy completely in the construction of his edifices. His orchestra moves in strangest and most unconventional curves, shoots with the violence of an exploding firearm, ambles like a palfrey, swoops like a bird. There are few who, at a first hearing of a Strauss poem, do not feel as though some wild and troubling and panic presence had leaned over the concert hall and bedeviled the orchestra. For, in his hands, it is no longer the familiar and terrorless thing it once had been, a thing about whose behavior one can be certain. It has become a formidable engine of steel and gold, vibrant with mad and unexpected things. Patterns leap and tumble out of it. Violin music launches swiftly into space, trumpets run scales, the tempi move with the velocity of express trains. It has become a giant, terrible bird, the great auk of music, that seizes you in its talons and spirals into the empyrean.

But it was what he seemed to promise to perform, to bring into being, even more than what he had already definitely accomplished, that spread about the figure of Strauss the peculiar radiance. It was Nietzsche who had made current the dream of a new music, a music that should be fiercely and beautifully animal, full of laughter, of the dry good light of the intellect, of "salt and fire and the great, compelling logic, of the light feet of the south, the dance of the stars, the quivering dayshine of the Mediterranean." The other composers, the Beethovens and Brahms and Wagners, had been sad, suffering, wounded men, men who had lost their divine innocence and joy in the shambles, and whose spiritual bodies were scarred, for all the muscular strength gained during their fights, by hunger and frustration and agony. Pain had even marred their song. For what should have been innocence and effortless movement and godlike joy, Mozartean coordination and harmony, was full of terrible cries, and convulsive, rending motions, and shrouding sorrow. And Nietzsche had dreamt of music of another sort. He had dreamt of a music that should be a bridge to the superman, the man whose every motion would be carefree. He had seen striding across mountain chains in the bright air of an eternal morning a youth irradiant with unbroken energy, before whom all the world lay open in vernal sunshine like a domain before its lord. He had seen one beside whom the other musicians would stand as convicts from Siberian prison camps who had stumbled upon a banquet of the gods. He had seen a young Titan of music, drunken with life and fire and joy, dancing and reeling and laughing on the top of the world, and with fingers amid the stars, sending suns and constellations crashing. He had caught sight of the old and eternally youthful figure of Indian Dionysus.

And even though Strauss himself could scarcely be mistaken for the god, nevertheless he made Nietzsche's dream appear realizable. He permitted one for an instant to perceive a musical realm in which the earth-fast could not breathe. He permitted one for an instant to hear ringing "the prelude of a deeper, mightier, perchance a more evil and mysterious music; a super-German music which does not fade, wither, and die away beside the blue and wanton sea and the clear Mediterranean sky; a music super-European, which would assert itself even amid the tawny sunsets of the desert; a music whose soul is akin

to the palm trees; a music that can consort and prowl with
great, beautiful, lonely beasts of prey; a music whose supreme
charm is its ignorance of Good and Evil." For he came with
some of the light and careless and arrogant tread, the intellectual sparkling, the superb gesture and port, of the musician of
the new race. The man who composed such music, one knew,
had been born on some sort of human height, in some cooler,
brighter atmosphere than that of the crowded valleys. For in
this music there beat a faster pulse, moved a lighter, fierier,
prouder body, sounded a more ironic and disdainful laughter,
breathed a rarer air than had beat and moved and sounded and
breathed in music. It made drunken with pleasant sound, with
full rich harmonies, with exuberant dance and waltz movements.
It seemed to adumbrate the arrival of a new sort of men, men of
saner, sounder, more athletic souls and more robust and cool
intelligences, a generation that was vitally satisfied, was less
torn and belabored by the inexpressible longings of the romantic world, a generation very much at home on the globe.
For it had none of the restless, sick desire of Wagner, none of
his excessive pathos, his heaviness and stiff grandeur. It had
come down off its buskins, was more easy, witty, diverting,
exciting, popular and yet cerebral. Though it was obviously the
speech of a complicated, modern man, self-conscious, sophisticated, nervous, product of a society perhaps not quite as free
and Nietzschean as it deemed itself, but yet cultivated and
illuminated and refined, it nevertheless seemed exuberantly
sound. The sweet, broad, diatonic idiom, the humor, the sleepy
Bavarian accent, the pert, naïve, little folk tunes it employed,
the tranquil, touching, childlike tones, the close of *Tod und
Verklärung,* with its wondrous unfolding of corolla upon
corolla, were refreshing indeed after all the burning chromaticism of Wagner, the sultry air of Klingsor's wonder-garden.

And this music glittered with the sun. The pitch of Wagner's
orchestra had, after all, been predominantly sober and sub-
dued. But in the orchestra of Strauss, the color gamut of the
plein-air painters got a musical equivalent. Those high and

brilliant tints, these shimmering, biting tones, make one feel as though Strauss made music with the paintbrush of a Monet or a Van Gogh. His trumpets are high and brilliant and silvery, his violins scintillant and electric, at moments winding a lazy, happy, smoke-blue thread through the sunburnt fabric of the score. His horns glow with soft, fruity timbres. The new sweetness of color which he attains in his songs, the pale gold of "Morgen," the rose of the "Serenade," the mild evening blue of "Traum durch die Dämmerung," shimmers throughout his orchestra scores. Never have wind instruments sounded more richly, dulcetly, than in that *Serenade für Dreizehn Bläser*. At a first hearing of *Also Sprach Zarathustra,* it seemed as though the very dayspring had descended into the orchestra to make that famous, brassy opening passage. For here, in the hand of Strauss, the orchestra begins to round out its form and assume its logical shape. The various families of instruments are made independent; often play separately. The shattering brass of which Berlioz had dreamt is realized. Violas d'amore, hecklephones, wind machines, are introduced into the band; the familiar instruments are used in unfamiliar registers. Through the tone poems of Strauss, the orchestral composer for the first time has a suitable palette, and can achieve a brilliance as great as that which the modern painter can attain.

Today, it is difficult to realize that Richard Strauss ever incensed such high hopes, that there was a time when he made appear realizable Nietzsche's mad dream of a modern music, and that for a while the nimbus of Dionysus burnt round his figure. Today it is difficult to remember that once upon a time Strauss seemed to the world the golden youth of music, the engineer of proud orchestral flights, the outrider and bannerman of his art. For it is long since he has promised to reveal the new beauty, the new rhythm, has seemed the wonderful start and flight toward some rarer plane of existence, some bluer ether, the friend of everything intrepid and living and young, the "arrow of longing for the superman." It is a long while since any gracious, lordly light has irradiated his person. In recent years he has become almost the very reverse of what he was, of what he gave so brave an earnest of becoming. He who was once so electric, so vital, so brilliant a figure has become dreary and outward and stupid, even. He who once seemed the champion of the new has come to fill us with the weariness of the struggle, with deep self-distrust and discouragement, has become a heavy and oppressive weight. He who once sought to express the world about him, to be the poet of the coming time, now seems inspired only by a desire to do the amazing, the surface thing, and plies himself to every ephemeral and shallow current of modern life. For Strauss has not only not deepened and matured and increased in stature; he has not even stood still, remained the artist that once he was. He has progressively and steadily deteriorated during the last decade. He has become a bad musician. He is the cruel, the great disappointment of modern music, of modern art. The dream-light has failed altogether, has made the succeeding darkness the thicker for the momentary illumination. Strauss today is seen as a rocket that sizzled up into the sky with many-colored blaze, and then broke suddenly and extinguished swiftly into the midnight.

It is not easy, even for those who were aware from the very first that Strauss was not the spirit "pardlike, beautiful and swift" and that there always were distinctly gross and insensitive particles in him, to recognize in the slack and listless person who concocts *Josephslegende* and the *Alpensinfonie,* the young and fiery composer, genius despite all the impurities of his style, who composed *Till Eulenspiegel* and *Don Quixote*; not easy, even though the contours of his idiom have not radically altered, and though in the sleepy facile periods of his later style one catches sight at times of the broad, simple diction of his earlier. For the later Strauss lacks pre-eminently and signally just the traits that made of the earlier so brilliant and engaging a figure. Behind the works of the earlier Strauss there was visible an intensely fierily experiencing being, a man who had powerful and poignant and beautiful sensations, and the gift of expressing them richly. Behind the work of the latter there is all too apparent a man who for a long while has felt nothing beautiful or strong or full, who no longer possesses the power of feeling anything at all, and is inwardly wasted and dull and spent. The one had a burning and wonderful pressure of speech. The other seems unable to concentrate energy and interest sufficiently to create a hard and living piece of work. The one seemed to blaze new pathways through the brain. The other steps languidly in roadways well worn. He is not even amusing any longer. The contriver of wonderful orchestral machines, the man who penetrated into the deathchamber and stood under the gibbet, has turned to toying with his medium, to imitating other composers, Mozart in *Der Rosenkavalier,* Handel in *Josephslegende,* Offenbach and Lully (a coupling that only Strauss has the lack of taste to bring about) in *Ariadne auf Naxos.* He has become increasingly facile and unoriginal, has taken to quoting unblushingly Mendelssohn, Tchaikovsky, Wagner, himself, even. His insensitivity has waxed inordinately, and led him to mix styles, to commingle dramatic and coloratura passages, to jumble the idioms of three centuries in a single work, to play all manner of pointless pranks with his art. His literary taste has grown increasingly uncertain. He who was once so careful in his choice of lyrics, and recognized the talents of such modern German poets as Bierbaum and Dehmel and Mackay, accepts librettos as dull and inartistic and precious as those with which Hofmannsthal is supplying him,* and lends his art to the boring buffooneries of *Der Rosenkavalier* and *Ariadne auf Naxos.* Something in him has bent and been fouled.†

* Rosenfeld modified this harsh criticism of Hugo von Hofmannsthal as a librettist many years later in the essay "The *Elektra* of Richard Strauss," *Discoveries of a Music Critic,* pp. 130–143. Despite some reservations about the opera's mixture of archaic Greek forms and Freudianism, he called it a "compact, powerful drama."

† Rosenfeld's judgment of Strauss's operas is fairly close to Stravinsky's acerbic comment, though it does not go to the Russian composer's extreme denial of merit: "I would like to admit all Strauss operas to whichever purgatory punishes triumphant banality. Their musical substance is cheap

One thing at least the Strauss of the tone poems indisputably was. He was freely, dazzlingly, daringly expressive. And this is what the Strauss of the last years thinly and rarely is. It is not Oscar Wilde's wax flowers of speech, nor the excessively stiff and conventionalized action of *Salome,* that bores one with the Strauss opera of that name. It is not even the libretto of *Der Rosenkavalier,* essentially coarse and boorish and insensitive as it is beneath all its powdered preciosity, that wearies one with Strauss's "musical comedy"; or the hybrid, lame, tasteless form of *Ariadne auf Naxos* that turns one against that little monstrosity. It is the generally inexpressive and insufficient music in which Strauss has vested them. The music of *Salome,* for instance, is not even commensurable with Wilde's drama. It was the evacuation of an obsessive desire, the revulsion from a pitiless sensuality that the poet had intended to procure through this representation. But Strauss's music, save in such exceptional passages as the shimmering, restless, nerve-sick opening page, or the beginning of the scene with the head, or certain other crimson patches, hampers and even negates the intended effect. It emasculates the drama with its pervasive prettiness, its lazy felicitousness where it ought to be monstrous and terrifying, its reminiscences of Mendelssohn, Tchaikovsky, and "Little Egypt." The lascivious and hieratic dance, the dance of the seven veils, is represented by a *valse lente.* Oftentimes the score verges perilously on circus music, recalls the sideshows at county fairs. No doubt, in so doing it weakens the odor exuded by Wilde's play. But if we must have an operatic *Salome,* it is but reasonable to demand that the composer in his music express the sexual cruelty and frenzy symbolized in the figure of the dancer. And the Salome of Strauss's score is as little the Salome of Wilde as she is the Salome of Flaubert or Beardsley or Moreau or Huysmans. One cannot help feeling her

---

and poor; it cannot interest a musician today." *Stravinsky in Conversation with Robert Craft* (London: Pelican Books, 1962), p. 89. This opinion, shared, incidentally, by Charles Ives, runs counter to the praise lavished on Strauss in most musical quarters today.

eminently a buxom, opulent Berliner, the wife, say, of the proprietor of a large department store; a heavy lady a good deal less *dämonisch* and "perverse" than she would like to have it appear. But there are moments when one feels as though Strauss's heroine were not even a Berliner, or of the upper middle class. There are moments when she is plainly Käthi, the waitress at the Münchner Hofbraühaus. And though she declares to Jokanaan that "it is his mouth of which she is enamored," she delivers the words in her own true-hearted, unaffected brogue.

Nor is *Elektra*, more sharp than *Salome* though it oftentimes is, the musical equivalent for the massive and violent forms of archaic Greek sculpture that Strauss intended it be. Elektra herself is perhaps more truly incarnate fury than Salome is incarnate luxury; ugliness and demoniacal brooding, madness and cruelty are here more sheerly powerfully expressed than in the earlier score; the scene of recognition between brother and sister is more large and touching than anything in *Salome*; Elektra's paean and dance, for all its closeness to a banal *cantilena*, its *tempo di valse* so characteristic of the later Strauss, is perhaps more grandiosely and balefully triumphant than the dancer's scene with the head. Nevertheless, the work is by no means realized. It is formally impure, a thing that none of the earlier tone poems are. Neither style nor shape are deeply felt. Both are superficially and externally conceived; and nothing so conclusively demonstrates it as the extreme ineffectuality of the moments of contrast with which Strauss has attempted to relieve the dominant mood of his work. Just as in *Salome* the more restless and sensual passages, lazily felt as they are, are nevertheless infinitely more significant than the intensely contrasting silly music assigned to the Prophet, so, too, in *Elektra*, the moments when Strauss is cruel, brutal, ugly are of a much higher expressiveness than those in which he has sought to write beautifully. For whereas in moments of the first sort the lions of the Mycenae gates do at times snarl and glower, in those of the second it is the Teutonic beer mug that makes itself felt.

Elektra laments her father in a very pretty and undistinguished melody, and entreats her sister to slay Klytemnaestra to the accompaniment of a sort of *valse perverse*. It is also in *tempo di valse* that Chrysothemis declares her need of wifehood and motherhood. As an organism the work does not exist.*

But even the expressiveness and considerability of *Salome* and *Elektra*, limited and unsatisfactory as they are, are wanting in the more recent works. With *Der Rosenkavalier*, Strauss seems to have reached a condition in which it is impossible for him to penetrate a subject deeply. No doubt he always was spotty, even though in his golden days he invariably fixed the inner informing binding rhythm of each of his works. But his last works are not only spotty, but completely spineless as well, invertebrate masses upon which a few jewels, a few fine patches, gleam dully. *Salome* and *Elektra* had at least a certain dignity, a certain bearing. *Der Rosenkavalier, Ariadne auf Naxos, Josephslegende,* and *Eine Alpensinfonie* are makeshift, slack, slovenly despite all technical virtuosity, all orchestral marvels. Everyone knows what the score of *Rosenkavalier* should have been, a gay, florid, licentious thing, the very image of the gallant century with its mundane amours and ribbons and cupids, its *petit-maîtres* and furbelows and billets-doux, its light emotions and equally light surrenders. But Strauss's music is singularly flat and hollow and dun, joyless and soggy, even though it is dotted with waltzes and contains the delightful introduction to the third act, and the brilliant trio. It has all the worst faults of the libretto. Hofmannsthal's "comedy for music," though gross and vulgar in spirit, and unoriginal in design, is full of a sort of clever preciosity, full of piquant details culled from eighteenth-century prints and memoirs. The

---

* In reassessing Strauss's music in his essay "The *Elektra* of Richard Strauss," *op. cit.*, Rosenfeld still believed that *Elektra* was not "a supremely clear and organic work of art," but he argued that "it is Strauss's strongest piece and incidentally his most prophetic, prefiguring much of the music of the generation of composers immediately successive to his own" and that it epitomized the "fatal exasperation and hysteria" which erupted in World War I.

scene of the coiffing is a print of Hogarth's translated to the stage; Rofrano's name "Octavian Maria Ehrenreich Bonaventura Fernand Hyazinth" is like an essay on the culture of the Vienna of Canaletto; the polite jargon of eighteenth-century aristocratic Austria spoken by the characters, with its stiff, courteous forms and intermingled French, must have been studied from old journals and gazettes. And Strauss's score is equally precious, equally a thing of erudition and cleverness. Mozart turned the imbecilities of Schickaneder to his uses; Weber triumphed over the ridiculous romancings of Helmine von Chezy. But Strauss follows Hofmannsthal helplessly, soddenly. Just as Hofmannsthal imitates Hogarth, so Strauss imitates Mozart, affects his style, his turns, his spirit; inserts a syrupy air in the style of Handel or Méhul in the first act; and jumbles Mozart with modern comic-opera waltzes, Handel with post-Wagnerian incantations. And like Hofmannsthal's libretto, the score remains a superficial and formless thing. The inner and coherent rhythm, the spiritual beat and swing, the great unity and direction, are wanting. "I have always wanted to write an opera like Mozart's, and now I have done it," Strauss is reported to have said after the first performance of *Der Rosenkavalier*. But *Der Rosenkavalier* is almost antipodal to *Don Giovanni* or to *Falstaff* or to *Die Meistersinger* or to any of the great comic operas. For it lacks just the thing the others possess abundantly, a strong lyrical movement, a warm emotion that informs the music bar after bar, scene after scene, act after act, and imparts to the auditor the joy, the vitality, the beauty of which the composers' hearts were full. It is a long while since Strauss has felt anything of the sort.

Had the new time produced no musical art, had no Debussy nor Scriabin, no Stravinsky nor Bloch put in appearance, one might possibly have found oneself compelled to believe the mournful decadence of Richard Strauss the inevitable development awaiting musical genius in the modern world. There exists a group, international in composition, which, above all other contemporary bodies, arrogates to itself the style of modernity. It is the group, tendrils of which reach into every great capital and center, into every artistic movement and cause, of the bored ones, the spoilt ones. The present system has lifted into a quasi-aristocratic and leisurely state vast numbers of people without background, without tradition or culture or taste. By reason of its largeness and resources, this group of people without taste, without interest, without finesse, has come to dominate in particular the world of art as the world of play, has come to demand distraction, sensation, excitement which its unreal existence does not afford it. Indeed, this band has come to give a cast to the whole of present-day life; its members pretend to represent present-day culture. It is with this group with its frayed sensibilities and tired pulses that Strauss has become increasingly identified, till of late he has become something like its court musician, supplying it with stimulants, awaking its curiosities, astonishing and exciting it with the superficial novelty of his works, trying to procure it the experiences it is so lamentably unable to procure itself. It is for it that he created the trumpery horrors, the sweet erotics of the score of *Salome*. It is for it that he imitated Mozart saccharinely in *Der Rosenkavalier;* mangled Molière's comedy; committed the vulgarities and hypocrisies of *Josephslegende*. And did no evidence roundly to the contrary exist, one might suppose this group to really represent modern life; that its modernity was the only true one; and that in expressing it, in conforming to it, Strauss was functioning in the only manner granted the contemporary composer. But since such evidence exists aplenty, since a dozen other musicians, to speak only of the practitioners of a single art, have managed to keep themselves immune and yet create beauty about them, to remain on the plane upon which Strauss began life, to persevere in the direction in which he was originally set, and yet live fully, one finds oneself convinced that the deterioration of Strauss, which has made him musical purveyor to this group, has not been the result of the pressure of outward and hostile circumstances. One finds oneself positively convinced that it was some inner weakness within himself that permitted the spoiled and ugly folk to seduce him from his road, and use him for their purposes.

And in the end it is as the victim of a psychic deterioration that one is forced to regard this unfortunate man. The thing that one sees happening to so many people about one, the extinction of a flame, the withering of a blossom, the dulling and coarsening of the sensibilities, the decay of the mental energies, seems to have happened to him, too. And since it happens in the lives of so many folk, why should it surprise one to see it happening in the life of an artist, and deflowering genius and ruining musical art? All the hectic, unreal activity of the later Strauss, the dissipation of forces, points back to such a cause. He declares himself in every action the type who can no longer gather his energies to the performance of an honest piece of work, who can no longer achieve direct, full, living expression, who can no longer penetrate the center of a subject, an idea. He is the type of man unfaithful to himself in some fundamental relation, unfaithful to himself throughout his deeds. Many people have thought a love of money the cause of Strauss's decay; that for the sake of gain he has delivered himself bound hand and foot into the power of his publishers, and for the sake of gain turned out bad music. No doubt, the love of money plays an inordinate role in the man's life, and keeps on playing a greater and greater. But it is probable that Strauss's desire for incessant gain is a sort of perversion, a mania that has gotten control over him because his energies are inwardly prevented from taking their logical course, and creating works of art. Luxury-loving as he is, Strauss has probably never needed money sorely. Some money he doubtlessly inherited through his mother, the daughter of the Munich beer brewer Pschorr; his works have always fetched large prices—his publishers have paid him as much as a thousand dollars for a single song; and he has always been able to earn great sums by conducting. No matter how lofty and severe his art might have become, he would always have been able to live as he chose. There is no doubt that he would have earned quite as much money with *Salome* and *Der Rosenkavalier* had they been works of high, artistic merit as he has earned with them in their present condition. The truth is that he has rationalized his unwillingness to go through the labor pains of creation by pretending to himself a constant and great need of money, and permitting himself to dissipate his energies in a hectic, disturbed, shallow existence, in a tremor of concert tours, guest-conductorships, money-making enterprises of all sorts, which leave him about two or three of the summer months for composition, and probably rob him of his best energies. So works leave his writing table half conceived, half executed. The score of *Elektra* he permits his publishers to snatch from him before he is quite finished with it. He commences composing *Der Rosenkavalier* before having even seen the third act. The third act arrives; Strauss finds it miserable. But it is too late. The work is half-finished, and Strauss has to go through with it. Composition becomes more and more a mechanical thing, the brilliant orchestration of sloppy, undistinguished music, the polishing up of details, the play of superficial cleverness which makes a score like *Der Rosenkavalier,* feeble as it is, interesting to many musicians.

And Richard Strauss, the one living musician who could with greatest ease settle down to uninterrupted composition, gets to his writing table in his apartment in Charlottenburg every evening at nine o'clock, that is, whenever he is not on duty at the Berlin Opera.

And always the excuses: "Earning money for the support of wife and child is not shameful," "I am going to accumulate a large enough fortune so that I can give up conducting entirely and spend all my time composing." But one can be sure that when Strauss soliloquizes, it is a different defense that he makes. One can be sure, then, that he justifies himself cynically, bitterly, grossly, tells himself that the game is not worth the candle, that greatness is a matter of advertisement, that only the values of the commercial world exist, that other success than the procurement of applause and wealth and notoriety constitutes failure. Why should you take the trouble to write good work that will bring you posthumous fame when without trouble you can write work that will bring you fame during your lifetime? The whole world is sham and advertisement and opportunism, is it not? Reputations are made by publishers and newspapers. Greatness is a matter determined by majorities. But impress the public, but compose works that will arouse universal comment, but break a few academic formulas and get yourself talked about, but write music that will surprise and seem wonderful at a first hearing, and your fame is assured. The important thing is to live luxuriously and keep your name before the public. In so doing one will have lived life as fully as it can be lived. And after one is dead, what does it all matter?

Yet, though the world be full of men whose spiritual energies have been lamed in kindred fashions, the terrible misadventure of Richard Strauss remains deeply affecting. However far the millions of bright spirits who have died a living death have fallen, their fall has been no farther than this man's. There can be no doubt of the completeness of Strauss's disaster. It is a long while since he has been much besides a bore to his once fervent admirers, an object of hatred to thousands of honest, idealistic musicians. He has completely, in his fifty-sixth year, lost the position of leadership, of eminence that once he had. Even before the war his operas held the stage only with difficulty. And it is possible that he will outlive his fame. One wonders whether he is not one of the men whose inflated reputations the war has pricked, and that a world will shortly wonder, before his two new operas, how it was possible that it should have been held at all by the man. Had he been the most idealistic, the most uncompromising of musicians he could not be less respected. Perhaps his last chance lay in the *Alpensinfonie*. Here was a ceremony that could have made him priest once again. Europe had reached a summit, humanity had had a vision. Before it lay a long descent, a cloudburst, the sunset of a civilization, another night. Could Strauss have once more girded himself, once more summoned the faith, the energy, the fire that created those first grand pages that won a world to him, he might have been saved. But it was impossible. Something in him was dead forever. And so, to us, who should have been his champions, his audiences, his work already seems old, part of the past even at its best, unreal except for a few of the fine symphonic works. To us, who once thought to see in him the man of the new time, he seems only the brave, sonorous trumpet call that heralded a king who never put in his appearance, the glare that in the East lights the sky for an instant and seems to promise a new day, but extinguishes again. He is indeed the false dawn of modern music.

Schoenberg

ARNOLD SCHOENBERG of Vienna is the great troubling presence of modern music. His vast, sallow skull lowers over it like a sort of North Cape. For with him, with the famous cruel five orchestral and nine piano pieces, we seem to be entering the arctic zone of musical art. None of the old beacons, none of the old stars, can guide us longer in these frozen wastes. Strange, menacing forms surround us, and the light is bleak and chill and faint. The characteristic compositions of Stravinsky and Ornstein, too, have no tonality, lack every vestige of a pure chord, and exhibit unanalyzable harmonies, and rhythms of a violent novelty, in the most amazing conjunctions. But they, at least, impart a certain sense of liberation. They, at least, bear certain witness to the emotional flight of the composer. An instinct pulses here, an instinct barbarous and unbridled, if you will, but indubitably exuberant and vivid. These works have a necessity. These harmonies have color. This music is patently speech. But the later compositions of Schoenberg withhold themselves, refuse our contact. They baffle with their apparently willful ugliness, and bewilder with their geometric cruelty and coldness. One gets no intimation that in fashioning them the composer has liberated himself. On the contrary, they seem icy and brain-spun. They are like men formed not out of flesh and bone and blood, but out of glass and wire and concrete.

They creak and groan and grate in their motion. They have all
the deathly pallor of abstractions.

And Schoenberg remains a troubling presence as long as one
persists in regarding these particular pieces as the expression of
a sensibility, as long as one persists in seeking in them the lyric
flight. For though one perceives them with the intellect one can
scarcely feel them musically. The conflicting rhythms of the
third of the *Three Pieces for Pianoforte* clash without generat-
ing heat, without, after all, really sounding. No doubt, there is
a certain admirable uncompromisingness, a certain Egyptian
severity, in the musical line of the first of the three. But if there
is such a thing as form without significance in music, might not
these compositions serve to exemplify it? Indeed, it is only as
experiments, as the incorporation in tone of an abstract and
intellectualized conception of forms, that one can at all comprehend them. And it is only in regarding him as primarily an
experimenter that the later Schoenberg loses his incomprehen-
sibility, and comes somewhat nearer to us.

There is much in Schoenberg's career that makes this explanation something more than an easy way of disposing of a
troublesome problem, makes it, indeed, eminently plausible.
Schoenberg was never the most instinctive and sensible, the
least cerebral and intellectualizing of musicians. For just as
Gustav Mahler might stand as an instance of musicianly temperament fatally outweighing musicianly intellect, so Arnold
Schoenberg might stand as an example of the equally excessive
outbalancing of sensibility by brain-stuff. The friendship of the
two men and their mutual admiration might easily be explained by the fact that each caught sight in the other of the
element he wanted most. No doubt, the works of Schoenberg's
early period, which extends from the songs, Opus 1, through the
Kammersymphonie, Opus 9, are full of a fervent lyricism, a
romantic effusiveness. *Gurrelieder,* indeed, opens wide the
floodgates of romanticism. But these compositions are somewhat
uncharacteristic and derivative. The early songs, for instance,
might have proceeded from the facile pen of Richard Strauss.
They have much of the Straussian sleepy warmth and sweet

harmonic color, much of the Straussian exuberance which at times so readily degenerates into the windy pride of the young bourgeois deeming himself a superman. It was only by accident that "Freihold" was not written by the Munich tone poet. The orchestral poem after Maeterlinck's *Pelléas* is also ultraromantic and post-Wagnerian. The trumpet theme, the *Pelléas* theme, for instance, is lineally descended from the "Walter von Stolzing" and *Parsifal* motives. The work reveals Schoenberg striving to emulate Strauss in the field of the symphonic poem; striving, however, in vain. For it has none of Strauss's glitter and point, and is rather dull and soggy. The great, bristling, pathetic climax is of the sort that has become exasperating and vulgar, rather than exciting, since Wagner and Tchaikovsky first exploited it. On the whole, the work is much less *Pelléas et Mélisande* than it is *Pelleas und Melisanda*. And the other works of this period, more brilliantly made and more opulently colored though they are, are still eminently of the romantic school. The person who declared ecstatically that assisting at a performance of the string sextet, *Verklärte Nacht,* resembled "hearing a new *Tristan,*" exhibited, after all, unconscious critical acumen. The great cantata, *Gurrelieder,* the symphonic setting of Jens Peter Jacobsen's romance in lyrics, might even stand as the grand finale of the whole post-Wagnerian, ultraromantic period, and represent the moment at which the whole style and atmosphere did its last heroic service. And even the *Kammersymphonie,* despite all the signs of transition to a more personal manner, despite the increased scholasticism of tone, despite the more acidulous coloration, despite the distinctly novel scherzo, with its capricious and fawnlike leaping, is not quite characteristic of the man.

It is in the String Quartet, Opus 7, that Schoenberg first speaks his proper tongue. And in revealing him, the work demonstrates how theoretical his intelligence is. No doubt, the D-minor Quartet is an important work, one of the most important of chamber compositions. Certainly, it is one of the great pieces of modern music. It gives an unforgettable and vivid sense of the voice, the accent, the timbre, of the hurtling, neurotic modern world; hints the coming of a free and subtle, bitter and powerful, modern musical art. As a piece of construction alone, the D-minor Quartet is immensely significant. The polyphony is bold and free, the voices exhibiting an independence perhaps unknown since the days of the madrigalists. The work is unified not only by the consolidation of the four movements into one, but as well by a central movement, a *Durchführung* which, introduced between the scherzo and the adagio, reveals the inner coherence of all the themes. There is no sacrifice of logic to the rules of harmony. Indeed, the work is characterized by a certain uncompromisingness and sharpness in its harmonies. The instrumental coloring is prismatic, all the registers of the strings being utilized with great deftness. Exclusive of the theme of the scherzo, which recalls a little overmuch the Teutonic banalities of Mahler's symphonies, the quality of the music is, on the whole, grave and poignant and uplifted. It has a scholarly dignity, a magistral richness, a chiaroscuro that at moments recalls Brahms, though Schoenberg has a sensuous melancholy, a delicacy and an Hebraic bitterness that the other has not. Like so much of Brahms, this music comes out of the silence of the study, though the study in this case is the chamber of a Jewish scholar more than that of a German. Were the entire work of the fullness and lyricism of the last two movements; were it throughout as impassioned as is the broad gray clamant germinal theme that commences the work and sweeps it before it, one might easily include the composer in the company of the masters of musical art.

Unfortunately, the magnificent passages are interspersed with unmusical ones. It is not only that the work does not quite "conceal art," that it smells overmuch of the laboratory. It is that portions of it are scarcely "felt" at all, are only too obviously carpentered. The work is full of music that addresses itself primarily to professors of theory. It is full of writing dictated by an arbitrary and intellectual conception of form. There is a great deal of counterpoint in it that exists only for the benefit of those who "read" scores, and that clutters the work. There are whole passages that exist only in obedience to

some scholastic demand for thematic inversions and deforma-
tions. There is an unnecessary deal of marching and counter-
marching of instruments, an obsession with certain rhythms
that becomes purely mechanical, an intensification of the contrapuntal pickings and peckings that annoy so often in the
compositions of Brahms. It is Schoenberg the intellectualist,
Schoenberg the Doctor of Music, not Schoenberg the artist, who
obtains here.

And it is he one encounters almost solely in the music of the
third period, the enigmatical little pieces for orchestra and
piano. It is he who has emerged victorious from the duel revealed by the D-minor Quartet. Those grotesque and menacing
little works are lineally descended from the intellectualized
passages of the great preceding one, are, indeed, a complete
expression of the theoretical processes which called them into
being. For while in the quartet the scholasticism appears to
have been superimposed upon a body of musical ideas, in the
works of the last period it appears well-nigh the generative
principle. These latter have all the airlessness, the want of
poetry, the frigidity of things constructed after a formula,
daring and brilliant though that formula is. They make it seem
as though Schoenberg had, through a process of consideration
and thought and study, arrived at the conclusion that the music
of the future would, in the logic of things, take such and such a
turn, that tonality as it is understood was doomed to disappear,
that part-writing would attain a new independence, that new
conceptions of harmony would result, that rhythm would attain
a new freedom through the influence of the new mechanical
body of man, and had proceeded to incorporate his theories in
tone. One finds the experimental and methodical at every turn
throughout these compositions. Behind them one seems invariably to perceive some one sitting before a sheet of music paper
and tampering with the art of music; seeking to discover what
would result were he to accept as harmonic basis not the major
triad but the minor ninth, to set two contradictory rhythms
clashing, or to sharpen everything and maintain a geometric

hardness of line. One always feels in them the intelligence
setting forth deliberately to discover new musical form. For all
their apparent freedom, they are full of the oldest musical
procedures, abound in canonic imitations, in augmentations,
and diminutions, in all sorts of grizzled contrapuntal maneu-
vers. They are head-music of the most uncompromising sort.
The *Five Orchestral Pieces* abound in purely theoretical combinations of instruments, combinations that do not at all sound.
Herzgewächse, the setting of the poem of Maeterlinck made
contemporaneously with these pieces, makes fantastic demands
upon the singer, asks the voice to hold high F *pppp,* to leap
swiftly across the widest intervals, and to maintain itself over a
filigree accompaniment of celesta, harmonium, and harp. But it
is in the piano music that the sonorities are most rudely
neglected. At moments they impress one as nothing more than
abstractions from the idiosyncrasies and mannerisms of the
works of Schoenberg's second period made in the hope of
arriving at definiteness of style and intensity of speech. They
smell of the synagogue as much as they do of the laboratory.
Beside the Doctor of Music there stands the Talmudic Jew, the
man all intellect and no feeling, who subtilizes over musical art
as though it were the Law.

The compositions of this period constitute an artistic retro-
gression rather than an advance. They are not "modern music"
for all their apparent stylistic kinship to the music of Stravinsky
and Scriabin and Ornstein. Nor are they "music of the past."
They belong rather more to the sort of music that has no more
relation with yesteryear than it has with this or next. They
belong to the sort that never has youth and vigor, is old the
moment it is produced. Their essential inexpressiveness makes
almost virtueless the characteristics which Schoenberg has carried into them from out his fecund period. The severity and
boldness of contour, so biting in the quartet, becomes almost
without significance in them. If there is such a thing as rhythm-
less music, would not the stagnant orchestra of the *Five Orchestral Pieces* exemplify it? The alternately rich and acidulous

color is faded; an icy green predominates. And, curiously enough, throughout the group the old romantic allegiance of the earliest Schoenberg reaffirms itself. Wotan with his spear stalks through the conclusion of the first of the *Three Pieces for Pianoforte*. And the second of the series, a composition not without its incisiveness, as well as several of the tiny *Six Piano Pieces*, Opus 19, recall at moments Brahms, at others Chopin, a Chopin of course cadaverous and turned slightly green.

It may be that by means of these experiments Schoenberg will gird himself for a new period of creativity just as once indubitably by the aid of experiments which he did not publish he girded himself for the period represented by the D-minor Quartet. It may be that after the cloud of the war has completely lifted from the field of art, and a normal interchange is re-established it will be seen that the monodrama, Opus 20, *Die Lieder des Pierrot Lunaire*, which was the latest of his works to obtain a hearing, was in truth an earnest of a new loosing of the old lyrical impulse so long incarcerated. But, for the present, Schoenberg, the composer, is almost completely obscured by Schoenberg, the experimenter. For the present, he is the great theoretician combating other theoreticians, the Doctor of Music annihilating doctor-made laws. As such, his usefulness is by no means small. He speaks with an authority no less than that of his adversaries, the other and less radical professors. He, too, has invented a system and a method; his *Harmonielehre*, for instance, is as irrefragable as theirs; he can quote scripture with the devil. He is at least demolishing the old constraining superstitions, and in so doing may exercise an incalculable influence on the course of music. It may be that many a musician of the future will find himself the better equipped because of Schoenberg's explorations. He is undoubtedly the most magistral theorist of the day. The fact that he could write at the head of his treatise on harmony, "What I have here set down I have learned from my pupils," independently proves him a great teacher. It is probable that his later music, the music of his puzzling "third period," will shortly come to be considered as simply a part of his unique course of instruction.

Gurrelieder

AN ARTIST'S EXPRESSION infrequently is completely individualized by the time of his twenty-seventh year, and that of Schoenberg was not exceptional. When in 1900 he began to set the
poetic cycle which the seraph of Danish literature, Jens Peter
Jacobsen, had formed from the legend of King Waldemar I of
Denmark and the fair Tove and called the songs of Gurre, the
castle with which the legend associated their tragic love, the
future heresiarch still was, regularly enough, under the domination of the expressions of his immediate predecessors. These
were the Wagnerian, the Straussian, the Brahmsian, and the
Mahleresque. His setting of *Gurrelieder* for giant orchestra,
choruses, and solo voices thus is largely traditional; like the
youthful work of other gifted composers, say, the Wagner of
The Flying Dutchman, the Strauss of *Don Juan,* the Stravinsky
of *L'Oiseau de Feu.* The giant cantata recalls the general
romanticism of the late nineteenth century, in particular the
rapture and the harmonic system of Wagner, the vasty means of
Mahler's choral symphonies and something of his melodic architectural form, Strauss's beefy contrapuntal effects and dramatic
emphasis, and Brahms's rich Lieder style. It actually is a sort of
Wagnerian music drama cast with Strauss's and Mahler's symphonic means in the form of a song cycle, for soloists and
chorus, preceded by a prelude and inclusive of two sizable
orchestral transitions, and not without distinct Brahmsian characteristics.

One tenor represents Waldemar, another Klaus the fool. The
soprano represents Tove; the mezzo the little wood dove; the
bass the peasant; the four-part male chorus, Waldemar's ghostly
henchmen. The work falls into three parts, lightly corresponding to the three parts of a symphony and the acts of an opera.
The first includes the songs of Waldemar and Tove expressing
their longing for each other, the songs vocal of their joy in
reunion, their nocturnal dialogue and premonitions of death

and of resurrection, and finally, after the first orchestral interlude, the song of the wood dove lamenting the death of Tove at
the hands of the jealous queen. The second part contains
Waldemar's denunciation and rejection of God. The third
embodies the demonic nocturnal hunt to which Waldemar and
his henchmen have been condemned, the choruses of the men
interspersed by the song of the frightened peasant, the jittery
soliloquy of the fool, the ghostly Waldemar's expression of his
sense of the dead Tove in the voice of the woods, in the regard
of the lake, in the laughing light of the stars: and finally the
play of the summer wind and the resurrection of the lovers in
the life of nature.

The composer of *Dreimals Sieben Lieder des Pierrot Lunaire*
is nonetheless clearly heralded, nay actually present, in *Gurrelieder;* as definitely present there as the composer of *Die
Walküre* in *Der Fliegende Holländer,* the composer of *Don
Quixote* in *Don Juan,* the composer of *Les Noces* in *L'Oiseau
de Feu.* The work, naturally enough, is unequal. The first four
songs in the first part have far less quality than the later ones;
and pages such as that of Waldemar's blasphemy, the macabre
hunting chorus, and the final salutation of the sunrise, reveal
more of ambition and striving than of power. The dreaminess
and the sweetness of some of the music is occasionally cloying.
And still, for all its weaknesses, its Wagnerian, Straussian,
Brahmsian echoes, *Gurrelieder* is a creation, the sonorous,
sumptuously colored embodiment of an original idea, full of
glowing poetic music, and doubtless has a future. The conception, to begin with, is a formal one. Each of the nineteen songs
composing the whole, a simple or double Lied form, is built up
structurally from its own melodic germ and is organically
related to the rest by the cyclic use of themes, by contrasts of
tonality and character, and by orchestral transitions of various
length. The work actually concludes with the chord in the
tonality with which it began. And Schoenberg's form is already
distinctive: and when we speak of his form as being already
distinctive, we are referring to the form of the older, the main

part of the *Gurrelieder*, written between 1900 and 1902, and not that of the close of the last section, including the *Sprechstimme*, the melodic use of the celesta, and the high, shrill, piercing sonorities; for that dates from 1910 and is therefore contemporaneous with the *Three Pieces*, Opus 11, and the work of the middle Schoenberg. Here, in the earliest parts of the score, we find him melodic and contrapuntal to a degree, even on the simplest and most Wagnerian pages. While his harmony is fairly Wagnerian, it is anything but slavishly so, displaying a considerable sensitivity. As for his melodic line, it frequently leaps over wide intervals, as in Tove's third song, and skips about nervously in the songs of the peasant and the fool. Instrumental sonorities are often used thematically, from Tove's second song onward. The instruments themselves frequently are employed soloistically, and examples of the oppositions of the sonorities of various orchestral families are anything but uncommon. And the individualized constituent forms and the grand one they build up communicate individual moods and an individual experience. If these moods and this experience are "romantic"; if *Gurrelieder*, like *Tristan*, constitutes with surging, rapturous, and dreamy page after page a "climate of love," it does so unhackneyedly. The erotic moods are tenderer, more penetrating and spiritualized than Wagner's relatively simple ones. Schoenberg's heroine, too, possibly in conformity with Jacobsen's idea, is much more feminine and shy than Wagner's heroic *amorosa*. The range of the moods also includes such fantastic and original variants as those of the bedeviled peasant, the dislocated and grotesque agonies of the fool, the Puckish humors of the "Summer Wind's Wild Chase." The very implicit experience, the vision of a vital progress by stages of personal love and personal loss to a selfless victorious absorption in the divine breath, the "life" of nature, while essentially romantic, is individual. And while the entire expression, like Wagner's, is rapturous and subjectively lyrical, it is rapturous to the verge of the ecstatic; and its psychographical and subjective lyricism borders on expressionism, on the ecstatically confessional. And it is a magical score, rich in the elusively mysterious, sensuous, melting, and bewitching sort of expressions which, drawn with a fineness no completely waking condition can achieve, flow from some enchantment in the subject itself and, abundant in the music of Schumann, of Wagner, of Debussy, are called poetical.

Need it be asseverated that these distinctive characteristics of *Gurrelieder* are the germs of those completely distinguishing and characterizing the later work, at least that part of it previous to the systematization of the twelve-tone technique? The plasticity of the *Gurrelieder*—what is it but the adumbration of the extraordinary plasticity of those later works, indicative of an intuition always connected with a form-feeling that works itself out with utter relentlessness, compression, and logicality, whether in the molds of the Lied form or in those of contrapuntal forms, the passacaglia, the canon, the inverted canon, or the *motus cancrizans?** The harmonic sensitivity, what is that but the indication of the sensitivity that was to produce the bewitching harmonic beauty of the characteristic atonal pieces, the third of the *Five Pieces for Orchestra,* "Der Wechselnder Akkord" in especial. The wide leaps and skips of the melodic line, are they indeed anything but the annunciation of the melodic line of the scherzo of the first *Kammersymphonie* and of *Das Buch der Hängenden Gärten,* the chamber operas, the song *Herzgewächse,* the *Three Times Seven Songs of Pierrot Lunaire?* For us, they are nothing if not prophetic; and for us, the thematic use of instrumental sonorities is equally so; also the soloistic use of instruments, triumphant first in the *Kammersymphonie* and then in all Schoenberg's instrumental pieces. And the oppositions of the sonorities of various instrumental families seem anticipatory of one of the traits of style most distinctly Schoenbergian. Equally so is the feeling communicated by *Gurrelieder.* The feelings expressed by the later music are those of exquisite, idealistic, not so

---

* Crablike or retrograde motion; repeating a melody backward.

largely neurotic as neurodynamic modern people—people who make tremendously prompt, deep, intense nervous responses. Tove herself is but an earlier version of the exquisite essence figuring in *Pierrot* as *eine weisse Wäscherin.** And the ideas which compose and relate these essences are those of the erotic experience. More consistently and continually than any other contemporary composer of worth, Schoenberg is the musician of the exquisite, the deep, and also the bitter and painful erotic adventure: a circumstance which connects his art with that of Beardsley, of Strindberg, of Rodin, and that of other great "decadents." Opus 15, the cycle of songs on poems derived from *Das Buch der Hängenden Gärten* by Stefan George, creates a "climate of love" even more subtly, more poignantly and inclusively than *Gurrelieder*. The monodrama *Erwartung* brings to biting, almost madly intense, expression the experience of the modern woman who, wandering beyond the walls of her little garden in search of her lover, finds him dead for the sake of another. And the other little music drama, *Die Glückliche Hand*—the hand of Venus—conveys the experience of an enamored artist who, physically disgusting to his partner, is crushed by her efforts to escape him. The *Serenade*, Opus 24, also expresses, with the help of the words of Petrarch, the experience of the rejected lover. Again, the moods of the later Schoenberg include many that, extensions of the tortured ones of the latter sections of *Gurrelieder*, approach the extreme of uneasiness, of torment and dolor; and the cantata's peasant, Klaus the fool, and the Puckish summer wind attain a kind of apotheosis in the extremely bizarre moods of the "youthful idealist," the moon-drunken dandy Pierrot Lunaire of the fantastic twenty-one songs. The later forms of expression are also extremely ecstatic, almost supremely so, and supremely confessional. Psychographical, subjectively lyrical music would seem to reach its most exalted pitch in these works: they make the composer seem one determined not to shrink from the most

* "A white laundress."

audacious articulations of inner movements, those of the unconscious itself, and the ultimate secrets of his own soul. And the
whole of the later music, with its many passages of the purest
lyrical expansion—for all its inclusion of pages of paper music
—constitutes the most poetic, glamorous music produced by any
living composer. That poetry is a fragile one, an exquisite one,
a sort of expression of the gleaming, evanescent moment of
feeling. *Pierrot Lunaire,* which contains this "Celtic magic"
perhaps more abundantly than any other one of Schoenberg's
works—it is perhaps its apex and one of those of modern music—
may even seem, with its elusive lights, surges, ecstasies, aromas, a
sort of Chinese jar filled with conserved flower petals, and thus
something of an anomaly in the present world. But it is not
certain that succeeding times will find it so and may not
conceive it as the crystallization of the finest Viennese, the *fin-
de-siècle* European sensibility, and find the place of the composer close to that of the other exquisite musical poets, Schumann, Wagner, Chopin, and Debussy.

Indeed so clear a prefigurement of the composer of all these
magical pieces does *Gurrelieder* give that it is difficult to
understand how musicians whose interest in their art is a
serious one could have contrived to assist at the first American
performance of the revelatory piece, under Stokowski's baton
early in 1932, and continue, for all the grossness of the production, unconvinced of the integrity of Schoenberg's entire output
up to the time of his systematization of the twelve-tone technique. That they should have come away as puzzled by the
system-making Schoenberg as they were before they heard the
cantata, is not a wonder. For *Gurrelieder* casts no light on him.
But that it should have failed to make them conscious of the
one man present from first to last in all of Schoenberg's pieces
confessing the dominance of sensibility, and failed to make
them recognize in the later atonal works, up to the *Serenade*
and the Suite, Opus 25, the logical developments of the germs
stirring in this first experiment with the larger means if not the
larger forms, verges upon the miraculous. For us, Schoenberg's

declaration at the time of the first performances of his songs on George's poems is unsurprising: "In these Lieder I have succeeded for the first time in approaching an ideal of expression and form that have hovered before me for years. Hitherto, I had merely not sufficient strength and sureness to realize that ideal. Now, however, I . . . have definitely started on my journey." For if we ourselves see anything in Schoenberg's career, it is nothing if not the development of a man according to the law of life which compels us, if we would live and grow, to become ever more fully and nakedly what we essentially are.

Schoenberg and Varèse

MEANWHILE, they played Europe and the New World off against each other at the International Guild. Schoenberg's *Serenade* began the program; Varèse's *Intégrales* ended it, and the interval was broad as the sea. It was delicate lacework sound against brute shrilling jagged music. It was the latest ghostly flowering of the romantic tradition against a polyphony not of lines, but of metallic cubical volumes. It was, essentially, the thinking introverted solitary against mass movement in which the individual goes lost; for the reason either piece did its author uncommon justice. Few works of Schoenberg traverse less writing for the eye than this new one, and breathe more thoroughly. The march which leads on the *Serenade* and then leads it off again may ultimately belong to the company of Schoenberg's paper pieces. But the rest of the little movements, the minuet, the variations, and the setting of Petrarch's sonnet Number 217, the "Dance Scene" and the "Song without Words," flow lightly; and bring within their small compass and in the familiar character of the *Serenade* a very personal quality of sound. The mood is serener than it was in *Pierrot Lunaire,* and the movement less languorous and less explosive. Nonetheless, the piece's quality is similarly half painful, half dreamy; characteristically Schoenbergian; the tone eerie and *sotto voce;*

the structure submitted to intense concentration. The nervous, excited strumming of the mandoline and guitar called for by the score has correspondences throughout the form. And like so much of Schoenberg the *Serenade* is fundamentally Brahmsian in feeling. The conservatism of the structure, the frequency of rhythmic repetitions, the symmetrical formation of motifs, themes, and entire sections, has been marked by the German aestheticians. Perfectly apparent to the layman is the brooding romanticism of the *melos*, particularly in the "Song without Words," and the spook-romanticism of the loose-jointed periods of the minuet and "Dance Scene." The characteristic undulant movement, the lyrical upheavals of the line, true, have been compressed by this ultramodern into minute spaces; stand immeasurably tightened, curtailed, and broken up. But they exist in Schoenberg as essentially as in Schumann, Wagner, and Brahms. That is the German, apparently, and the European in touch with a past. Schoenberg is the carrier-on, the continuator of his predecessors' line of advance. Despite the architectural preoccupation distinguishing him from the great mass of his artistic ancestors, from Brahms, even, Schoenberg is the romanticist of today; as Stravinsky justly if unkindly denominated him. He is the singer *par excellence* of the individual, the proud, solitary, brooding soul; the lover *par excellence* of the singular, the *raffiné*, the precious in musical expression; of the strange and unwonted in harmony and mood. The sudden entirely unheralded high F, *pianpianissimo*, which squeaks in the singer's voice toward the close of the song *Herzgewächse*: what is it but a very extreme example of Schoenberg's characteristic processes? To a degree the *Serenade* approaches the humanistic ideal a little more closely than *Pierrot Lunaire* and *Herzgewächse*, less descriptive and macabre and perverse as it is. But the divergence is insignificant. Jewelry and feeling of rarity remain; and with those aspects of romanticism, its more permanent attractive ones. Like his masters, Schoenberg is busied in a rigorous search for his own truth, for his own naturalness, and uncompromisingly bends the inherited means of music to parallel his way of feeling. The *Serenade* is the work of a truthseeker, not satisfied with conventions, and actively developing the suppleness, copiousness, and precision of his medium. To be sure, there is a novelty in Schoenberg's approach. His touch is less warm, his emotional frontage narrower than the great romanticists'. He is the man of his hour, and that hour is a difficult and tortured one, less communicable than its forerunners, isolating its members in moody loneliness and semimystical adventure. Schoenberg's music sounds as exquisite, shadowy, and remote as Paul Klee's painting looks. Brahms shudders like a ghost. But the ghost has the old gravity and sentiment, and wears Wagnerian plumes, besides.

Passing from the *Serenade* to *Intégrales* is like passing from the I-ness to the it-ness of things; from a hypersensitive unworldly feeling to a sense of strident material power; and from a traditional expression to one which is independent, and rooted as largely in life as in Berlioz and Stravinsky. Varèse stems from the fat European soil quite as directly as Schoenberg does. The serious approach, the scientific curiosity, of what of the nineteenth century remained on the Continent, is active in him and his audacious art. Besides Varèse is somewhat of a romanticist. For all his extreme aural sensitivity to the ordinary phenomena and perception of the prodigious symphony of the city and port of New York, he has a tendency to seize upon life in terms of the monstrous and the elemental. *Amériques*, the first of his characteristic "machines," resembles Brontosaurus, the nasty hungry *Fresser*, waddling filthy, stinking, and trumpeting through a mesozoic swamp. Fafner was an elf in comparison. That is the Berlioz influence: it is significant that Varèse first appeared before the American public in the capacity of conductor of the Frenchman's prodigious *Requiem*. But his romantic aspects are balanced by more humanistic ones. Varèse has derived his idiom through direct perception, and used it in interests other than those of descriptivity. He has never imitated the sounds of the city in his works, as he is frequently supposed to have done. His music is much more in the nature of penetration. He will tell you how much the symphony of New York differs from that of Paris: Paris' being noisier, a succession of shrill, brittle hissing sounds, New York's on the contrary, quieter, for the mere reason that it is incessant, enveloping the New Yorker's existence as the rivers the island of Manhattan. He works with those sonorities merely because he has come into relation with American life, and found corresponding rhythms set free within himself. It is probable that at the moments in which Varèse is compelled to give form to his feelings about life, sensations received from the thick current of natural sound in which we dwell, push out from the storehouses of the brain as organic portions of an idea.

His feeling is equally preponderantly unromantic. It is much more a feeling of life massed. There are those who will say, of course, that *Intégrales* is merely cubical music. To a definite degree, Varèse's polyphony is different from the fundamentally linear polyphony of Stravinsky's art. His music is built more vertically, moves more to solid masses of sound, and is very rigorously held in them. Even the climaxes do not break the cubism of form. The most powerful pronouncements merely force sound into the air with sudden violence, like the masses of two impenetrable bodies in collision. The hardness of edge and impersonality of the material itself, the balance of brass, percussion and woodwind, the piercing golden screams, sudden stops and lacunae, extremely rapid *crescendi* and *diminuendi*, contribute to the squareness. The memorable evening of its baptism, *Intégrales* resembled nothing so much as shining cubes of freshest brass and steel set in abrupt pulsing motion. But for us, they were not merely metallic. They were the tremendous masses of American life, crowds, city piles, colossal organizations; suddenly set moving, swinging, throbbing by the poet's dream; and glowing with a clean, daring, audacious, and majestic life. Human power exulted anew in them. Majestic skyscraper chords, grandly resisting and moving volumes, ruddy sonorities, and mastered ferocious outbursts cried it forth. For the first time in modern music, more fully even than in the first section of *Le Sacre,* one heard an equivalent Wotan's spear music. But this time, it had something to do not with the hegemony of romantic Germany, but with the vast forms of the democratic, communistic new world.

Without the juxtaposition of the *Serenade, Intégrales* would have been a great experience adding to a growing prestige. But that evening the Atlantic rolled. The opposition of the two works precluded such concepts as "Schoenberg's music" and "music by Varèse." One saw two kinds of music, apart as two continents, and based a thousand leagues from each other. Far to the east one saw romanticism rooted in the individualism of western Europe, romanticism that indeed was the gentle old European life. And close, there lay the new humanism, the hard, general spirit, rooted in the massive communal countries: Russia and the United States, itself an integral portion of all one meant saying "the new world" and "America."

Wozzeck

THE MUSICAL WORLD may think to perceive in the isolation in which members of the Viennese group about Schoenberg have been living with their intimates and their pupils, acquainted each, it has been asserted, with at most eleven persons outside his actual family, the sign of their divorce from common humanity and self-indulgent concentration of interest in a private world; and choose to detect in the apparently fantastic monotonal system, the twelve-tone technique original among them, the proof of a retreat from life. Yet it is a fact that out of this secluded group there has come a dramatic work beautifully and broadly expressive, through the new musical form developed among its members, of the psyche and the world of one of the most tragic of contemporary human types. This is the *Wozzeck* of Alban Berg,* himself one of the principal creators

* This essay was written before Berg's death [author's note].

in the *cénacle,* and indubitably Schoenberg's most gifted pupil. And the piece proves that the insulation of the components of the Viennese coterie is merely apparent and actually the state of self-sufficiency, of indifference to the politics of art, and of utter concentration upon the formal and aesthetic problems crowding in upon them, in which the complete feeling of life leaves pure artists.

The book of this deeply moving musical drama is made up of fifteen of the twenty-three brief scenes of the tragi-grotesque play of *Woyzeck* or *Wozzeck,* the little masterpiece in which Georg Büchner, a prematurely deceased member of the Young German school of the 1830's and a revolutionary who expressed the tragedy of revolutions in his drama *Dantons Tod,* arraigned the existing social idea through sympathy with the underdog. The action half realistically, half symbolistically, represents the catastrophe of a poor soldier in a provincial German garrison during a time of peace; but the relation of the crude action to the facts of poverty, of human savagery and stupidity, generalizes it into a symbol of the experience not only of the "little man" but of the fine but incomplete and defenseless individual in an unspiritual society. Franz Wozzeck, the protagonist, is weak not only because of his ignorance, his poverty, and his low social status, but because of the circumstance that his sensitive mind is a half-developed individual's. As Dr. Willi Reich points out in his excellent analysis, Wozzeck has an unclear sense of the primeval unity of his being and a childlike intuition of the life of the all-mother, and he has begun to judge for himself and to judge himself. But his half-awakened individualism only renders him helpless against the humiliations he has to endure from the powers of the world and the repressions of military servitude; and under his humiliations and repressions, assisted by his own inner weakness, his intuitions become delusions, and he ends as a murderer and a suicide. These oppressive half-external, half-internal powers are satirically represented by Büchner in the form of a caricature of a captain, a military doctor, and a drum major, so that the whole of Wozzeck's spiritual as well as material environment appears in a grotesquely comic light. Through the figure of the captain we perceive the force of a fear-engendered Philistine morality; through that of the doctor, the inhuman coldness of materialistic science, inimical to man and his soul; and through that of the drum major, the brute in the male. All these part real and part symbolic as well as half-external and half-interior forces grind Wozzeck under and deride him. The military doctor, a scoundrel, performs medical experiments upon him—Wozzeck submitting because the few *groschen* the doctor pays him help support his girl and their illegitimate child. The drum major seduces the girl, actually half abandoned by the helpless Wozzeck. The captain, himself tormented by the military doctor, maliciously opens Wozzeck's eyes upon the intrigue. Faced with the final humiliation of having to share the object of his love with another, the desperate soldier stabs the girl and drowns himself in a pond.

The fifteen scenes drawn by Berg from this mordant little tragi-grotesque have been organized by him in the form of three acts of five scenes apiece, constituting respectively an Exposition, a Crisis, and a Catastrophe; and in this shape they have been made contributory to a music drama intensifying Büchner's idea with a power that sets the product beside the most aesthetic works bequeathed the lyric theater since Wagner—*Pelléas, Le Coq d'Or,* and *Elektra.* The composer has freshly felt the oppressive world of the underdog. His atonal material is deeply infused with the terrible experience and its tormented moods. And he had conceived his score in sympathy with the dramatist, reinforcing *his* work in the way permitted by it. The dramatist had called for incidental music in the forms of military marches, folk songs and choruses, and dances of various kinds. Again, his play is episodic, inviting musical connections of the short scenes. And its realism, in spirit not so much that of the nineteenth as of the expressionistic twentieth century, almost invites a musical reinforcement of the action itself. For, figurative of inarticulate characters, it allows these personages to exhibit their feelings and their conscious, semi-conscious, and wholly unconscious motives in brittle, ejaculatory, sometimes entirely irrational, words and phrases and sentences resembling those of persons under fearful emotional stress, thus by its very illyricality offering music the opportunity of purveying lyric and choragic expressions and augmenting the dramatic expression in the way most naturally its own. And Berg's score performs the three chores consciously and unconsciously left to music by Büchner. It supplies the realistic incidental music. It connects the little scenes with interludes. It supplements the verbal and dramatic expressions with music that lyrically expresses the tormented feelings and states of the protagonists and that choragically renders the sentiments of an ideal spectator moved by the vision of their unnecessary suffering; particularly in the great orchestral epilogue, which, placed before the final scene and recapitulative of the thematic material of the score, seems to cry to the heavens the pity of the waste of the human being, and to men the need of a humane world.

And it presents its entire contribution, popular incidental music and all, in the shape of formalized symphonic music. Retaining to a certain extent the Wagnerian technique of the leitmotiv, Berg has rejected the porridgelike Wagnerian form of the music drama, conceiving his score in the framework of forms drawn from absolute music—suites, passacaglias, themes with variations, fugues, sonata forms, inventions, etc.—and integrating his material in these traditional molds solidly, sustainedly, sometimes with a refreshing musicianly length of breath. Perhaps not all of these formalizations of his are equally distinguished or unified among themselves from the point of view of style. Berg is one of the genial contemporary Europeans, a student of Schoenberg's quite worthy of comparison with his puissant teacher. All of his works, his String Quartet and Chamber Symphony no less than his *Wozzeck,* introduce us to expressions of a live sensibility, a genuine lyricism and eloquence, and a fire nobly held in rein: the possible effect of the combination of Germanic feeling and fervor with Viennese elegance. One is tempted to call Berg's temperament simpler than Schoenberg's,

more sensuous and warm and romantic: and he is armed with a
deal of this master's prodigious technique. But he is also a little
less powerful than Schoenberg, and his expression tends more to
run in grooves dug by the music of Debussy and *Tristan* than
Schoenberg's does. He is less sure of his style than his master,
less evenly inspired. Thus, just as in the material of *Wozzeck,*
one sometimes hears echoes of the *Ring* and of *Pelléas,* one
sometimes finds the score recalling, as in the great orchestral
epilogue, the mannerisms of Puccini and Strauss. Still, these
pages are venial sins, not really blemishing. The music as a
whole sounds very rich; and the innumerably many fruits of
exquisite feeling and discretion audible in it, to a degree amply
compensate for the occasional secondary passages. Besides, much
of *Wozzeck* is prime: the passacaglia, for example, the variations, indeed the majority of the scenes and interludes; and all
of it with sure eloquence reinforces, interprets, and generalizes
the dramatic idea. We never find the composer sacrificing
emotion or the interests of the drama to the traditional musical
organisms in which he has cast his score. The vocal medium, a
mixture of song proper and Schoenbergesque speech-song, conforms realistically to the drama of the words and situations.
And through Berg's constant application of the musical principle of variation in conformity to the dramatic movement, the
traditional forms remain sensitively, pointedly psychographic
and representative of the developments of the tragedy. The
score as a whole is capitally expressive, particularly in the soft,
descending, dragging progressions accompanying the deep depression into which the laden Wozzeck is thrown by the voices
of nature at twilight, in the stuttering rhythm to which the
horrified tavern guests awaken to the blood stains on the
deranged man's hands, in the sibilant chromatic harmonies in
sevenths that follow the suicide in the stilly pond, and in the
dance scene with its unforgettable communication of a world
from which all color and joy have fled.

Besides, the various absolute musical forms have been applied to the text with a sense of their dramatic relevancy. The
five-part binary form, a symphony, underpins the entire second

act, itself representative of the growing difference between Wozzeck and Marie. The music of the first act, exposing Wozzeck's relationship to his environment, begins in the form of a suite, continues first as a rhapsody, then as a military march and cradle song, then as a passacaglia, and ends as an *andante affetuoso quasi rondo;* and each of these forms, too, has its dramatic symbolism. The suite, for example, which is made up of archaic dance patterns such as gavottes, gigues, and sarabandes, underlies Wozzeck's conversation with the captain, the representative of church and state. The passacaglia mordantly intonates the scene exposing the doctor and his fixed idea; the military march and cradle song, the scene exhibiting Marie's excitement over the soldiery and her loneliness with her child. The last act, again, is made up of five inventions, through which a reiterated low B-flat, an organ point, accompanies the mounting obsession of the murderous impulse; and like the preceding forms, the inventions are appropriate to the action. The very final scene, where Marie's boy innocently plays while other children run in with the news of the discovery of her dead body, is coupled with a *perpetuum mobile,* itself poignantly expressive of the sense of the unending meaningless motion called "life" with which the tragedy leaves one. Thus a pronouncedly successful attempt to solve the problem of form in the musical drama with the means of absolute music, an important proof that a large work can be built up atonally and with the twelve-tone technique of the Viennese group, and one of the solid achievements of modern music, *Wozzeck* has expressed the gray and terrible world where the "little man," the underdog, lives, suffers, and perishes alone, unseen, unheard: and thus idealistically given the modern world a potential social ligament. For the essence of the character himself, we repeat, is the underdog's in the widest sense. It is that of half the fine people we know. And it is that of all the people all over the world who, half-individualized members of an unspiritual society, suffer, break, and perish, struggling to hold the bit of infinity that is the patrimony of the human creature.

II

Impressionism, Primitivism,
and Neoclassicism

Berlioz

THE COURSE OF TIME, that has made so many musicians recede from us and dwindle, has brought Berlioz the closer to us and shown him great. The age in which he lived, the decades that followed his death, found him unsubstantial enough. They recognized in him only the projector of gigantic edifices, not the builder. His music seemed scaffolding only. Though a generation of musicians learned from him, came to listen to the proper voices of the instruments of the orchestra because of him, though music became increasingly pictural, ironic, concrete because he had labored, his own work still appeared ugly with unrealized intentions. If he obtained at all as an artist, it was because of his frenetic romanticism, his bizarreness, his Byronic postures, traits that were after all minor and secondary enough in him. For those were the only of his characteristics that his hour could understand. All others it ignored. And so Berlioz remained for half a century simply the composer of the extravagant *Symphonie Fantastique* and the brilliant *Harold in Italy*, and, for the rest, a composer of brittle and arid works, barren of authentic ideas, "a better litterateur than musician." However, with the departure of the world from out the romantic house, Berlioz has rapidly recovered. Music of his that before seemed ugly has gradually come to have force and significance. Music of his that seemed thin and gray has suddenly become satisfactory and red. Composers as eminent as Richard Strauss, conductors as conservative as Weingartner, critics as sensitive as Romain Rolland have come to perceive his vast strength and importance, to express themselves concerning him in no doubtful language. It is as though the world had had to move to behold Berlioz, and that only in a day germane to him and among the men his kin could he assume the stature rightfully his, and live.

For we exist today in a time of barbarian inroads. We are beholding the old European continent of music swarmed over by Asiatic hordes, Scyths and Mongols and Medes and Persians, all the savage musical tribes. Once more the old arbitrary barrier between the continents is disappearing, and the classic traits of the West are being mingled with those of the subtle, sensuous, spiritual East. It is as if the art of music, with its new scales, its new harmonies, its new coloring, its new rhythmical life, were being revolutionized, as if it were returning to its beginnings. It is as if some of the original impulse to make music were reawakening. And so, through this confusion, Berlioz has suddenly flamed with significance. For he himself was the rankest of barbarians. A work like the *Requiem* has no antecedents. It conforms to no accepted canon, seems to obey no logic other than that of the rude and powerful mind that cast it forth. For the man who could write music so crude, so sheerly strong, so hurtling, music innocent of past or tradition, the world must indeed have been in the first day of its creation. For such a one forms must indeed have had their pristine and undulled edge and undiminished bulk, must have insisted themselves sharply and compellingly. The music has all the uncouthness of a direct and unquestioning response to such a vision. Little wonder that it was unacceptable to a silver and romantic epoch. The romanticists had aspired to paint vast canvases, too. But the vastness of their canvases had remained a thing of intention, a thing of large and pretentious decoration. Berlioz' music was both too rude and too stupendous for their tastes. And, in truth, to us as well, who have felt the great cubical masses of the moderns and have heard the barbarian tread, the sense of beauty that demanded the giant blocks of the *Requiem* music seems still a little a strange and monstrous thing. It seems indeed an atavism, a return to modes of feeling that created the monuments of other ages, of barbarous and forgotten times. Well did Berlioz term his work "Babylonian and Ninevitish"! Certainly it is like nothing so much as the cruel and ponderous bulks, the sheer, vast tombs and ramparts and terraces of Khorsabad and Nimrud, bare and oppressive under the sun of Assyria. Berlioz must have harbored some elemental demand for form inherent in the human mind but buried and forgotten until it woke to life in him again. For there is a truly primitive and savage power in the imagination that could heap such piles of music, revel in the shattering fury of trumpets, upbuild choragic pyramids. Here, before Stravinsky and Ornstein, before Moussorgsky, even, was a music barbarous and radical and revolutionary, a music beside which so much of modern music dwindles.

It has, primarily, some of the nakedness, some of the sheerness of contour, toward which the modern men aspire. In the most recent years there has evidenced itself a decided reaction from the vaporous and fluent contours of the musical impressionists, from the style of *Pelléas et Mélisande* in particular. Men as disparate as Schoenberg and Magnard and Igor Stravinsky have been seeking, in their own fashion, the one through a sort of mathematical harshness, the second through a Gothic severity, the third through a machinelike regularity, to give their work a new boldness, a new power and incisiveness of design. Something of the same sharpness and sheerness was attained by Berlioz, if not precisely by their means, at least to a degree no less remarkable than theirs. He attained it through the nakedness of his melodic line. The music of the *Requiem* is almost entirely a singularly powerful and characteristic line. It is practically unsupported. Many persons pretend that Berlioz wanted a knowledge of harmony and counterpoint. Certainly his feeling for harmony was a very rudimentary one, in nowise refined beyond that of his predecessors, very simple when compared to that of his contemporaries, Chopin and Schumann. And his attempts at creating counterpoint, judged from the first movement of *Harold in Italy,* are clumsy enough. But it is questionable whether this ignorance did not stand him in good stead rather than in bad; and whether, in the end, he did not make himself fairly independent of both these musical elements. For the *Requiem* attains a new sort of musical grandeur from its sharp, heavy, rectangular, rhythmically powerful melodic line. It voices through it a bold, naked, immense language. With Baudelaire, Berlioz could have said, "L'énergie c'est le grâce suprême." For the beauty of this his masterpiece lies in just the delineating power, the characteristic of this crude, vigorous, unadorned melody. Doubtless to those still baffled by its nudity, his music appears thin. But if it is at all thin, its thinness is that of the steel cable.

And it has the rhythmical vivacity and plenitude that characterizes the newest musical art. If there is one quality that unites in a place apart the Stravinskys and Ornsteins, the Blochs and Scriabins, it is the fearlessness and exuberance and savagery with which they pound out their rhythms. Something long buried in us seems to arise at the vibration of these fierce, bold, clattering, almost convulsive strokes, to seek to gesticulate and dance and leap. And Berlioz possessed this elemental feeling for rhythm. Schumann was convinced on hearing the *Symphonie Fantastique* that in Berlioz music was returning to its beginnings, to the state where rhythm was unconstrained and irregular, and that in a short while it would overthrow the laws which had bound it so long. So, too, it seems to us, despite all the rhythmical innovations of our time. The personality that could beat out exuberantly music as rhythmically various and terse and free must indeed have possessed a primitive naïveté and vitality and spontaneity of impulse. What manifestation of unbridled will in that freedom of expression! Berlioz must have been blood brother to the savage, the elemental creature who out of the dark and hidden needs of life itself invents on his rude musical instrument a mighty rhythm. Or, he must have been like a powerful and excited steed, chafing his bit, mad to give his energy rein. His blood must forever have been craving the liberation of turgid and angular and irregular beats, must forever have been crowding his imagination with new and compelling combinations, impelling him to the movements of leaping and marching. For he seems to have found in profusion the accents that quicken and lift and lance, found them in all varieties, from the brisk and delicate steps of the ballets in *La Damnation de Faust* to the large, far-flung momentum that drives the choruses of the *Requiem* mountain high; from the mad and riotous finales of the *Harold* symphony and the *Symphonie Fantastique* to the red, turbulent, and *canaille* march rhythms, true music of insurgent masses, clangorous with echoes of tocsins and barricades and revolutions.

But it is in his treatment of his instrument that Berlioz seems most closely akin to the newest musicians. For he was the first to permit the orchestra to dictate music to him. There had, no doubt, existed skillful and sensitive orchestrators before him, men who were deeply aware of the nature of their tools, men who, like Mozart, could scarcely repress their tears at the sound of a favorite instrument, and wrote marvelously for flutes and horns and oboes and all the components of their bands. But matched with his, their knowledge of the instrument was patently relative. For, with them, music had on the whole a general timbre. Phrases which they assigned, say, to violins or flutes can be assigned to other instruments without doing the composition utter damage. But in the works of Berlioz music and instruments are inseparable. One cannot at all rearrange his orchestration. Though the phrases that he has written for bassoon or clarinet might imaginably be executed by other instruments, the music would perish utterly in the substitution. What instrument but the viola could appreciate the famous *Harold* theme? For just as in a painting of Cézanne's the form is inseparable from the color, is, indeed, one with it, so, too, in the works of Berlioz and the moderns the form is part of the sensuous quality of the band. When Rimsky-Korsakov uttered the pronouncement that a composition for orchestra could not exist before the orchestration was completed, he was only phrasing a rule upon which Berlioz had acted all his life. For Berlioz set out to learn the language of the orchestra. Not only did he call for new instruments, instruments that have eventually become integral portions of the modern bands, but he devoted himself to a study of the actual natures and ranges and qualities of the old, and wrote the celebrated treatise that has become the textbook of the science of instrumentation. The thinness of much of his work, the feebleness of the overture to

Benvenuto Cellini, for instance, results from his inexperience in the new tongue. But he had not to practice long. It was not long before he became the teacher of his very contemporaries. Wagner owes as much to Berlioz' instrumentation as he owes to Chopin's harmony.

But for the new men, he is more than teacher. For them he is like the discoverer of a new continent. Through him they have come to find a new fashion of apprehending the world. Out of the paintbox that he opened, they have drawn the colors that make us see anew in their music the face of the earth. The tone poems of Debussy and the ballets of Ravel and Stravinsky, the scintillating orchestral compositions of Strauss and Rimsky and Bloch, could scarcely have come to be had not Berlioz called the attention of the world to the instruments in which the colors and timbres in which it is steeped, lie dormant.

And so the large and powerful and contained being that, after all, was Berlioz has come to appreciation. For behind the fiery, the volcanic Berlioz, behind the Byronic and fantastical composer, there was always another, greater man. The history of the art of Berlioz is the history of the gradual incarnation of that calm and majestic being, the gradual triumph of that grander personality over the other, up to the final unclosing and real presence in *Roméo* and the *Mass for the Dead.* The wild romanticist, the lover of the strange and the lurid and the grotesque who created the *Symphonie Fantastique,* never, perhaps, became entirely abeyant. And some of the salt and flavor of Berlioz' greater, more characteristic works, the tiny musical particles, for instance, that compose the "Queen Mab" scherzo in *Roméo,* or the bizarre combination of flutes and trombones in the *Requiem,* macabre as the Orcagna frescoes in Pisa, are due to his fantastical imaginings. But, gradually, the deeper Berlioz came to predominate. That deeper spirit was a being that rose out of a vast and lovely cavern of the human soul, and was clothed in stately and in shining robes. It was a spirit that could not readily build itself out into the world, so large and simple it was, and had to wait long before it could find a worthy portal. It managed only to express itself partially, fragmentarily, in various transformations, till, by change, it found in the idea of the *Mass for the Dead* its fitting opportunity. Still, it was never entirely absent from the art of Berlioz, and in the great clear sense of it gained in the *Requiem* we can perceive its various and ever-present substantiations, from the very beginning of his career.

It is in the overture to *King Lear* already, in that noble and gracious introduction. From the very beginning, Berlioz revealed himself a proud and aristocratic spirit. Even in his most helpless moments, he is always noble. He shows himself possessed of a hatred for all that is unjust and ungirt and vulgar. There is always a largeness and gravity and chastity in his gesture. The coldness is most often simply the apparent coldness of restraint; the baldness, the laconism of a spirit that abhorred loose, ungainly manners of speech. Even the frenetic and orgiastic finales of the *Harold* and *Fantastic* symphonies are tempered by an athletic steeliness and irony, are pervaded, after all, by the good dry light of the intellect. The greater portion of the *Harold* is obviously, in its coolness and neatness and lightness, the work of one who was unwilling to dishevel himself in the cause of expression, who outlined his sensations reticently rather than effusively, and stood always a little apart. The *Corsair* overture has not the wild, rich balladry of that of the *Flying Dutchman,* perhaps. But it is full of the clear and quivering light of the Mediterranean. It is, in the words of Hans von Bülow, "as terse as the report of a pistol." And it flies swiftly before a wind its own. The mob scenes in *Benvenuto Cellini* are bright and brisk and sparkling, and compare not unfavorably with certain passages in *Petrouchka*. And, certainly, *Roméo* manifests unforgettably the fineness and nobility of Berlioz' temper. "The music he writes for his love scenes," someone has remarked, "is the best test of a musician's character." For, in truth, no type of musical expression gives so ample an opportunity to all that is latently vulgar in him to produce itself. And one has but to compare the "Garden Scene" of

Roméo with two other pieces of music related to it in style, the second act of *Tristan* and the *Romeo* of Tchaikovsky, to perceive in how gracious a light Berlioz' music reveals him. Wagner's powerful music hangs over the garden of his lovers like an oppressive and sultry night. Foliage and streams and the very moonlight pulsate with the fever of the blood. But there is no tenderness, no youth, no delicacy, no grace in Wagner's love passages. Tchaikovsky's, too, is predominantly lurid and sensual. And while Wagner's at least is full of animal richness, Tchaikovsky's is morbid and hysterical and perverse, sets us amid the couches and draperies and pink lampshades instead of out under the nighttime sky. Berlioz', however, is full of a still and fragrant poesy. His is the music of Shakespeare's lovers indeed. It is like the opening of hearts dumb with the excess of joy. It has all the high romance, all the ecstasy of the unspoiled spirit. For Berlioz seems to have possessed always his candor and his youth. Through three hundred years men have turned toward Shakespeare's play, with its Italian night and its balcony above the fruit-tree tops, in wonder at its youthful loveliness, its delicate picture of first love. In Berlioz' music, at last, it found a worthy rival. For the musician, too, had within him some of the graciousness and highness and sweetness of spirit the poet manifested so sovereignly.

But it is chiefly in the *Requiem* that Berlioz revealed himself in all the grandeur and might of his being. For in it all the aristocratic coolness and terseness of *La Damnation de Faust* and of *Harold en Italie,* all the fresco-like calm of *Les Troyens à Carthage,* find their freest, richest expression. "Were I to be threatened with the destruction of all that I have ever composed," wrote Berlioz on the eve of his death, "it would be for that work that I would beg life." And he was correct in the estimation of its value. It is indeed one of the great edifices of tone. For the course of events which demanded of Berlioz the work had supplied him with a function commensurate with his powers, and permitted him to register himself immortally. He was called by his country to write a mass for a commemoration service in the church of the Invalides. That gold-domed building, consecrated to the memory of the host of the fallen, to the countless soldiers slain in the wars of the monarchy and the republic and the empire, and soon to become the tomb of Napoleon, had need of its officiant. And so the genius of Berlioz arose and came. The *Requiem* is the speech of a great and classic soul, molded by the calm light and fruitful soil of the Mediterranean. For all its "Babylonian and Ninevitish" bulk, it is full of the Latin calm, the Latin repose, the Latin resignation. The simple tone, quiet for all its energy, the golden sweetness of the "Sanctus," the naked acceptance of all the facts of death, are the language of one who had within him an attitude at once primitive and grand, an attitude that we have almost come to ignore. Listening to the Mass, we find ourselves feeling as though some *vates* of a Mediterranean folk were come in rapt and lofty mood to offer sacrifice, to pacify the living, to celebrate with fitting rites the unnumbered multitudes of the heroic dead. There are some compositions that seem to find the common ground of all men throughout the ages. And to the company of such works of art, the grand *Mass for the Dead* of Hector Berlioz belongs.

Still, the commission to write the *Requiem* was but a momentary welcoming extended to Berlioz. The age in which he lived was unprepared for his art. It found itself better prepared for Wagner. For Wagner's was nearer the older music, summed it up, in fact. So Berlioz had to remain uncomprehended and unhoused. And when there finally came a time for the music of Wagner to retreat, and another to take its place, Berlioz was still half buried under the misunderstanding of his time. And yet, with the Kassandra of Eulenberg,* Berlioz could have said at the moment when it seemed as though eternal night were about to obscure him forever:

> *Einst treibt der Frühling uns in neuer Blüthe*
> *Empor ans Licht; Leben, wir scheiden nicht,*

* Herbert Eulenberg (1876–1949), German playwright.

Denn ewig bleibet, was in uns erglühte
*Und drängt sich ewig wieder auf zum Licht!**

For the likeness so many of the new men bear him has provided us with a wonderful instance of the eternal recurrence of things.

Moussorgsky

THE MUSIC of Moussorgsky comes up out of a dense and livid ground. It comes up out of a ground that lies thickly packed beneath our feet, and that is wider than the widest waste, and deeper than the bottomless abysses of the sea. It comes up from a soil that descends downward through all times and ages, through all the days of humankind, down to the very foundations of the globe itself. For it grows from the flesh of the nameless, unnumbered multitudes of men condemned by life throughout its course to misery. It has its roots where death and defeat have been. It has its roots in all bruised and maimed and frustrate flesh, in all flesh that might have borne a god and perished barren. It has its root in every being who has been without sun, in every being who has suffered cold and hunger and disease, and pierces down and touches every voiceless woe, every defeat that man has ever known. And out of that sea of mutilated flesh it rises like low, trembling speech, halting and inarticulate and broken. It has no high, compelling accent, no eloquence. And yet, it has but to lift its poor and quavering tones, and the splendor of the world is blotted out, and the great, glowing firmament is made a sorrowful gray, and, in a single instant, we have knowledge of the stern and holy truth, know the terrible floor upon which we tread, know what man

---

* "Once in new bloom, spring brings us
  Upwards to the light; life, we are not leaving,
  Because what has shone once in us remains forever
  And drives forever up again to the light."

has ever suffered, and what our own existences can only prove to be.

For it is the cry of one possessed and consumed in every fiber of his being by that single consciousness. It is as though Moussorgsky, the great, chivalric Russian, the great, sinewy giant with blood aflame for gorgeousness and bravery and bells and games and chants, had been all his days the Prince in *Khovanshchina* to whom the sorceress foretells: "Disgrace and exile await thee. Honors and power and riches will be torn from thee. Neither thy past glory nor thy wisdom can save thee. Thou wilt know what it is to want, and to suffer, and to weep the tears of the hopeless. And so, thou wilt know the truth of this world." It is as though he had heard that cry incessantly from a million throats, as though it had tolled in his ears like a bourdon until it informed him quite, and suffused his youth and force and power of song. It is as though his being had been opened entirely in orientation upon the vast, sunless stretches of the world, and distended in the agony of taking up into himself the knowledge of those myriad broken lives. For it is the countless defeated millions that live again in his art. It is they who speak with his voice. Better even than Walt Whitman, Moussorgsky might have said:

> Through me, many long dumb voices,
> Voices of the interminable generations of prisoners and
>   slaves,
> Voices of the diseas'd and despairing and of thieves and
>   dwarfs,
> Voices of cycles of preparation and accretion—

It as as though he had surrendered himself quite to them, had relinquished to them his giant Russian strength, his zest of life, his joy, had given them his proud flesh that their cry and confession might reach the ears of the living.

Sometimes, Moussorgsky is whole civilizations discarded by life. Sometimes, he is whole cultures from under which the earth has rolled, whole groups of human beings who stood silently and despairingly for an instant in a world that care-lessly flung them aside, and then turned and went away. Sometimes he is the brutal, ignorant, helpless throng that kneels in the falling snow while the conquerors, the great ones of this world, false and true alike, pass by in the torchlight amid fanfares and hymns and acclamations and speak the fair, high words and make the kingly gestures that fortune has assigned to them. Sometimes he is even life before man. He is the dumb beast devoured by another, larger; the plants that are crowded from the sunlight. He knows the ache and pain of inanimate things. And then, at other moments, he is a certain forgotten individual, some obscure, nameless being, some crea-ture, some sentient world like the monk Pimen or the Innocent in *Boris Godunov,* and out of the dust of ages a halting, inarticulate voice calls to us. He is the poor, the aging, the half-witted; the drunken sot mumbling in his stupor; the captives of life to whom death sings his insistent, luring songs; the half-idiotic peasant boy who tries to stammer out his declaration of love to the superb village belle; the wretched fool who weeps in the falling snowy night. He is those who have never before spoken in musical art, and now arise, and are about us and make us one with them.

But it is not only as content that they are in this music. This music is they, in its curves and angles, in its melody and rhythms, in its style and shape. There are times when it stands in relation to other music as some being half giant, half day-laborer, might stand in the company of scholars and poets and other highly educated and civilized men. The unlettered, the uncouth, the humble, the men unacquainted with eloquence are in this music in very body. It pierces directly from their throats. No film, no refinement on their speech, no art of music removes them from us. As Moussorgsky originally wrote these scores, their forms are visible on page after page. When his music laughs it laughs like barbarians holding their sides. When it weeps, it weeps like some little old peasant woman crouching and rocking in her grief. It has all the boisterousness and hoarseness of voices that sound out of peasant cabins and are lodged in men who wear birch-bark shoes and eat coarse food and suffer cold and hunger. Within its idiom there are the croonings and wailings of thousands of illiterate mothers, of people for whom expression is like a tearing of entrails, like a terrible birth-giving. It has in it the voices of folk singing in fairs, of folk sitting in inns; exalted and fanatical and mystical voices; voices of children and serving maids and soldiers; a thousand sorts of uncouth, grim, sharp speakers. The plaint of Xenia in *Boris Godunov* is scarcely more than the underlining of the words, the accentuation of the voice of some simple girl uttering her grief for someone recently and cruelly dead. There are moments when the whole of *Boris Godunov*, machinery of opera and all, seems no more elegant, more artful and refined than one of the simpler tunes cherished by common folk through centuries, passed from generation to generation and assumed by each because in moments of grief and joy and longing and ease it brought comfort and solace and relief. This music is common Russia singing. It is Russia speaking without the use of words. For like the folk song, it has within it the genius and values of the popular tongue. Moussorgsky's style is blood brother to the spoken language, is indeed as much the Russian language as music can be. In the phrase of Jacques Rivière, "it speaks in words ending in *ia* and *schka,* in humble phrases, in swift, poor, suppliant terms." Indeed, so unconventional, so crude, shaggy, utterly inelegant, are Moussorgsky's scores, that they offend in polite musical circles even today. It is only in the modified, "corrected," and indubitably castrated versions of Rimsky-Korsakov that *Boris* and *Khovanshchina* maintain themselves upon the stage. This iron, this granite and adamantine music, this grim, poignant, emphatic expression will not fit into the old conceptions. The old ones speak vaguely of "musical realism," "naturalism," seeking to find a pigeonhole for this great quivering mass of life.

No doubt the music of Moussorgsky is not entirely iron-gray. Just as, in the midst of *Boris,* there occurs the gentle scene between the Czar and his children, so scattered through this stern body of music there are light and gay colors, brilliant and joyous compositions. Homely and popular and naïve his melodies and rhythms always are, little peasant girls with dangling braids, peasant lads in gala garb, colored balls that are thrown about, singing games that are played to the regular accompaniment of clapping palms, songs about ducks and parrakeets, dances full of shuffling and leaping. Even the movements of the sumptuous "Persian Dances" in *Khovanshchina* are singularly naïve and simple and unpretentious. Sometimes, however, the full gorgeousness of Byzantine art shines through this music, and the gold-dusty modes, the metallic flatness of the pentatonic scale, the mystic twilit chants and brazen trumpet calls make us see the mosaics of Ravenna, the black and gold icons of Russian churches, the aureoled saints upon bricked walls, the minarets of the Kremlin. There is scarcely an operatic scene more magnificent than the scene of the coronation of Czar Boris, with its massive splendors of pealing bells and clarion blares and the caroling of the kneeling crowds. Then, like Boris himself, Moussorgsky sweeps through in stiff, blazoned robes, crowned with the domed, flashing Slavic tiara. And yet through all these bright colors, as through the darker, sadder tones of the greater part of his work, there comes to us that one anguished, overwhelming sense of life, that single great consciousness. The gay rich spots are but part of it, intensify the great somber mass. Their simplicity, their childlikeness, their innocence, are qualities that are perceived only after suffering. The sunlight in them is the gracious, sweet, kindly sunlight that falls only between nights of pain. The bright and chivalric passages of *Boris,* the music called forth by the memories of feudal Russia, and the glory of the Czars, give a deeper, stranger, even more wistful tone to the great gray pile of which they are a part. *Khovanshchina* is never so much the tragedy, the monument to beings and cultures superseded and cast aside in the relentless march of life, as in the scene when Prince Ivan Khovansky meets his death. For at the moment that the old boyar, and with him the old order of Russia, goes to his doom, there is intoned by his followers the sweetest melody that Moussorgsky wrote or could write. And out of that hymn to the glory of the perishing house there seems to come to us all the pathos of eternally passing things, all the wistfulness of the last sunset, all the last greeting of a vanished happiness. More sheerly than any other moment, more even than the infinitely stern and simple prelude that ushers in the last scene of *Boris* and seems to come out of a great distance and sum up all the sadness and darkness and pitifulness of human existence, that scene brings into view the great bleak monolith that the work of Moussorgsky really is, the great consciousness it rears silently, accusingly against the sky. As collieries rear themselves, grim and sinister, above mining towns, so this music rears itself in its Russian snows, and stands, awful and beautiful.

And, of late, the single shaft has outtopped the glamorous Wagnerian halls. The operas of Moussorgsky have begun to achieve the eminence that Wagner's once possessed. To a large degree, it is the change of times that has advanced and appreciated the art of Moussorgsky. Although *Boris* saw the light at the same time as *Götterdämmerung*, and although Moussorgsky lies chronologically very near the former age, he is far closer to us in feeling than is Wagner. The other generation, with its pride of material power, its sense of well-being, its surge toward mastery of the terrestrial forces, its need of luxury, was unable to comprehend one who felt life a grim, sorrowful thing, who felt himself a child, a crone, a pauper, helpless in the terrible cold. For that was required a less naïve and confident generation, a day more sophisticated and disabused and chastened. And so Moussorgsky's music, with its poor and uncouth and humble tone, its revulsion from pride and material grandeur and lordliness, its iron and cruelty and bleakness, lay unknown and neglected in its snows. Indeed, it had to await the coming of *Pelléas et Mélisande* in order to take its rightful place. For while Moussorgsky may have influenced Debussy artistically, it was Debussy's work that made for the recognition and popularization of Moussorgsky's. For the music of Debussy is the delicate and classical and voluptuous and aristocratic expression of the same consciousness of which Moussorgsky's is the severe, stark, barbaric; the caress as opposed to the pinch. Consequently, Debussy's art was the more readily comprehensible of the two. But, once *Pelléas* was produced, the assumption of *Boris* was inevitable. Moussorgsky's generation had arrived. The men who felt as he, who recognized the truth of his spare, metallic style, his sober edifices, had attained majority. A world was able to perceive in the music of the dead man its symbol.

But it is by no means alone the timeliness of Moussorgsky that has advanced him to his present position. It is the marvelous originality of his art. He is one of the most completely and nobly original among composers, one of the great inventors of form. The music of Moussorgsky is almost completely treasure-trove. It is not the development of any one thing, the continuation of a line, the logical outcome of the labors of others, as the works of so many even of the greatest musicians are. It is a thing that seems to have fallen to earth out of the arcana of forms like some meteorite. At the very moment of Wagner's triumph and of the full maturity of Liszt and Brahms, Moussorgsky composed as though he had been born into a world in which there was no musical tradition, a world where, indeed, no fine musical literature, and only a few folk songs and orthodox liturgical chants and Greek Catholic scales existed. Toward musical theory he seems to have been completely indifferent. Only one rule he recognized, and that was, "Art is a means of speech between man and man, and not an end." He was self-taught, and actually invented an art of music with each step of composition. And what he produced, though it was not great in bulk, was novel with a newness that is one of the miracles of music. Scarcely a phrase in his operas and songs moves in a conventional or unoriginal curve. The songs of Moussorgsky are things that can be recognized in each of their moments, so deeply and completely distinctive they are. There is not a bar of the collection called *Sans Soleil* that is not richly and powerfully new. The harmonies sound new, the melodies are free and strange and expressive, the forms are solid and weighty as bronze and iron. They are like lumps dug up out of the earth. The uttermost simplicity obtains. And every stroke is decisive and meaningful. Moussorgsky seems to have crept closer to life than most artists, to have seized emotions in their nakedness and sharpness, to have felt with the innocence of a child. One of his collections is entitled *La Chambre d'Enfants*. And that surprise and wonder at all the common facts of life, the sharpness with which the knowledge of death comes, character- ize not alone this group, but all the songs. He is throughout them the child who sees the beetle lie dead, and who expresses his wonder and trouble directly from his heart with all the sharpness of necessary speech. So much other music seems indirect, hesitating, timorous, beside these little forms of granite.

And then, Moussorgsky's operas, *Boris* in particular, are dramatically swifter than most of Wagner's. He never made the mistake the master of Bayreuth so frequently made, of subordi- nating the drama to the music, and arresting the action for the sake of a "Waldweben" or a "Charfreitagszauber." The little scenes of Pushkin's play spin themselves off quickly through the music; the action is reinforced by a skeleton-like form of music, by swift vivid tonal etchings, by the simplest, directest pictur- ings. Musical characterization is of the sharpest; original ideas pile upon each other and succeed each other without ado. The score of *Boris*, slim as it is, is a treasure house of inventions, of some of the most perfect music written for the theater. Few operatic works are musically more important, and yet less pretentious. And *Khovanshchina*, fragmentary though it is, is almost no less full of noble and lovely ideas. These fragments, melodies, choruses, dances are each of them real inventions, wonderful pieces caught up in nets, the rarest sort of beauties. A deep, rich glow plays over these melodies. Their simplicity is the simplicity of perfectly felicitous inventions, of things sprung from the earth without effort. They are so much like folk tunes that one wonders whether they were not produced hundreds of years ago and handed down by generations of Russians. One of them even, the great chorus in the first scene, might stand as a sort of national anthem for Russia. Others, like the instrumental accompaniment to the first entrance of Prince Ivan Khovansky, are some of those bits that represent a whole culture, a whole tradition and race.

These pieces are the children of an infinitely noble mind. There is something in those gorgeous melodies, those magnificent cries, those proud and solemn themes of which both *Boris* and *Khovanshchina* are full, that makes Wagner seem plebeian and bourgeois. Peasantlike though the music is, reeking of the soil, rude and powerful, it still seems to refer to a mind of a prouder, finer sort than that of the other man. The reticence, the directness, the innocence of any theatricality, the avoidance of all that is purely effective, the dignity of expression, the salt and irony, the round, full ring of every detail are good and fortifying after the scoriac inundations of Wagner's genius. The gaunt gray piles, the metallic surfaces, the homelinesses of Moussorgsky, are more virile, stronger, more resisting than Wagner's music. Only folk aristocratically sure of themselves can be as gay and light at will. If there is anything in modern music to be compared with the sheer, blunt, powerful volumes of primitive art it is the work of Moussorgsky. And as the years pass, the man's stature and mind become more immense, more prodigious. One has but to hearken to the accent of the greater part of modern music to gauge in whose shadow we are all living, how far the impulse coming from him has carried. The whole living musical world, from Debussy to Bloch, from Stravinsky to Bartók, has been vivified by him. And, certainly, if any modern music seems to have the resisting power that beats back the centuries and the eons, it is his pieces of bronze and ironware and granite. What the world lost when Modest Moussorgsky died in his forty-second year we shall never know.

But, chiefest of all, his music has the grandeur of an essentially religious act. It is the utterance of the profoundest spiritual knowledge of a people. Moussorgsky was buoyed by the great force of the Russian charity, the Russian humility, the Russian pity. It was that great religious feeling that possessed the man who had been a foppish guardsman content to amuse ladies by strumming them snatches of *Il Trovatore* and *La Traviata* on the piano, and gave him his profound sense of reality, his knowledge of how simple and sad a thing human life is after all, and made him vibrate so exquisitely with the suffering inherent in the constitution of the world. It gave his art its color, its character, its tendency. It filled him with the unsentimental, warm, animal love that made him represent man faithfully and catch the very breath of his fellows as it left their bodies. Certainly, it was from his race's dim, powerful sense of the sacrament of pain that his music flows. He himself confessed that it was the sense of another's inarticulate anguish, sympathy with a half-idiotic peasant boy stammering out his hopeless love, that first stirred the poet within him and led him to compose. The music of defeat, the insistent cry of the world's pain, sound out of his music because the Russian folk has always known the great mystery and reality and good of suffering, has known that only the humble, only those who have borne defeat and pain and misfortune can see the face of life, that sorrow and agony can hallow human existence, and that while in the days of his triumph and well-being man is a cruel and evil being, adversity often makes to appear in him divine and lovely traits. Dostoevski was never more the Russian prophet than when he wrote *The Idiot,* and uttered in it his humble thanksgiving that through the curse of nature, through the utter uselessness of his physical machine, through sickness and foolishness and poverty, he had been saved from doing the world's evil and adding to its death. And Moussorgsky is the counterpart of the great romancer. Like the other, he comes in priestly and ablutionary office. Like the other, he expresses the moving, lowly god, the god of the low, broad forehead and peasant garb, that his people bears within it. Both prose and music are manifestations of the Russian Christ. To Europe in its late hour he came as emissary of the one religious modern folk, and called on men to recognize the truth and reform their lives in accordance with it. He came to wrest man from the slavery of the new gigantic body he had begotten, to wean him from lust of power, to pacify and humble him. Once more he came to fulfil the Old Testamentary prophets. The evangel of Tolstoi, the novels of Dostoevski, the music of Moussorgsky are the new gospels. In Moussorgsky, music has given the new world its priest.

Debussy

DEBUSSY'S MUSIC is our own. All artistic forms lie dormant in the soul, and there is no work of art actually foreign to us, nor can such a one appear, in all the future ages of the world. But the music of Debussy is proper to us, in our day, as is no other, and might stand before all time our symbol. For it lived in us before it was born, and after birth returned upon us like a release. Even at a first encounter the style of *Pelléas* was mysteriously familiar. It made us feel that we had always needed such rhythms, such luminous chords, such limpid phrases, that we perhaps had even heard them, sounding faintly, in our imaginations. The music seemed as old as our sense of selfhood. It seemed but the exquisite recognition of certain intense and troubling and appeasing moments that we had already encountered. It seemed fashioned out of certain ineluctable, mysterious experiences that had budded, ineffably sad and sweet, from out our lives, and had made us new, and set us apart, and that now, at the music's breath, at a half-whispered note, at the unclosing of a rhythm, the flowering of a cluster of tones out of the warm still darkness, were arisen again in the fullness of their stature and become ours entirely.

For Debussy is of all musicians the one amongst us most fully. He is here, in our midst, in the world of the city. There is about him none of the unworldliness, the aloofness, the superhumanity that distances so many of the other composers from us. We need not imagine him in exotic singing robes, nor in classical garments, nor in any strange and outmoded and picturesque attire, to recognize in him the poet. He is the modern poet just because the modern civilian garb is so naturally his. He is the normal man, living our own manner of life. We seem to know him as we know ourselves. His experiences are but our own, intensified by his poet's gift. Or, if they are not already ours, they will become so. He seems almost ourselves as he passes through the city twilight, intent upon some errand upon which we, too, have gone, journeying a road which we ourselves have traveled. We know the room in which he lives, the windows from which he gazes, the moments which come upon him there in the silence of the lamp. For he has captured in his music what is distinguished in the age's delight and tragedy. All the fine sensuality, all the eastern pleasure in the infinite daintiness and warmth of nature, all the sudden, joyous discovery of color and touch that made men feel as though neither had been known before, are contained in it. It, too, is full of images of the "earth of the liquid and slumbering trees," the "earth of departed sunset," the "earth of the vitreous pour of the full moon just tinged with blue." It is full of material loveliness, plies itself to innumerable dainty shells—to the somnolence of the southern night, to the hieratic gesture of temple dancers, to the fall of lamplight into the dark, to the fantastic gush of fireworks, to the romance of old mirrors and faded brocades and Saxony clocks, to the green young panoply of spring. And just as it gives again the age's consciousness of the delicious robe of earth, so, too, it gives again its sense of weariness and powerlessness and oppression. The nineteenth century had been loud with blare and rumors and the vibration of colossal movements, and man had apparently traversed vast distances and explored titanic heights and abysmal depths. And yet, for all the glare, the earth was darker. The light was miasmic only. The life of man seemed as ever a brief and sad and simple thing, the stretching of impotent hands, unable to grasp and hold; the interlacing of shadows; the unclosing, a moment before night-fall, of exquisite and fragile blossoms. The sense of the infirmity of life, the consciousness that it had no more than the significa-tion of a dream with passing lights, or halting steps in the snow, or an old half-forgotten story, had mixed a deep wistfulness and melancholy into the very glamour of the globe, and become heavier itself for all the sweetness of earth. And Debussy has fixed the two in their confusion.

He has permeated music completely with his impressionistic sensibility. His style is an image of this our pointillistically feeling era. With him impressionism achieves a perfect musical form. Structurally, the music of Debussy is a fabric of exquisite and poignant moments, each full and complete in itself. His wholes exist entirely in their parts, in their atoms. If his phrases, rhythms, lyric impulses, do contribute to the formation of a single thing, they yet are extraordinarily independent and significant in themselves. No chord, no theme, is subordinate. Each one exists for the sake of its own beauty, occupies the universe for an instant, then merges and disappears. The harmonies are not, as in other compositions, preparations. They are apparently an end in themselves, flow in space, and then change hue, as a shimmering stuff changes. For all its golden earthiness, the style of Debussy is the most liquid and im-palpable of musical styles. It is forever gliding, gleaming, melting; crystallizing for an instant in some savory phrase, then moving quiveringly onward. It is well-nigh edgeless. It seems to flow through our perceptions as water flows through fingers. The iridescent bubbles that float upon it burst if we but touch them. It is forever suggesting water—fountains and pools, the glistening spray and heaving bosom of the sea. Or, it shadows forth the formless breath of the breeze, of the storm, of per-fumes, or the play of sun and moon. His orchestration invari-ably produces all that is cloudy and diaphanous in each instru-ment. He makes music with flakes of light, with bright motes of pigment. His palette glows with the sweet, limpid tints of a Monet or a Pissarro or a Renoir. His orchestra sparkles with iridescent fires, with divided tones, with delicate violets and argents and shades of rose. The sound of the piano, usually but the ringing of flat colored stones, at his touch becomes fluid, velvety, and dense, takes on the properties of satins and liqueurs. The pedal washes new tint after new tint over the keyboard. "Reflets dans l'Eau" has the quality of sheeny blue satin, of cloud pictures tumbling in gliding water. Blue fades to green and fades back again to blue in the middle section of "Homage à Rameau." Bright, cold moonlight slips through "Et la lune descend sur le temple qui fut"; ruddy sparks glitter in "Mouvement" with its Petrouchka-like joy; the piano is liquid and luminous and aromatic in "Cloches à Travers les Feuilles."

Yet there is no uncertainty, no mistiness in his form, as there is in that of some of the other impressionists. His music is classically firm, classically precise and knit. His lyrical, shimmering structures are perfectly fashioned. The line never hesitates, never becomes lost nor involved. It proceeds directly, clearly, passing through jewels and clots of color, and fusing them into the mass. The trajectory never breaks. The music is always full of its proper weight and timbre. It can be said quite without exaggeration that his best work omits nothing, neglects nothing, that every component element is justly treated. His little pieces occupy a space as completely as the most massive and grand of compositions. A composition like "Nuages," the first of the three *Nocturnes* for orchestra, while taking but five minutes in performance, outweighs any number of compositions that last an hour. *L'Après-midi d'un Faune* is inspired and new, marvelously, at every measure. The three little pieces that comprise the first set of *Images* for piano will probably outlast half of what Liszt has written for the instrument. *Pelléas* will someday be studied for its miraculous invention, its classical moderation and balance and truth, for its pure diction and economical orchestration, quite as the scores of Gluck are studied today.

For Debussy is, of all the artists who have made music in our time, the most perfect. Other musicians, perhaps even some of the contemporary, may exhibit a greater heroism, a greater staying power and indefatigability. Nevertheless, in his sphere he is every inch as perfect a workman as the greatest. Within his limits he was as pure a craftsman as the great John Sebastian in his. The difference between the two is the difference of their ages and races, not the difference of their artistry. For few composers can match with their own Debussy's perfection of taste, his fineness of sensibility, his poetic rapture and profound awareness of beauty. Few have been more graciously rounded and balanced than he, have been, like him, so fine that nothing which they could do could be tasteless and insignificant and without grace. Few musicians have been more nicely sensible of their gift, better acquainted with themselves, surer of the character and limitations of their genius. Few have been as perseverantly essential, have managed to sustain their emotion and invention so steadily at a height. The music of Debussy is full of purest, most delicate poesy. Perhaps only Bach and Moussorgsky have as invariably found phrases as pithy and inclusive and final as those with which *Pelléas* is strewn, phrases that with a few simple notes epitomize profound and exquisite emotions, and are indeed the word. There are moments in Debussy's work when each note opens a prospect. There are moments when the music of *Pelléas,* the fine fluid line of sound, the melodic moments that merge and pass and vanish into one another, become the gleaming rims that circumscribe vast dark-ling forms. There are portions of the drama that are like the moments of human intercourse when single syllables unseal deep reservoirs. The tenderness manifest here is scarcely to be duplicated in musical art. And tenderness, after all, is the most intense of all emotions.

A thousand years of culture live in this fineness. In these perfect gestures, in this grace, this certainty of choice, this justice of values, this simple, profound, delicate language, there live on thirty generations of gentlefolk. Thirty generations of cavaliers and dames who developed the arts of life in the mild and fruitful valleys of "the pleasant land of France" speak here.

The gentle sunlight and gentle shadow, the mild winters and mild summers of the Ile de France, the plentiful fruits of the earth, the excitement of the vine, contributed to making this being beautifully balanced, reserved, refined. The instruction and cultivation of the classic and French poets and thinkers, Virgil and Racine and Marivaux, Catullus and Montaigne and Chateaubriand, the chambers of the Hôtel de Rambouillet, the gardens and galleries of Versailles, the immense drawing room of eighteenth-century Paris, helped form this spirit. In all this man's music one catches sight of the long foreground, the long cycles of preparation. In every one of his works, from the most imposing to the least, from the String Quartet and *Pelléas* to the gracile, lissome little waltz, "La Plus que Lente," there is manifest the Latin genius nurtured and molded and developed by the fertile, tranquil soil of France.

And in his art, the gods of classical antiquity live again. Debussy is much more than merely the sensuous Frenchman. He is the man in whom the old pagan voluptuousness, the old untroubled delight in the body, warred against so long by the black brood of monks and transformed by them during centuries into demoniacal and hellish forms, is free and pure and sweet once more. They once were nymphs and naiads and goddesses, the quartet and *L'Après-midi d'un Faune* and "Sirènes." They once wandered through the glades of Ionia and Sicily, and gladdened men with their golden sensuality, and bewitched them with the thought of "the breast of the nymph in the brake." For they are full of the wonder and sweetness of the flesh, of flesh tasted deliciously and enjoyed not in closed rooms, behind secret doors, and under the shameful pall of the night, but out in the warm, sunny open, amid grasses and scents and the buzzing of insects, the waving of branches, the wandering of clouds. The quartet is alive, quivering with light, and with joyous animality. It moves like a young fawn; spins the gayest, most silken, most golden of spider webs; fills one with the delights of taste and smell and sight and touch. In the most glimmering, floating of poems, *L'Après-midi d'un Faune,* there is caught magically by the climbing, chromatic flute, the drowsy pizzicati of the strings, and the languorous sighing of the horns, the atmosphere of the daydream, the sleepy warmth of the sunshot herbage, the divine apparition, the white wonder of arms and breasts and thighs. The lento movement of *Ibéria* is like some drowsy, disheveled gypsy. Even "La Plus que Lente" is full of the goodness of the flesh, is like some slender young girl with unclosing bosom. And in "Sirènes," something like the eternal divinity, the eternal beauty of woman's body, is celebrated. It is as though on the rising, falling, rising, sinking tides of the poem, on the waves of the glamorous feminine voices, on the aphrodisiac swell of the sea, the white Anadyomene herself, with her galaxy of Tritons and naiads, approached earth's shores once more.

If any musical task is to be considered as having been accomplished, it is that of Debussy. For he wrote the one book that every great artist writes. He established a style irrefragably, made musical impressionism as legitimate a thing as any of the great styles. That he had more to make than that one contribution is doubtful. His art underwent no radical changes. His style was mature already in the quartet and in *Proses Lyriques,* and had its climax in *Pelléas,* its orchestral deployment in *Nocturnes* and *La Mer* and *Ibéria,* its pianistic expression in the two volumes of *Images* for pianoforte. Whatever the refinement of the incidental music to *Le Martyre de Saint-Sébastien,* Debussy never really transgressed the limits set for him by his first great works. And so, even if his long illness caused the deterioration, the hardening, the formularization, so evident in his most recent work, the sonatas, the *Épigraphes, En Blanc et Noir,* and the "Berceuse Héroïque," and deprived us of much delightful art, neither it nor his death actually robbed us of some radical development which we might reasonably have expected. The chief that he had to give he had given. What his age had demanded of him, an art that it might hold far from the glare and tumult, an art into which it could retreat, an art which could compensate it for a life become too cruel and

demanding, he had produced. He had essentially fulfilled himself.

The fact that *Pelléas* is the most eloquent of all Debussy's
works and his eternal sign does not, then, signify that he did
not grow during the remainder of his life. A complex of
determinants made of his music drama the fullest expression of
his genius, decreed that he should be living most completely at
the moment he composed it. The very fact that in it Debussy
was composing music for the theater made it certain that his
artistic sense would produce itself at its mightiest in the work.
For it entailed the statement of his opposition to Wagner. The
fact that it was music conjoined with speech made it certain
that Debussy, so full of the French classical genius, would
through contact with the spoken word, through study of its
essential quality, be aided and compelled to a complete realization of a fundamentally French idiom. And then Maeterlinck's
little play offered itself to his genius as a unique auxiliary. It,
too, is full of the sense of the shadowiness of things that
weighed upon Debussy, has not a little of the accent of the time.
This "vieille et triste légende de la forêt"* is alive with images,
such as the old and somber castle inhabited by aging people
and lying lost amid sunless forests, the rose that blooms in the
shadow underneath Mélisande's casement, Mélisande's hair that
falls farther than her arms can reach, the black tarn that broods
beneath the castle vaults and breathes death, Golaud's anguished search for truth in the prattle of the child, that could
not but call a profound response from Debussy's imagination.
But, above all, it was the figure of Mélisande herself that made
him pour himself completely into the setting of the play. For
that figure permitted Debussy to give himself completely in the
creation of his ideal image. The music is all Mélisande, all
Debussy's love-woman. It is she that the music reveals from the
moment Mélisande rises from among the rocks shrouded in
the mystery of her golden hair. It is she the music limns from the

---

* " 'The sad, ancient legend of the forest.' "

very beginning of the work. The entire score is but what a man might feel toward a woman that was his, and yet, like all women, strange and mysterious and unknown to him. The music is like the stripping of some perfect flower, petal upon petal. There are moments when it is all that lies between two people, and is the fullness of their knowledge. It is the perfect sign of an experience.

And so, since Debussy's art could have no second climax, it was in the order of things that the works succeeding upon his masterpiece should be relatively less important. Nevertheless, the ensuing poems and songs and piano pieces, with the exception of those written during those years when Debussy could have said with Rameau, his master, "From day to day my taste improves. But I have lost all my genius," are by little less perfect and astounding pieces of work. His music is like the peaks of a mountain range, of which one of the first and nearest is the highest, while the others appear scarcely less high. And they are some of the bluest, the loveliest, the most shining that stretch through the region of modern music. It will be long before humankind has exhausted their beauty.

Ravel

RAVEL AND DEBUSSY are of one lineage. They both issue from what is deeply, graciously temperate in the genius of France. Across the span of centuries, they touch hands with the men who first expressed that silver temperance in tone, with Claude Le Jeune, with Rameau and Couperin and the other clavecinists. Undiverted by the changes of revolutionary times, they continue, in forms conditioned by the modern feeling for color, for tonal complexity, for supple and undulant rhythm, the high tradition of the elder music.

Claude Le Jeune wrote motets; the eighteenth-century masters wrote gavottes and rigadoons, forlanas and chaconnes, expressed themselves in courtly dances and other set and severe

forms. Ravel and Debussy compose in more liberal and naturalistic fashion. And yet, the genius that animates all this music is
single. It is as though all these artists, born so many hundred
years apart from each other, had contemplated the pageant of
their respective times from the same point of view. It is as
though they faced the problems of composition with essentially
the same attitudes, with the same demands and reservations.
The new music, like the old, is the work of men above all
reverent of the art of life itself. It is the work of men of the sort
who crave primarily in all conduct restraint, and who insist on
poise and good sense. They regard all things humanly, and
bring their regard for the social values to the making of their
art. Indeed, the reaction of Debussy from Wagnerism was
chiefly the reaction of a profoundly socialized and aristocratic
sensibility outraged by overemphasis and unrestraint. The men
of whom he is typical throughout the ages never forget the
world and its decencies and its demands. And yet they do not
eschew the large, the grave, the poignant. The range of human
passions is present in their music, too, even though many of
them have not had gigantic powers, or entertained emotions as
grand and intense as the world-consuming, world-annihilating
mysticism of a Bach, for instance. But it is shadowed forth more
than stated. If many of them have been deeply melancholy, they
have nevertheless taken counsel with themselves, and have said,
with Baudelaire: "Sois sage, ô ma douleur, et tiens-toi plus
tranquille."* All expression is made in low, aristocratic tone, in
grisaille. Most often it achieves itself through a silvery grace. It
is normal for these men to be profound through grace, to be
amusing and yet artistically upright. It is normal for them to
articulate nicely. High in their consciousness there flame always
the commandments of clarity, of delicacy, of precision. Indeed,
so repeatedly have temperaments of this character appeared in
France, not only in her music, but also in her letters and other
arts, from the time of the Pléiade, to that of Charles Louis

* " 'Be good, my sorrow, and stay more quiet.' "

Philippe and André Gide and Henri de Régnier, that it is difficult not to hold theirs the centrally, essentially French tradition, and not to see in men like Rabelais only the Frank, and in men like Berlioz only the atavism to Gallo-Roman times.

But it is not only the spirit of French classicism that Ravel and Debussy inherit. In one respect their art is the continuation of the music that came to a climax in the works of Haydn and Mozart. It is subtle and intimate, and restores to the auditor the great creative role assigned to him by so much of the music before Beethoven. The music of Haydn and Mozart defers to its hearer. It seeks deliberately to enlist his activity. It relies for its significance largely upon his contribution. The music itself carries only a portion of the composer's intention. It carries only enough to ignite and set functioning the auditor's imagination. To that person is reserved the pleasure of fathoming the intention, of completing the idea adumbrated by the composer. For Haydn and Mozart did not desire that the listener assume a completely passive attitude. They had too great a love and respect of their fellows. They were eager to secure their collaboration, had confidence that they could comprehend all that the music intimated, regarded them as equals in the business of creation. But the music written since their time has forced upon the hearer a more and more passive role. The composers arrogated to themselves, to varying extents, the greater part of the activity; insisted upon giving all, of doing the larger share of the labor. The old intimacy was lost; with Wagner the intellectual game of the leitmotiv system was substituted for the creative exercise. The art of Ravel and Debussy returns to the earlier strategy. It makes the largest effort to excite the creative imagination, that force which William Blake identified with the Saviour Himself. It strives continually to lure it into the most energetic participation. And because Ravel and Debussy have this incitement steadily in view, their music is a music of few strokes, comparable indeed to the pictural art of Japan which it so often recalls. It is the music of suggestion, of sudden kindlings, brief starts and lines, small forms. It never insists. It only pricks. It instigates, begins, leaves off, and then continues, rousing to action the hearer's innate need of an aim and an order and meaning in things. Its subtle gestures, its brief, sharp, delicate phrases, its quintessentiality, are like the thrusting open of doors into the interiors of the conscience, the opening of windows on long vistas, are like the breaking of light upon obscured memories and buried emotions. They are like the unsealing of springs long sealed, suffering them to flow again in the night. And for a glowing instant, they transform the auditor from a passive receiver into an artist.

And there is much besides that Ravel and Debussy have in common. They have each been profoundly influenced by Russian music, *Daphnis et Chloé* showing the influence of Borodin, *Pelléas et Mélisande* that of Moussorgsky. Both have made wide discoveries in the field of harmony. Both have felt the power of outlying and exotic modes. Both have been profoundly impressed by the artistic currents of the Paris about them. Both, like so many other French musicians, have been kindled by the bright colors of Spain, Ravel in his orchestral rhapsody, in his one-act opera *L'Heure Espagnole* and in the piano piece in the collection *Miroirs* entitled "Alborada del Gracioso," Debussy in *Ibéria* and in some of his preludes. Indeed, a parallelism exists throughout their respective works. Debussy writes *Homage à Rameau;* Ravel, *Le Tombeau de Couperin.* Debussy writes *Le Martyre de Saint-Sébastien;* Ravel projects an oratorio, *Saint-François d'Assise.* Ravel writes the "Ondine" of the collection entitled *Gaspard de la Nuit;* Debussy follows it with the "Ondine" of his second volume of preludes. Both, during the same year, conceive and execute the idea of setting to music the lyrics of Mallarmé entitled "Soupir" and "Placet Futile." Nevertheless, this fact constitutes Ravel in nowise the imitator of Debussy. His work is by no means, as some of our critics have made haste to insist, a counterfeit of his elder's. Did the music of Ravel not demonstrate that he possesses a sensibility quite distinct from Debussy's, in some respects less fine, delicious, lucent, in others perhaps even more deeply engaging; did it not represent a distinct development from Debussy's art in a direction quite its own, one might with justice speak of a discipleship. But in the light of Ravel's actual accomplishment, of his large and original and attractive gift, of the magistral craftsmanship that has shown itself in so many musical forms, from the song and the sonatine to the String Quartet and the orchestral poem, of the talent that has revealed itself increasingly from year to year, and that not even the war and the experience of the trenches has driven underground, the parallelism is to be regarded as necessitated by the spiritual kinship of the men, and by their contemporaneity.

And, certainly, nothing so much reveals Ravel the peer of Debussy as the fact that he has succeeded so beautifully in manifesting what is peculiar to him. For he is by ten years Debussy's junior, and were he less positive an individuality, less original a temperament, less fully the genius, he could never have realized himself. There would have descended upon him the blight that has fallen upon so many of the younger Parisian composers less determinate than he and like himself made of one stuff with Debussy. He, too, would have permitted the art of the older and well-established man to impose upon him. He, too, would have betrayed his own cause in attempting to model himself upon the other man. But Debussy has not swerved nor hampered Ravel any more than has his master, Gabriel Fauré. He is too sturdily set in his own direction. From the very commencement of his career, from the time when he wrote the soft and hesitating and nevertheless already very personal "Pavane pour une Infante Défunte," he has maintained himself proudly against his great collateral, just as he has maintained himself against what is false and epicene in the artistic example of Fauré. Within their common limits, he has realized himself as essentially as Debussy has done. Their music is the new and double blossoming of the classical French tradition. From the common ground, they stretch out each in a different direction, and form the greater contrast to each other because of all they have in common.

The intelligence that fashioned the music of Debussy was one completely aware, conscious of itself, flooded with light in its most secret places, set foursquare in the whirling universe. Few artists have been as sure of their intention as Debussy always was. The man could fix with precision the most elusive emotions, could describe the sensations that flow on the borderland of consciousness, vaguely, and that most of us cannot grasp for very dizziness. He could write music as impalpable as that of the middle section of *Ibéria,* in which the very silence of the night, the caresses of the breeze, seem to have taken musical flesh. Before the body of his work, so clear and lucid in its definition, so perfect in its organization, one thinks perforce of a world created out of the flying chaos beneath him by a god. We are given to know precisely of what stuff the soul of Debussy was made, what its pilgrimages were, in what adventure it sought itself out. We know precisely wherein it saw reflected its visage, in "water stilled at even," in the angry gleam of sunset on wet leaves, in wild and headlong gypsy rhythms, in moonfire, shimmering stuffs and flashing spray, in the garish lights and odors of the Peninsula, in rain fallen upon flowering parterres, in the melancholy march of clouds, the golden pomp and ritual of the church, the pools and gardens and pavilions reared for its delight by the delicate Chinese soul, in earth's thousand scents and shells and colors. For Debussy has set these adventures before us in their fullness. Before he spoke, he had dwelt with his experiences till he had plumbed them fully, till he had seen into and around and behind them clearly. And so we perceive them in their essences, in their eternal aspects. The designs are the very curve of the ecstasy. They are sheerly delimited. The notes appear to bud one out of the other, to follow each other out of the sheerest necessity, to have an original timbre, to fix a matter never known before, that can never live again. Every moment in a representative composition of Debussy's is logical and yet new. Few artists have more faultlessly said what they set out to say.

Ravel is by no means as perfect an artist. He has not the clear self-consciousness, the perfect recognition of limits. His music has not the absolute completeness of Debussy's. It is not that he is not a marvelous craftsman, greatly at ease in his medium. It is that Ravel dares, and dares continually; seeks passionately to bring his entire body into play; aspires to plenitude of utterance, to sheerness and rigidity of form. Ravel always goes directly through the center. But compare his *Rapsodie Espagnole* with Debussy's *Ibéria* to perceive how direct he is. Debussy gives the circumambient atmosphere, Ravel the inner form. Between him and Debussy there is the difference between the Apollonian and the Dionysiac, between the smooth, level, contained, perfect, and the darker, more turbulent, passionate, and instinctive. For Ravel has been vouchsafed a high grace. He has been permitted to remain, in all his manhood, the child that once we all were. In him the powerful and spontaneous flow of emotion from out the depths of being has never been dammed. He can still speak from the fullness of his heart, cry his sorrows piercingly, produce himself completely. Gracious and urbane as his music is, proper to the world of modern things and modern adventures and modern people, there is still a gray, piercing lyrical note in it that is almost primitive, and reflects the childlike singleness and intensity of the animating spirit. The man who shaped not only the deliberately infantine *Ma Mère l'Oye*, but also things as quiveringly simple and expressive and songful as "Oiseaux Tristes," as "Sainte," as "Le Gibet," or the "Sonatine," as the passacaglia of the *Trio* or the vocal interlude in *Daphnis et Chloé*, has a pureness of feeling that we have lost. And it is this crying, passionate tone, this directness of expression, this largeness of effort, even in tiny forms and limited scope, that, more than his polyphonic style or any other of the easily recognizable earmarks of his art, distinguishes his work from Debussy's. The other man has a greater sensuousness, completeness, inventiveness perhaps. But Ravel is full of a lyricism, a piercingness, a passionateness, that much of the music of Debussy successive to *Pelléas* wants. We understand

Ravel's music, in the famous phrase of Beethoven, as speech "vom Herz—zu Herzen."*

And we turn to it gratefully, as we turn to all art full of the "sense of tears in mortal things," and into which the pulse of human life has passed directly. For there are times when he is close to the bourne of life, when his art is immediately the orifice of the dark, flowering, germinating region where lie lodged the dynamics of the human soul. There are times when it taps vasty regions. There are times when Ravel has but to touch a note, and we unclose; when he has but to let an instrument sing a certain phrase, and things which lie buried deep in the heart rise out of the dark, like the nymph in his piano poem, dripping with stars. The music of *Daphnis,* from the very moment of the introduction with its softly unfolding chords, its far, glamorous fanfares, its human throats swollen with songs, seems to thrust open doors into the unplumbed caverns of the soul, and summon forth the stuff to shape the dream. Little song written since Weber set his horns a-breathing, or Brahms transmuted the witchery of the German forest into tone, is more romantic. Over it might be set the invocation of Heine:

> *Steiget auf, ihr alten Traüme!*
> *Oeffne dich, dur Herzenstor!†*

Like the passage that ushers in the last marvelous scene of his great ballet, it seems to waken us from the unreal world to the real, and show us the face of the earth, and the overarching blue once more.

And Ravel is at once more traditional and more progressive a

---

* " 'From the heart to other hearts.' "
† "Rise, you old dreams!
  Open up, gates of the heart!"

A lyric by Heine in which the poet sits in the ruins and thinks of splendid times past, of pine trees, brooks, larks, medieval ladies and tournaments. The poem is permeated by a pleasurable melancholy as Death conquers all.

composer than Debussy. One feels the past most strongly in him. Debussy, with his thoroughly impressionistic style, is more the time. No doubt there is a certain almost Hebraic melancholy and sharp lyricism in Ravel's music which gives some color to the rumor that he is Jewish. And yet, for all that, one feels Rameau become modern in his sober, gray, dainty structures, in the dryness of his black. In *Le Tombeau de Couperin*, Ravel is the old clavecinist become contemporary of Scriabin and Stravinsky, the old clavecinist who had seen the projectiles fall at Verdun and lost a dozen friends in the trenches. He finds it easy, as in some of his recent songs, to achieve the folktone. If it is true that he is a Jew, then his traditionalism is but one more brilliant instance of the power of France to adopt the children of alien races and make them more intensely her own than some of her proper offspring. In no other instance, however, not in that of Lully nor in that of Franck, has the transfusion of blood been so successful. Ravel is in nowise treacherous to himself. There must be something in the character of the French nation that makes of every Jew, if not a son, yet the happiest and most faithful of stepchildren.

And as one feels the past more strongly in Ravel, so, too, one finds him in certain respects even more revolutionary than Debussy. For while the power of the latter flagged in the making of strangely MacDowellesque preludes, or in the composition of such ghosts as *Gigues* and *Jeux* and *Khamma*, Ravel has continued increasingly in power, has developed his art until he has come to be one of the leaders of the musical evolution. If there is a single modern composition which can be compared to *Petrouchka* for its picture of mass-movement, its pungent naturalism, it is the "Feria" of the *Rapsodie Espagnole*. If there is a single modern orchestral work that can be compared to either of the two great ballets of Stravinsky for rhythmical vitality, it is *Daphnis et Chloé*, with its flaming Dionysiac pulses, its "pipes and timbrels," its wild ecstasy. The same delicate clockwork mechanism characterizes *L'Heure Espagnole*, his *opéra bouffe*, that characterizes *Petrouchka* and *Le Rossignol*. A piano poem like "Scarbo" rouses the full might of the piano, and seems to bridge the way to the music of Leo Ornstein and the age of steel. And Ravel has some of the squareness, the sheerness and rigidity for which the ultramodern are striving. The liquescence of Debussy has given away again to something more metallic, more solid and unflowing. There is a sort of new stiffness in this music. And in the field of harmony Ravel is steadily building upon Debussy. His chords grow sharper and more biting; in *Le Tombeau de Couperin* and the minuet on the name of Haydn there is a harmonic daring and subtlety and even bitterness that is beyond anything attained by Debussy, placing the composer with the Stravinskys and the Schoenbergs and the Ornsteins and all the other barbarians.

And then his ironic humor, as well, distinguishes him from Debussy. The humor of the latter was, after all, light and whimsical. That of Ravel, on the other hand, is extremely bitter. No doubt, the "icy" Ravel, the artist "à qui l'absence de sensibilité fait encore une personalité,"* as one of the Quirites termed him, never existed save in the minds of those unable to comprehend his reticence and delicacy and essentiality. Nevertheless, besides his lyrical, dreamy, romantic temper, he has a very unsentimental vein, occurring no doubt, as in Heine, as a sort of corrective, a sort of compensation, for the pervading sensibleness. And so we find the tender poet of the "Sonatine" and the String Quartet and *Miroirs* writing the witty and mordant music of *L'Heure Espagnole;* setting the bitter little *Histoires Naturelles* of Jules Renard for chant, writing in *Valses Nobles et Sentimentales* a slightly ironical and disillusioned if smiling and graceful and delicate commentary to the season of love, projecting a music drama on the subject of Don Quixote. Over his waltzes Ravel maliciously sets a quotation from Henri de Regnier: "Le plaisir délicieux et toujours nouveau d'une occupation inutile."† With Casella, he writes a musical *à la manière de,* parodying Wagner, d'Indy, Chabrier,

* " 'Whose lack of sensitivity is itself a kind of personality.' "
† " 'The delicious and ever-fresh pleasure of a useless occupation.' "

Strauss, and others most wittily. Something of Erik Satie, the clown of music, exists in him, too. And probably nothing makes him so inexplicable and irritating to his audiences as his ironic streak. People are willing to forgive an artist all, save only irony.

What the future holds for Maurice Ravel is known only to the three Norns. But, unless some unforeseen accident occur and interrupt his career, it can only hold the most brilliant rewards. The man seems surely bound for splendid shores. He is only in the forty-fifth year of his life, and though his genius was already fresh and subtle in the quartet, written as early as 1903, it has grown beautifully in power during the last two decades. The continued exploration of musical means has given his personality increasingly free play, and has unbound him. The gesture of the hand has grown swifter and more commanding. The instruments have become more obedient. He has matured, become virile and even magistral. The war has not softened him. He speaks as intimately as ever in *Le Tombeau de Couperin*. Already one can see in him one of the most delightful and original musical geniuses that have been nourished by the teeming soil of France. It is possible that the future will refer to him in even more enthusiastic tone.

Stravinsky

THE NEW STEEL ORGANS of man have begotten their music in *Le Sacre du Printemps*. For with Stravinsky, the rhythms of machinery enter musical art. With this his magistral work a new chapter of music commences, the spiritualization of the new body of man is manifest. Through Debussy, music had liquefied, become opalescent and impalpable and fluent. It had become, because of his sense, his generation's sense, of the infirmity of things, a sort of symbol of the eternal flux, the eternal momentariness. It had come to body forth all that merges and changes and disappears, to mirror the incessant departures and evanescences of life, to shape itself upon the infinitely subtle play of light, the restless, heaving, foaming surface of the sea, the impalpable racks of perfume, upon gusts of wind and fading sounds, upon all the ephemeral wonder of the world. But through Stravinsky, there has come to be a music stylistically well-nigh the reverse of that of the impressionists. Through him, music has become again cubical, lapidary, massive, mechanistic. Scintillation is gone out of it. The delicate, sinuous melodic line, the glamorous sheeny harmonies, are gone out of it. The elegance of Debussy, the golden sensuality, the quiet, classic touch, are flown. Instead, there are come to be great, weighty, metallic masses, molten piles and sheets of steel and iron, shining adamantine bulks. Contours are become grim, severe, angular. Melodies are sharp, rigid, asymmetrical. Chords are uncouth, square clusters of notes, stout and solid as the pillars that support roofs, heavy as the thuds of triphammers. Above all, there is rhythm, rhythm rectangular and sheer and emphatic, rhythm that lunges and beats and reiterates and dances with all the steely perfect tirelessness of the machine, shoots out and draws back, shoots upward and shoots down, with the inhuman motion of titanic arms of steel. Indeed, the change is as radical, as complete, as though in the midst of moonlit noble gardens a giant machine had arisen swiftly from the ground and inundated the night with electrical glare and set its metal thews and organs and joints relentlessly whirring, relentlessly functioning.

And yet, the two styles, Debussy's and Stravinsky's, are related. Indeed, they are complementary. They are the reactions to the same stimulus of two fundamentally different types of mind. No doubt, between the two men there exist differences besides those of their general fashions of thinking. The temper of Debussy was profoundly sensuous and aristocratic and contained. That of Stravinsky is nervous and ironic and violent. The one man issued from an unbroken tradition, was produced by generations and generations of gentlemen. The other is one of those beings who seem to have been called into existence solely by the modern way of life, by express trains and ocean greyhounds, by the shrinkage of continents and the vibration of the twentieth-century world. But the chief difference, the difference that made *Le Sacre du Printemps* almost antithetical to *Pelléas et Mélisande,* is essentially the divergence between two cardinal manners of apprehending life. Debussy, on the one hand, seems to be of the sort of men in whom the center of conscience is, figuratively, sunken; one of those who have within themselves some immobility that makes the people and the things about them appear fleeting and unreal. For such, the world is a far distant thing, lying out on the rims of consciousness, delicate and impermanent as sunset hues or the lights and gestures of the dream. The music of Debussy is the magistral and classic picture of this distant and glamorous procession, this illusory and fantastical and transparent show, this thing that changes from moment to moment and is never twice the same, and flows away from us so quickly. But Stravinsky, on the other hand, is in the very midst of the thing so distant from the other man. For him, the material world is very real, sharp, immediate. He loves it, enjoys it, is excited by its many forms. He is vividly responsive to its traffic. Things make an immediate and biting impression on him, stimulate in him pleasure and pain. He feels their edge and knows it hard, feels their weight and knows it heavy, feels their motion in all its violence. There is in Stravinsky an almost frenetic delight in the processes that go on about him. He goes through the crowded thoroughfares, through cluttered places, through factories, hotels, wharves, sits in railway trains, and the glare and tumult and pulsation, the engines and locomotives and cranes, the whole mad phantasmagoria of the modern city, evoke images in him, inflame him to reproduce them in all their weight and gianthood and mass, their blackness and luridness and power. The most vulgar things and events excite him. The traffic, the restlessness of crowds, the noise of vehicles, of the clatter of horses on the asphalt, of human cries and calls sounding above the street-bass, a couple of organ grinders trying to outplay each other, a brass band coming down the avenue, the thunder of a railway train hurling itself over leagues of steel, the sirens of steamboats and locomotives, the overtones of factory whistles, the roar of cities and harbors, become music to him. In one of his early orchestral sketches, he imitates the buzzing of a hive of bees. One of his miniatures for string quartet bangs with the beat of the wooden shoes of peasants dancing to the snarling tones of a bagpipe. Another reproduces the droning of the priest in a little chapel, recreates the scene almost cruelly. And the score of *Petrouchka* is alive marvelously with the rank, garish life of a cheap fair. Its bubbling flutes, seething instrumental caldron, concertina rhythms and bright, gaudy colors conjure up the movement of the crowds that surge about the amusement booths, paint to the life the little flying flags, the gestures of the showmen, the bright balloons, the shooting galleries, the gypsy tents, the crudely stained canvas walls, the groups of coachmen and servant girls and children in their holiday finery. At moments one can even smell the sausages frying.

For Stravinsky is one of those composers, found scattered all along the pathway of his art, who augment the expressiveness of music through direct imitation of nature. His imagination seems to be free, bound in nowise by what other men have adjudged music to be, and by what their practice has made it seem. He comes to his art without prejudice or preconception of any kind, it appears. He plays with its elements as capriciously as the child plays with paper and crayons. He amuses himself with each instrument of the band careless of its customary uses. There are times when Stravinsky comes into the solemn con-clave of musicians like a gamin with trumpet and drum. He disports himself with the infinitely dignified String Quartet, makes it do light and acrobatic things. There is one interlude of *Petrouchka* that is written for snare drums alone. His work is incrusted with cheap waltzes and barrel organ tunes. It is gamy and racy in style; full of musical slang. He makes the orchestra imitate the quavering of an old hurdy-gurdy. Of late he has written a ballet for eight clowns. And he is reported to have said, "I should like to bring it about that music be performed in streetcars, while people get out and get in." For he finds his greatest enemy in the concert room, that rut that limits the play of the imagination of audiences, that fortress in which all of the intentions of the men of the past have established themselves, and from which they dominate the musical present. The concert room has succeeded in making music a drug, a sedative, has created a "musical attitude" in folk that is false, and robbed musical art of its power. For Stravinsky music is either an infection, the communication of a lyrical impulse, or nothing at all. And so he would have it performed in ordinary places of congregation, at fairs, in taverns, music halls, streetcars, if you will, in order to enable it to function freely once again. His art is pointed to quicken, to infect, to begin an action that the listener must complete within himself. It is a sort of musical shorthand. On paper, it has a fragmentary look. It is as though Stravinsky had sought to reduce the elements of music to their sharpest and simplest terms, had hoped that the "development" would be made by the audience. He seems to feel that if he cannot achieve his end, the communication of his lyrical impulse, with a single strong motif, a single strong movement of tones, a single rhythmic start, he cannot achieve it at all. So we find him writing songs, the three Japanese lyrics, for instance, that are epigrammatic in their brevity; a piece for string quartet that is played in fifty seconds; a three-act opera that can be performed in thirty minutes.

But it is no experiment in form that he is making. He seems to bring into music some of the power of the Chinese artists who, in the painting of a twig, or of a pair of blossoms, represent the entire springtide. He has written some of the freshest, most rippling, delicate music. Scarcely a living man has written more freshly or humorously. April, the flowering branches, the snowing petals, the clouds high in the blue, are really in the shrilling little orchestra of the Japanese lyrics, in the green, gurgling flutes and watery violins. None of the innumerable Spring Symphonies, Spring Overtures, Spring

Songs, are really more vernal, more soaked in the gentle sunshine of spring, are more really the seed-time, than the six naïve piping measures of melody that introduce the figure of the *Sacre* entitled "Rondes Printanières." No doubt, in venturing to write music so bold and original in aesthetic, Stravinsky was encouraged by the example of another musician, another Russian composer. Moussorgsky, before him, had trusted in his own innocence instead of in the wisdom of the fathers of the musical church, had dared obey the promptings of his own blood and set down chords, melodies, rhythms, just as they sang in his skull, though all the world rise up to damn him. But the penning of music as jagged, cubical, barbarous as the prelude to the third act of Stravinsky's little opera, *The Nightingale,* or as naked, uncouth, rectangular, rocklike, polyharmonic, headlong, as some of that of *Le Sacre du Printemps* required no less perfect a conviction, no less great a self-reliance. The music of Stravinsky is the expression of an innocence comparable indeed to that of his great predecessor. *Le Sacre du Printemps* is what its composer termed it. It is "an act of faith."

And so, free of preconceptions, Stravinsky was able to let nature move him to imitation. Just as Picasso brings twentieth-century nature into his still lives, so the young composer brings it into his music. It is the rhythm of machinery that has set Stravinsky the artist free. All his life he has been conscious of these steel men. Mechanical things have influenced his art from the beginning. It is as though machinery had revealed him to himself, as though sight of the functioning of these metal organisms, themselves but the extension of human bones and muscles and organs, had awakened into play the engine that is his proper body. For, as James Oppenheim has put it in the introduction to *The Book of Self,* "Man's body is just as large as his tools, for a tool is merely an extension of muscle and bone; a wheel is a swifter foot, a derrick a greater hand. Consequently, in the early part of the century, the race found itself with a new gigantic body." It is as though the infection of the dancing, lunging, pumping piston rods, walking beams, drills, has awakened out of Stravinsky a response and given him his power to beat out rhythm. The machine has always fascinated him. One of his first original compositions, written while he was yet a pupil of Rimsky-Korsakov's, imitates fireworks, distinguishes what is human in their activity, in the popping, hissing, exploding, in the hysterical weeping of the fiery fountains, the proud exhibitions and sudden collapses of the pinwheels. It is the machine, enemy of man, that is pictured by *The Nightingale,* that curious work of which one act dates from 1909, and two from 1914. Stravinsky had the libretto formed on the tale of Hans Christian Andersen which recounts the adventures of the little brown bird that sings so beautifully that the Emperor of China bids it to his court. Stravinsky's nightingale, too, comes to the palace and sings, and all the ladies of the entourage fill their mouths with water in the hopes of better imitating the warbling of the songster. But then there enter envoys bearing the gift of the Emperor of Japan, a mechanical nightingale that amuses the court with its clockwork antics. Once more the emperor commands the woodland bird to sing. But it is flown. In his rage the emperor banishes it from his realm. Then Death comes and sits at the emperor's bedside, and steals from him crown and scepter, till, of a sudden, the nightingale returns, and sings, and makes Death relinquish his spoils. And the courtiers who come into the imperial bedchamber expecting to find the monarch dead, find him well and glad in the morning sunshine.

And in his two major works, *Petrouchka* and *Le Sacre du Printemps,* Stravinsky makes the machine represent his own person. For the actions of machinery woke first in the human organism, and Stravinsky intensifies consciousness of the body by referring these motions to their origin. *Petrouchka* is the man-machine seen from without, seen unsympathetically, in its comic aspect. Countless poets before Stravinsky have attempted to portray the puppet-like activities of the human being, and *Petrouchka* is but one of the recent of innumerable stage shows that expose the automaton in the human soul. But the puppet show of Stravinsky is singular because of its musical accompaniment. For more than even the mimes on the stage, the orchestra is full of the spirit of the automaton. The angular, wooden gestures of the dolls, their smudged faces, their entrails of sawdust, are in the music ten times as intensely as they are upon the stage. In the score of *Petrouchka* music itself has become a little mannikin in parti-colored clothes, at which Stravinsky gazes and laughs as a child laughs at a funny doll, and makes dance and tosses in the air, and sends sprawling. The score is full of the revolutions of wheels, of delicate clockwork movements, of screws and turbines. Beneath the music one hears always the regular, insistent, maniacal breathing of a concertina. And what in it is not purely mechanistic nevertheless completes the picture of the world as it appears to one who has seen the man-machine in all its comedy. The stage pictures, the trumpery little fair, the tinsel and pathetic finery of the crowds, the dancing of the human ephemeridae a moment before the snow begins to fall, are stained marvelously deeply by the music. The score has the colors of crudely dyed, faded bunting. It has indeed a servant girl grace, a coachman ardor, a barrel organ, tintype, popcorn, fortuneteller flavor.

Le Sacre, on the other hand, is the man-machine viewed not from without, and unsympathetically, but from within. So far, it is Stravinsky's masterwork, the completest and purest expression of his genius. For the elements that make for the originality of style of *Petrouchka* and the other of Stravinsky's representative compositions, in this work attain a signal largeness and powerfulness. The rhythmic element, already fresh and free in the scherzo of *L'Oiseau de Feu* and throughout *Petrouchka*, attains virile and magistral might in it, surges and thunders with giant vigor. The instrumentation, magical with all the magic of the Russian masters in the earlier ballets, here is informed by the sharpness, hardness, nakedness which is originally Stravinsky's. Besides, the latter work has the thing hitherto lacking somewhat in the young man's art—grandeur and severity and ironness of language. In it he stands com-

pletely new, completely in possession of his powers. And in it
the machine operates. Ostensibly, the action of the ballet is laid
in prehistoric times. Ostensibly, it figures the ritual with which
a tribe of Stone Age Russians consecrated the spring. Something
of the sort was necessary, for an actual representation of machines, a ballet of machines, would not have been as grimly
significant as the angular, uncouth gestures of men, would by
no means have as nakedly revealed the human engine. Here, in
the choreography, every fluid, supple, curving motion is sup-
pressed. Everything is angular, cubical, rectilinear. The music
pounds with the rhythm of engines, whirls and spirals like
screws and flywheels, grinds and shrieks like laboring metal.
The orchestra is transmuted to steel. Each movement of the
ballet correlates the rhythms of machinery with the human
rhythms which they prolong and repeat. A dozen mills pulsate
at once. Steam escapes; exhausts breathe heavily. The weird
orchestral introduction to the second scene has all the oppressive silence of machines immobile at night. And in the hurtling
finale the music and the dancers create a figure that is at once
the piston and a sexual action. For Stravinsky has stripped away
from man all that with which specialization, differentiation,
have covered him, and revealed him again, in a sort of cruel
white light, a few functioning organs. He has shown him a
machine to which power is applied, and which labors in blind
obedience precisely like the microscopic animal that eats and
parturates and dies. The spring comes; and life replenishes
itself; and man, like seed and germ, obeys the promptings of the
blind power that created him, and accomplishes his predestined
course and takes in energy and pours it out again. But, for a
moment, in *Le Sacre du Printemps,* we feel the motor forces,
watch the naked wheels and levers and arms at work, see the
dynamo itself.

The ballet was completed in 1913, the year Stravinsky was
thirty-one years old. It may be that the work will be succeeded
by others even more original, more powerful. Or it may be that
Stravinsky has already written his masterpiece. The works that

he has composed during the war are not, it appears, strictly new developments. Whatever enlargement of the field of the string quartet the three little pieces which the Flonzaleys played here in 1915 created, there is no doubt that it was nothing at all to compare with the innovation in orchestral music created by the great ballet. And, according to rumor, the newest of Stravinsky's work, the music-hall ballet for eight clowns,* and the work for the orchestra, ballet, and chorus entitled *Les Noces,* are by no means as bold in style as *Le Sacre,* and resemble *Petrouchka* more than the later ballet. But, whatever Stravinsky's future accomplishment, there can be no doubt that with this one work, if not also with *Petrouchka,* he has secured a place among the true musicians. It is doubtful whether any living composer has opened new musical land more widely than he. For he has not only minted music anew. He has reached a point ahead of us that the world would have reached without him. That alone shows him the genius. He has brought into music something for which we had long been waiting, and which we knew must one day arrive. To us, at this moment, *Le Sacre du Printemps* appears one of those compositions that mark off the musical miles.

Thanks to the International Guild: A Musical Chronicle

1. *Preamble*

EDGAR VARÈSE and Carlos Salzedo, operating under the name, the International Composers' Guild, maintained a hatchery for musical bacilli where in glass boxes new combinations and voices, aesthetics and world feelings germinated. Twice or

* No such work was ever written, unless Rosenfeld was referring to *L'Histoire du Soldat.*

thrice a year doctor and assistant doctor went about their secret forcing-house examining the queer little growths and culling those apparently possessing the power of life. Then a concert was arranged, and the small experiments let into the world. During some five years, 1922–1927, these genial musicians made their periodic deliveries of musical germs; and so infectious were certain cultures that today we dwell among horizons of art, hence of the world, thrust back by them. (Again the advantage of permitting creative spirits to conduct artistic organizations stands evident. In the hands of the artist, the institution becomes a means of expression second only to his own work; another instrument for the affirmation of his day; the instrumentality of the work of his fellows producing in the director something of the disinterestedness and serious approach characterizing high scientific spheres.)

Like other hatcheries, Varèse and Salzedo's produced its chickens with two heads, its vocalizing sturgeons and strange composite bugs. The buzz of life was not unvaryingly strong on the International's Sunday nights in Aeolian Hall, ever the Cave of Winds. Affirmativeness led the two radicals to pledge their Guild to discoveries, disclosure of the new in vision, personality, and method; and since Americas are not to be revealed at will, certain of their releases had a sterile curiosity, a purely speculative interest. Still, the professional, inquisitive, experimental tension invariably persisted. A responsiveness to the hour, a spirit of initiative, promptitude, and willingness which we in New York still tend to associate with Parisian circles, combined as it was with an artistic standard of performance, distinguished even the Guild's dullest parties from those of rival organizations. The Society of the Friends of Music declared itself a musical museum beside the Guild. Pro Arte evidently was another depot for modern French work; and the League of Composers a social function where the performance of music served the ambitions of mediocrities; handsomely dressed people conversed up and down the aisles; and music preluded to an apotheosis of personal projections and chicken salad in close quarters. Occasionally, the net gain of an International Sunday evening was no more than an amusing suggestion, like the one provided the evening Henry Cowell demonstrated with the Amerindian thunder-stick, and found the tone of primitive American godwardness. At other times, it was merely the promise of a new musical geography; as the evening when the program introduced music by a Chilean, an Italian from Crete, a Negro from Mississippi, and a Mexican born, bred, and resident in the city of Mexico; and the voices and racial backgrounds of Acario Cotapos, Massimo Zanotti-Bianco, William Grant Still, and Carlos Chavez queer-colored the musical future. Frequently, the rewards were magnificent and memorable. Many of them, the single concert appearance of little Florence Mills, for example, enshrined their moments. Others, such as the presentations of *Les Noces, Renard, Hyperprism,* and *Intégrales,* and, in second line, the introductions of Ruggles, Hindemith, Rudhyar,* Webern, and Chavez, established new musical values; and were cardinal in producing here in New York an audience capable of receiving a fresh musical expression at the creative moment. Perhaps essentially critical, our time possesses a stomach for art sounder and robuster, a level of taste superior to the last two centuries'; and much of the advance is due to the work of the experimental stations of which 291 Fifth Avenue† is perhaps the most, and the International Composers' Guild not the least, important. To review the experiences for which we have to thank the association of Varèse and Salzedo is therefore not only to appreciate a number of the more significant compositions and composers discovered during the last years, and to define the main lines of musical advance. It is also to make the growth in taste, elevatory to

* Dane Rudhyar (Daniel de Chennevière; 1895–   ), an American composer, painter, philosopher, poet, author of a book on Debussy.

† 291 Fifth Avenue, Alfred Stieglitz' art gallery, was for ten years (1907–1917) not only a showplace for experimental painters, sculptors, and photographers, but a meeting place for *avant-garde* artists of all persuasions. Marsden Hartley and Georgia O'Keefe were two painters whose work became known through Stieglitz' efforts.

planes of subtler, wider understanding, more positive and our own.

2. Renard

THERE IS A PROPRIETY in beginning this little chronicle of recent developments in music with an account of the Stravinsky pieces played by the International Composers' Guild. While it is doubtful whether Stravinsky is a creator and form-finder of the first water; and while his most recent, classicizing compositions make us wonder whether he is not a sort of musical *agent provacateur,* gaining the confidence of the creative wing only at the strategic moment to sell out to the stand-patters; there is no doubt that the recent revulsion from musical romanticism to humanism was made largely under his leadership. That of Satie was, after all, more theoretical. The scores Stravinsky produced between 1914 and 1920, beautifully conveyed the new orientation, the new humanistic conception of the material of music and its treatment. The composer of *Renard, Les Noces, L' Histoire du Soldat,* the *Symphonies for Wind Instruments,* and other less ambitious pieces, was eminently one of those gifted individuals whose personal road coincides with the general. The direction of human society, with its new mass-life, communism, impersonality, was paralleled by some anti-individualism in his own desires; and the two reacted upon and strengthened one another. Having begun as an ultraromantic, descriptive, precious composer influenced by the Russian romanticism of Rimsky and the aristocratic French romanticism—impressionism—of Debussy, he found himself increasingly uninterested by that individualistic spirit, its "respiration of Bayreuth," jewelry, and pictoriality; and increasingly drawn toward dryer, preciser, more absolute musical forms; and moved to relinquish the expression of the singular, the subjective, and the remote in favor of the commonplace, the external, even the banal. The general experience was again full of interest: John Smith, and what happened to Mary; and Stravinsky's embodiments of it were more plastic than his great romantic pieces, *Petrouchka* and *Le Sacre du Printemps*. These had been a trifle too "intellectual," too subservient to the literary conception, wanting the great line and relentless logic. The form was piecemeal, leaning upon the stage. But the new works were more independent; and quite as full as their immediate predecessors of the brilliant ideas, rhythms and colorations, tones of "the moment," which had made Stravinsky the most interesting of living composers.

Renard, the first important Stravinsky composition offered by the Guild, is the first of these expressions of the new humanism. An animal fable for male voices and small orchestra, it represents a complete break with the direction of the romantic past that still held Stravinsky during the time he wrote *Petrouchka* and *Le Sacre*. Like all revolutionary acts, *Renard* flowed from tendencies astir well before the performer's birth. It is fruit of established tradition, that of the Russian nationalistic school. The Russian Five not only used demotic musical idioms. All of them, and Moussorgsky in particular, had before them the ideal of a popular, primitive, and robust art, expressive of the common experiences of humanity and free in spirit as well as idiom from grandiosity and preciousness. Tolstoi inveighing against the superb, godlike spirit of Wagner; and setting up as models of art the bare naïve representations of peasant fairs, was merely carrying to a fanatical extreme the essentially communal, humanistic, perhaps even Christian feeling of Russia. This aesthetic, Stravinsky inherited by temperament and as pupil of Rimsky-Korsakov; and we find him embodying it in several works preceding *Renard*. *Petrouchka* to a degree is humanistic, disillusioned, even primitivistic, in Moussorgsky's intention. Its idiom is based on the musical expressions of the populace, folk songs and dances and barrel organ tunes; and the interlude for snare drum alone is characteristic of the color of the work, deliberately bunting and booths, coachmen and nursemaids, concertinas, fifes, and the atmosphere of a gingerbread fair. In *Le Sacre du Printemps* too Stravinsky aimed at a primitivism; embodying not the modern masses but the human past; the herd life surviving in man's unconscious. Here melody, harmony, and rhythm are deliberately brutal, angular, inarticulate, expressive of the human strata where the individual does not exist, and life is blind instinct and swarm-being. For all its romanticism *Le Sacre* is the first communist ballet. The peculiar tone color of *Renard,* the "village band" music for trumpet, cymbal, and drum opening and closing of the little farce, and the huzzahing and falsetting of the singers, therefore are not without grand precedents in Stravinsky's own art.

What distinguishes *Renard* from its predecessors, is the fact that it is better formed than they, and of a healthier temper. Humanistic and disabused in idea, it is self-definitive, and free from the traces of romanticism and preciousness which compromise the spirit of the great ballets. Both *Petrouchka* and *Le Sacre* lean to a degree on literary and mimetic ideas for their meanings. *Petrouchka* is not without descriptivity. Jewelry of a kind, a love of the singular harmony and the rare color, flashes through the deliberately humble material. Besides, the humor is essentially romantic. The puppet hero is a last incarnation of the important, unhoused, romantic ego, while the music expresses the pathos and irony of election and superiority-inferiority. Though *Le Sacre* embodies a common experience, the common life of man, it seizes upon it in terms of the monstrous and the remote, and by means of a music that points back to the faëry of Rimsky-Korsakov. The music of *Renard* nonetheless is as pure in form as in popularity. It is not piecemeal; does not lean on literary or mimetic ideas; and is not descriptive. It merely fixes the general mood of the cruel and comic animal *fabliau* it embodies. By virtue of its independence it is nonetheless able, even in concert form, to bathe us in the atmosphere of the rude side show, and set us amid the birchbark shoes and red grinning faces of Russian peasants and children. Preciosity is entirely out of the picture. No harmony or instrumental effect calls attention to itself. The rhythms snap and accelerate with a certain ease. Shrill, robust, homely, and rough to threadbareness, the music has a uniform and appropriate coloration; recalling both peasant improvisations and the cantatas of Bach, so notably regular in their instrumental hues. The savage humor is free of romantic irony. It is not the Master of the Show, but human nature, universal nature, that is satirized in the self-complacency of the cock sunning himself upon his perch and caressing himself with his little guardian doodle-do, in the hypocrisy of mother fox disguised as a nun and entreating master cock to come down and be confessed, in the lamentations of the poor cock in the hands of the crafty wretch, and in the fatal curiosity of the latter when cat and goat began their serenade. Perhaps *Renard* is not the greatest Stravinsky. It has the scope of neither *Petrouchka*, *Le Sacre*, or *Les Noces*. The musical ideas are not striking; and there are brittle and even dull pages among its gleeful, sportive ones. But unlike its predecessors it builds up. And beneath the savagery, there is much health. Ultimately, it is health that interests.

3. *Les Noces*

DOMINANT IN *Renard*, the new method triumphed in *Les Noces*, with *Le Sacre* one of the capital pieces of modern music. *Les Noces* is humanistic like *Renard*, but a larger, more powerful and complicated expression; moving us not with the indirection and irony, savagery, and burlesque of the animal fable, but with feeling in its simple, immediate form. This is to say that *Signori* Brutality and Sentimentality, twin eccentric halves of emotional disconnection, must find the music respectively saccharine and cold. The raucous, strident, willful note is well out of it, and the ungirt, facile, unrestrained one out of it as well. But where there is capacity for direct relation, sensation, emotion, and sentiment, the vibrance must gratify. Indeed, so justly does the work convey the proportion of robustness and tenderness, impersonality and secret warmth which inform our best experience, that one can well have the illusion that *Les Noces* is "it."

Stravinsky calls from the four pianos and the little battery a simultaneously metallic, frosty, and dense quality of sound. Bell tones permeate the instrumental medium, flat Kremlin chimes, clock strokes, tzings of Chinese temple gongs: bell tones always bright, sharp, high up in air, quickly muffled and cut off as peals in Europe on certain gaudies. A scattering of cloudy pages throws the robustious brilliance into relief; and the movingly spaced series of clangorous chords, struck at the end, seems merely to gather and decisively hold the firm rich quality of white metals, nickel, silver, and steel, felt throughout the score.

Reserve, austerity of strength, characterizes the entire medium; the human no less than the instrumental. Chorus and soli sound somewhat as the voices in *Renard*, clamant, severe, half impersonal, bare of nuances, and with a strangely satisfying liturgical monotony. In section four, the ribald wedding festival, shouted tones of speech and falsetto singing thrust their dry and burlesque timbers into the broad rigid flow, lightening it; but the entire effect is of a running fresco of uniform, loud, lively, not too sensitive hard sound, expressive of whole, unnervous and not too intuitive people.

Frankly conceived as the exploitation of a material, a medium, *Les Noces* affects us directly as sonority, leaning on no visual or literary idea. It is wholly an expressive play of rigid lines and volumes. None of Stravinsky's pieces, neither *Renard* nor the *Symphonies for Wind Instruments*, stands more the object existing outside the artist, in its own right. Here, the music is the action; and, played with a ballet or without one, carries the intent. Various moods traverse it as the ritual of the peasant marriage unfolds, and the bride dresses, the bridegroom leaves his house, the parents relinquish their children, and the new couple ceremoniously bed. But the different moods, barbaric gaiety and sadness, tenderness and ribaldry remain structural carriers of the central quality. The very style has the cool fire of objectivity. There is abuse of *ostinato*, but drunken rhythmic stuff, compulsive wild dancebeats and cubic jerks and accents are given, with an elegance Stravinsky has not equaled.

The score is clearly, transparently written for all its poly-harmony and polyrhythmicality; solid with the telling counter-point of the later Stravinsky, and cumulative in its effect. No dry rasping passages break the brisk, never precipitous move-ment of the four conjoined sections, each very slightly larger in volume than the last. The vasty clock-strokes of the solemn conclusion round and resolve the well-sustained initial impulse.

These items distinguish *Les Noces* from Stravinsky's earlier peak, the intrinsically romantic consecration. The ultimately differentiating trait nonetheless is the fact that *Les Noces,* unlike the *Sacre* with its monstrosity of proportion, and fearful feeling of an alien, excessive and tigerish nature, is entirely human in scale. Through it we find ourselves in a world rela-tive and proportionate to man, before a portal not too vasty for him and adjusted to his size. This is the region that concerns him and is his proper study. We hear the voices of the human being as the drive of sex selection gives him themes: voices of virginal fear and painful manumission and majoration; an-cestral promptings; orgiastic suggestions; tenderness from the untouched depths, and the heart of decision in which blind transmitted energies gather themselves for a new thrust into the unknown. We feel Man; and not, as in *Le Sacre,* human bacilli, pistons, brainless bobbing organisms that dance when power is applied to them, and make machine-like, involuntary gestures and motions. The humanity whose impulses are embodied in *Les Noces* remain a rudimentary, unindividualizing horde. Personality is not yet present; in any case it is not the indi-vidual aspects of his peasants and people that have interested the composer. Still, the music has a voluntariness, a decisiveness, a species of active virtue different from the fatalistic and passive spirit of *Le Sacre*. There, it is the earth that does; fecundating herself with the blood of man. He is scarcely separated from her; in all things her unconscious child. In *Les Noces* there is still a sacrifice and a death. A man and woman die so that a new life made of them both may begin. But, still blind, still half-conscious, man consents. What spirit of choice, concentration, willingness in the series of dire bell-strokes cutting bride and groom off from their past and rounding the piece! *Amor fati!* and with the spirit of consent, choice, selection, freedom, and Man are here.

4. *We Question Stravinsky*

STRAVINSKY was a good thirty minutes late for rehearsal the afternoon I interviewed him. The handful of musicians assembled for *Renard* and *Ragtime* sat or strolled languidly about on the atticky bare stage of Carnegie Hall. The horn player amused himself by blowing the cantilene from *Der Trompeter von Säckingen* into the cavernous auditorium with fearful emphasis, while at irregular intervals a humorous someone struck loud banal chords on the piano. There would be no opportunity of speaking with Stravinsky before the rehearsal, I saw, regretting the time I would have to wait in order to get my interview. Then Stravinsky came rapidly onto the stage from the wings, a metallic insect all swathed in hat, spectacles, muffler, overcoat, spats, and walking stick; and accompanied by three or four secretarial, managerial personages. The man was an electric shock. In a minute business was upon the entire assemblage. There was a sound of peremptory orders; the group on the platform was in its chairs underneath the conductor's stand; a little personage who looked like someone in a Moscow Art Theatre performance rushed forward to the composer and started stripping him of his coats and helping him into a pink sweater-vest; Carlos Salzedo appeared at the keyboard of the piano; and Stravinsky, simultaneously resembling a bug, Gustav Mahler, and a member of the Russian Ballet, began rehearsing. If he had been late, there was no laggardliness in his mind at all. Never a doubt as to exactly what it was he wanted and the means to arrive at his end! He himself might not be able to play all the instruments assembled before him; still he could tell the musicians how they could get the effects wanted. The bassoonist had some difficulty with the high notes. Stravinsky told him how he could reach them. At the moment when the bass drum enters, Stravinsky stopped the orchestra. "Deeper," he said in German. The drummer struck again. "No," said Stravinsky, "it must sound the way it does in the circus. You will need a heavier drumstick." In passages of complicated rhythm, he stopped the orchestra, sang the measure very quietly, and then left the musicians to play it after him. Once there was a dispute. He stuck his nose into the score, read a few bars carefully, then said to the instrumentalist, "You must make it this way" and sang the notes. Most of his talking was done in German, but he spoke French with Salzedo, Russian with one of the men, and indicated the passages by numbers given in very correct English. By the time ten minutes were elapsed I was comfortably enjoying the spectacle and oblivious of delay. The man was abrupt, impatient, energetic, but never ironic either of himself or of his interlocutors; most exemplary in his relations with the players. It was apparent they were working out a little problem together, and Stravinsky had some suggestions which might enable them all to solve it. A kind of interest radiated from him to the musicians, who began entering into the spirit of the animal comedy, and kindling him in return. He commenced singing the words in Russian, even danced a little in his pink sweater up on the conductor's stand. Certainly, at the more startling dramatic entrances, his two feet leaped together off the ground. His arms at all times mimed the rhythmic starts and jerks, till one could actually perceive where his music came from. Renard the Fox, there was no doubt, was himself, grinning from behind his glasses in ferocious joy, and plucking a feather out of the silly vain old cock with every accent of the drunken score.

When the rehearsal was over, I followed Salzedo (quite as admirable a friend as he is a musician), and was presented. The little Stanislavsky type was helping on with coats and hat; and I found myself before an oval, olive, excessively sensitive face from out some fine old Chinese print, and a man who sat at once nervous, intelligent, and master of himself. I heard myself saying in French that I had some questions which I wanted to ask him, and that I regretted I spoke French and German equally badly; and was relieved to hear Stravinsky answering quietly that we would converse in the language we both spoke. Several Steinway piano movers having taken possession of the stage, we retreated with Salzedo to the first rows of the parterre, and across the backs of the chairs I began explaining to him that I had heard he had said he was striving to keep all personal emotion out of his music, that I was puzzled by the expression, and wanted to know more of what he meant.

He measured me a moment, then said suddenly, "We are going to exchange roles. It is I who am going to interview you. I want you to begin by telling me exactly what it is *you* mean by 'personal emotion.'"

I laughed. "But, Mr. Stravinsky, *I* am not a genius."

"Neither am I," he retorted. Then after a moment, "Suppose you went out and narrowly escaped being run over by a trolley car. Would you have an emotion?"

"I should hope so, Mr. Stravinsky."

"So should I. But if I went out and narrowly escaped being run over by a trolley car, I would not immediately rush for some music paper and try to make something out of the emotion I had just felt. You understand."

"Yes, of course. But it would cease being personal as soon as one began. However, Mr. Stravinsky, do you impose an intellectual theory of emotion or non-emotion upon yourself when you compose?"

"Intellectual theory," he snorted, as if I had wished to accuse him of cretinism, "certainly not! I don't think I go to work twice in the same fashion. Besides, what is all this about personal emotion? All emotion goes back to the personal equation. What is emotional for one man is not emotional for another. But there are certain artists who go out before the world and commence crying," and here he raised his arms while a look of disgust passed over his face, "'Oh, I am such a great man, such a great artist! I have all these wonderful feelings and these wonderful experiences. I see God, the whole, and Heaven knows what else.'"

"That's mere impotence." Here he shot a glance at me.

"What I am trying to find out, is whether you have any kind of idea that certain things which we call feeling, or the heart, or the soul, are passing out of life? You know, there are certain people who are trying to strike the scientific attitude in living, and working without pity, without sympathy, without desire, even——"

"That's utterly absurd," he interrupted, "the very thing which you are afraid of, and try to repress—that's the very thing which is going to seize you in the end. Anyway, the form of the repression is equivalent to the form of the expression. But of course there is romanticism, and perhaps that is going out of life. But in their very effort to escape from romanticism, people are committing the most grotesque errors. Take Schoenberg, for example. Schoenberg is really a romantic at heart who would like to get away from romanticism. He admires Aubrey Beardsley! Just think—he considers Aubrey Beardsley wonderful! It's unbelievable, isn't it? But even the romantic composers aren't as 'romantic' as people have tried to make them. Schumann, for instance. I know I could play Schumann for people so that he wouldn't have that particular sort of sentimentalism which we don't admire today. But then people would say it wasn't Schumann."

As he finished the speech, I became aware of another voice, redolent of purest Avenue A, pouring into my ear, "Say, young feller, you got to get out of here if you don't want to get run over," and found a grand piano guided by several piano-moving huskies, bearing down on me. By the time I had climbed over the backs of several seats and gotten into Stravinsky's row, the train of the conversation had been interrupted. This time I began by asking him whether he told himself stories or saw pictures while he composed.

He looked at me a little maliciously and shot out, "Is this a confession you are demanding of me?"

"Oh, Mr. Stravinsky, I'm very raw, I see——"

"Well, if it is a confession you are demanding, here is the answer, No! No! A thousand times, no!"

"But when you compose, is there not something which guides you? A feeling of form? A sense of rhythm? Aren't you seeking to draw a line about something which you feel has an existence prior to your effort of composition?"

"I see what you mean," he said. "These are questions about which the whole world is thinking. What interests me most of all is construction. What gives me pleasure is to see how much of my material I can get into line. I want to see what is coming. I am interested first in the melody, and the volumes, and the instrumental sounds, and the rhythm. It is like this. It is like making love to a woman." Here he glanced about, perceived Mrs. Salzedo sitting a few rows back, apologized humorously for the Gallicism, and then resumed, "You find yourself, you don't know how, in possession of, say, four bars of music. Well, the real musician is the one who knows what there is to be done with these four bars; knows what he can make out of them. Composition really comes from the gift of being able to see what your material is capable of."

"But, suppose, Mr. Stravinsky, I hear one of your compositions, and certain images of the world, or of condition, come into my mind. Do you feel that I am reading something into your creations which does not exist there?"

"But, my dear sir, who is the interpreter here? It is you. That is for you, and not for me, to say."

"You see, the first time I ever heard the *Sacre,* I saw machinery and industrial landscapes——"

He interrupted. "Who conducted it the first time you ever heard it?"

"Monteux."

He nodded his head, satisfied. "Monteux does it very well, very well. Monteux has the right idea of the *Sacre.*"

"Then let me ask you one more question, Mr. Stravinsky. Do you think any work, any work of today, I mean, which is genuinely living, can fail to interpret to us elements of the daily life, say our relationships with people?"

He sat reflective a moment. "Perhaps not," he said. "I don't know. We don't know what the creative moment is made up of. It may even be anecdotal. You see I myself have not the same feeling against what is purely anecdotal as against what is either picturesque or literary. I feel there is a difference, and I am perfectly willing to acknowledge that certain bits of the *Sacre* have an anecdotal interest. But not picturesque. And in the main, the interest is architectural. That is all. When people hear my *Octuor* and especially my piano concerto, they are sure to talk about 'back to Bach.' But that is not what I mean. The material of Bach's day was, let us say, the size of this hall. The material of our day," and here he lifted the crook'd head of his cane, "is about the size of this. But I feel we in our day are working with our material in the spirit of Bach, the constructive spirit; and I think that what we give, though perhaps smaller in comparison, is in its concentration and economy an equivalent for the immense structures of Bach."

Many conversations come to rest with the name of the cantor of the Thomas School: this one was one of them. As we went through the door giving on the passageway, and while Salzedo was talking to Stravinsky about the music of Varèse, a young fellow who had been listening to the conversation from a little distance rushed up to the composer, declared he admired his work, and begged to be allowed to shake his hand. There was a half-embarrassed moment, Stravinsky bowing like an oriental potentate, and doubtlessly enjoying, for the thousandth time, the sweetest of all homages, that of young people.

I, however, was still puzzled. Had I missed my good opportunity?

5. *"Igor, Tu N'est Qu'un Villain!"* *

AFTER HAVING BEEN READILY PENETRABLE, Stravinsky's aims had become puzzling. Once he had written music and said nothing. He had been an intuitive musician; ironic, undoubtedly, but moved by and addressed to, sensibility. Now, the world was full

* " 'Igor, you're nothing but a scoundrel!' "

of his words, statements, theories, analyses, and apologies. The man had grown theoretical, and the music had grown dumb. There was much talk of "pure" musicality, redolent of Picasso's "pure" pictiveness. All artistic problems were to be solved by "pure" means. A composer was to write music, a painter to paint pictures. There was also a deal of ado about the eschewal of "personal emotion"; and some more concerning the correspondences between musical form and the machine, resting on coordination of parts, perfect functionality, and unimpeded watch-movement. The questions put the composer by myself go to show how puzzling when first aired these simple ideas were; now we know they signify the greenness of the grass. What darkened them was, I dare say, not so much my simplicity, as the fact they transformed into conscious aims things unconsciously, intuitively pursued by humanistic artists. Also the fact that the music they appeared to explain was not entirely open to intuition; and not very important. Had it been open, and as worthy as *Le Sacre,* the *Symphonies, Les Noces,* and *L'Histoire du Soldat,* no one, I am sure, saving the professors, would have paid attention to them. Certainly not myself, always aware of Nietzsche's warning that of all Wagnerian exegists, the one least to be regarded was Wagner himself. In any case, they would not have puzzled.

Now, the prime concerns in this case, the Piano Concerto, the *Octuor for Wind Instruments,* the Piano Sonata, and *Serenade,* and the much "advertised" *Oedipus Rex* left and continue to leave one fumbling for their bourne and reason. Not merely because of their archaicism. The archaicizing tendency of music in itself is neither good nor bad. It is as old as the score of *Die Meistersinger;* and although not inevitably bound up with humanism, is frequently its concomitant: witness, its presence in the relatively humanistic *Die Meistersinger,* and its absence in the ultraromantic *Tristan.* Of late, it has produced excellent results through certain German moderns, Hindemith and Schoenberg in particular. Not, however, through Stravinsky. His adaptations of the forms of Handel, Bach, Pergolesi, Clementi, Bellini, Cimarosa, Czerny, and others, turn one from all "movement back to" anybody; probably for the reason that the conceptions are not clear. Some fine music there is in all these later pieces of his: rigid, strong, pleasantly dry and magnificently sonorous music, cast in Bachian, Handelian eighteenth-century forms of chorale and fugue. All avoid the deadwood of musical art, descriptiveness, romantic string-vibration (the concerto is written for piano and brass, woodwinds, and percussion, the *Octuor* for brass and woodwinds) ; and all have something of the pure spontaneous movement, the structurality, the wit and the serenity which satisfy today. There is some feeling, perhaps even "personal emotion" in the second movement of the concerto, charmingly modeled on the slow movements of Bach's concerti and sonatas. The chorale in the *Octuor,* with its softly blent brass and wood, is a sustained ethereal magnificence. Passages of speedy cursive counterpoint appear in the concerto; Jocasta's antique grand air in *Oedipus* is rich and moving; the instrumental combinations of these late works are robust and interesting, particularly in the concerto, with its puffing, jazzy brass. In the *Octuor,* the sonorities are not quite as happily balanced, witness the first entrance of the horns and trumpets.

This recent music is not sensual; does not excite the passions. Predominantly reflective, it has been conceived and set down in the best of taste. What is *Oedipus Rex* other than a triumph of good manner? The brutal, hot, uncouth is excluded from this version of the old, cruel, magnificently worked out tale of helpless blood-guilt. The music is undeluded, unemphatic, architectural. The musician has attempted to solve all his problems musically, striving for externality and thingness. Eschewing pictorialness and descriptivity, Stravinsky's "oratorio" flows agreeably, never hot-colored or grandiose (in the Wagnerian sense) , or sensational; bearing evidence of thought and consideration in every bar. No doubt but Stravinsky has found "subtle and probably unprecedented ways of uniting the instruments and the chorus." A most intelligent performance! A lesson in manners; a counsel of humility, sobriety, and piety! Only, it doesn't move! It is like an illustration, amusing the reflective faculties; not mobilizing the mind, the thinking body. Like all its predecessors, it compels no fresh experience. The region to which all living, rooted works repair in us and which repays the visit with gratitude and loyalty, is never touched by it. We listen, intellectually concerned, delighted sometimes by some felicity of style or form, and irritated by an unslaked thirst. The head alone is involved; and who wants everything done through the head? What is musical in us wants to hear, and is not to be interested by comments, even by Stravinsky's. And if they were merely Stravinsky's! *His* analysis, criticism couched in music, might be tolerable. But who cares for Cocteau's? We want *Oedipus,* either Sophocles plus or nothing; certainly not the coquetry of a feeble, posturing Parisian.

What has happened; turning Igor Stravinsky into Mr. Modernsky; making one recall Debussy's slapstick "Igor, tu n'est qu'un villain!" Was it not actually in the effort to discover this that I went to interview the man, wishing to gain at their source the confidence denied me by the works themselves? I did not suspect my motive, and asked random questions; now, however, it is clear to me that there was an unconscious question and that it was this: what has happened? Just as well it was not articulated at that time! It would not have been answered. Stravinsky, I believe, would merely have spoken a little more fully of his new architectural interest, of his anti-nationalism and anti-orientalism; and not without a certain justice, since these orientations do lie at the root of his adventures in archaicism. But he would not have revealed their dynamism, the forces concealed behind their prim intellectualistic masks; and that was the object of my inquiry. He could not; since their very power over him, and his own intellectualistic delusion of the "all-power" of thought, flowed just from an aversion to roots, dynamics: forces in and without himself. That, indeed, was what had happened: Stravinsky had turned against his own roots! The psychology of the *émigré* had developed in him: the spirit of the man not so much the physical exile as the exile from his early associations and the past alive in him; indeed from his own body.—This, curiously enough, came to me across the pages not of a Stravinsky score, but of a T. S. Eliot criticism: something about Chapman or Crashaw, Dryden or Marlowe; I've forgotten whom. In any case, in recognizing the analogy between Eliot's bookishness and Stravinsky's cerebralism and archaicism, I saw behind the scene; assisting at the birth of an hybrid style and defective classicism, neither Russian nor western nor Stravinsky. In flying from his early associations and the past alive in him, the *émigré* becomes mere head. For purposes of life, this head has to manufacture itself a body. It has to make the foreign its own; willfully identifying itself with that which makes the foreigner at home in his foreignness. Since this is early association and the living past, the *émigré* is unconsciously moved to identify himself with the forms assumed by them, sole contact possible to heads. He gradually becomes a fanatic of manners; called to defend his adopted country's culture and high tradition; more Catholic than the Pope, more royalist than the king; the intellectual knowledge, possession, appreciation of that past becoming subjectively potent symbols of identification. The extreme English nicety of Henry James, his lamentations over a departed aristocracy, furnish the perfect instance. Another is to be found in T. S. Eliot's combination of head-rhythms with peevish bookishness and a puritanic cult for classic English expression divorced from a corresponding interest in the poetic personalities and the human adventure. A third, alas! is the cerebralism and archaicism of the recent Stravinsky.

A spiritual exile from Russia, forced to take root in western Europe, Stravinsky has perforce sought to assimilate principles of a tradition foreign to him. If others, notably the Germans, are able to archaicize, to go "back to Bach," it is for the reason that the archaic, northern, Protestant idiom is in their blood, in their early experience; reaching them in living transmission through Wagner and Reger. Not to the Russian; since the stuff of art must long accumulate in the unconscious and lie ripening there, before it becomes fluent and malleable.

Hence, too, the theoretical camouflage: the aprioristic reasoning. Still, even in rootlessness, Stravinsky remains the man of his time. Pressing need of justification through identification with some traditional, established value, is absurdly common. In past years, men sought it through religion. Weighted with a sense of moral guilt, they felt themselves damned, weeping for the sinful will organized in them; and dreamed of bathing themselves clean within a fountain filled with blood. *Nous avons passé tout ça.** Yet substitute for the word "salvation" the word "aestheticism," or "structurality," "impersonality," "classicism," and you will see there is no new thing underneath the moon. Instead of ethical guilt there is aesthetic guilt. Men groan with the dark sense of artistic damnation. Emotionalism, sentimentality, sensuality are the unforgivable sins. Men tremble that their works are not acceptable to posterity as forms suspended in a void; tormenting themselves whether grace has elected them one of the hundred and forty-four thousand saints composing the main, the Cezannesque trunk of art, or whether they are predestined mere branches, twigs, and leaves? In nightmares knowing themselves romanticists, they feel the whole anguish of the pit. Or, perceiving Aristotle and the old Chinese, Bach, Cezanne, and Spinoza in aesthetic glory at the right hand of God, they yearn to wash fatal inferiority away in the faultless essence of the motets of Orlando di Lasso, the *terze rime* of Dante, and the frescoes on the Sistine ceiling. American critics run to be spanked by oriental humbugs, and preach to sinners about prose, intellectuality, and the mechanics of art. We are indeed a "lost" generation!

The rooted expression *is* justification. Now, Stravinsky had his roots. *Renard, Les Noces,* and the *Symphonies* were in his own tradition and in the humanistic track. Hence it is not

* "We've been through all that."

reasonable to suppose that a better adjustment will put him in touch with his own background again. Meanwhile, it is fortunate that even his neoclassical works are not without their contribution, even though it be more a thing of intention than of accomplishment. They are architectural in conception; and the new birth of the architectural interest has considerably deepened and enlarged the field of music. It is a part of the profound, world-wide development of the mind enabling man to think quickly through shapes, lines, and rhythms; responsible for the interest of "abstract" art, literature, and music. Something therefore is to be learned from Stravinsky's experiments. They are not ungrateful exercises, Moscheles* perhaps more than Czerny.† Indeed, we have already to thank them for increased capacity to recognize the prevalency of the architectural interest among the ultramodern composers, and to distinguish those most happily responsive to it. The taste we have for Hindemith, for example, is largely due to Stravinsky.

The Evolution of Stravinsky

THE LOWER PART of the scene was wrapped in green darkness during the American stage première of the *Oedipus Rex* of Cocteau and Stravinsky, given by the Philadelphia Orchestra under Dr. Stokowski, with the assistance of the stage designer Robert Edmond Jones, and Mme. Matzenauer, Mr. Paul Althouse, and the Harvard University Glee Club, at the Metropolitan in the winter of 1930. Robed in blue, the chorus was massed upon a low grandstand rather to the left of the stage, with the soloists in their midst. The unseen Speaker commenced: "Without knowing it, Oedipus is at cross-purposes with the forces which spy on us from the further side of the

---

* Ignaz Moscheles (1794–1870), virtuoso pianist, a friend of Mendelssohn's.

† Karl Czerny (1791–1857), Austrian pianist (a pupil of Beethoven's), and composer of exacting technical studies for the piano.

grave. From the day of his birth they have been watching him to set a snare for him into which he shall fall." As the music began monotonously and hopelessly muttering a rune of the cruel Powers, into the luminous upper half of the scene there rose, as from out the humanity cowering at its base, a gaunt, twelve-foot effigy of Oedipus the King. And in the course of the nightmarelike drama petrified in music, one after another equally tall and garish puppets of Creon, Teresias, Jocasta, and the other dramatis personae appeared beside it. At the moment of the catastrophe, the message of Jocasta's suicide, it vanished; then, while the orchestra and the chorus cried out of their darkness in horror and terror of the ferocious gods, a hideous effigy of the blinded, naked, outcast Oedipus rose on high, and dwindling beneath the weight of his pitiless fate, descended, extinguishing like a suddenly defective electric wire. For a last time the chorus and the drums monotonously muttered their hopeless rune.

No Greek drama had been presented to us. The antique tragedy had conceived of fate as a subtle concordance of character and circumstance. The classic Oedipus was not the puppet of an entirely external destiny. His catastrophe to a decided degree was the consequence of his own violence. The king who dashed out his eyes in his despair and shame was the violent son of a violent father, who had introduced sodomy into Greece, the offspring of an overbearing, high-handed family that disobeyed and sought to outwit the gods, and as little a passive victim as the Shakespearean Macbeth. If he walked into any "trap," it was one in nowise separate from himself. Certainly the antique destiny, in Aeschylus and in Sophocles, at least, invariably remained the daughter of the discords, the deceptions, and the ignorances of gods and of men, never the action of hostile powers upon helpless creatures.

No: what had been presented was a much blacker, more primitive conception of the relations of gods and human beings, one that, ever latent in the European mind, periodically rises from it in all its fearfulness. It represents gods jealous of and hostile to man, and man inevitably their enemy and their victim. Man has committed a sin, the original sin. He has been born: he has emerged from the night whose power he has defied and whose peace he has broken. But the gods are the stronger. Man is ultimately unconscious, and life involves him in evil upon evil: till at last, in awareness of his guilt, and broken in power and pride, he sinks, shattered, into the night from which he blindly rose. And behind the action of the Cocteau-Stravinsky *Oedipus Rex* one felt the ineradicable past deed whose inevitable consequence the catastrophe was, not half so much the blind parricide and incest as the event of birth itself; and read and heard from the forms the expression of the deep, irrational feeling of his original, inexpiable guilt that, lodged in man, mutters continually within him, and rises and overwhelms him in his hours of weakness and defeat; and the might of the Night itself that holds him by this hook.

The oratorio-opera proved one of the most pessimistic and bitter of the messages of a composer who, distinguished by the pessimism and bitterness of his experience, is easily the greatest of personal forces in the contemporary musical world: the author of a mass of compositions extremely dynamic in form, including some of the world's most swiftly moving, starkly and intensely expressive pieces; of a half-dozen ballet scores which have restored to the choreographic form an importance comparable to that which Wagner returned to the music drama; and the immediate cause of a majority of the changes that have occurred in the cast and character of creative music during the last two decades. *Oedipus* also reinforced the feeling of disappointment the productions of Stravinsky immediately anterior to it had roused.

The very first of his individual compositions, the ballets *Petrouchka* and *Le Sacre du Printemps,* which he composed during the milling period immediately preceding the outbreak of the World War for the Diaghilev ballet, instantly had revealed the advent of a young composer with a fresh, very pungent, material sense. These extraordinary scores of the young Stravinsky, and to an extent the shortly subsequent *Renard* and *Les Noces,* were, partially, outcrops of the nationalistic movement of Russian music represented during the nineteenth century by the compositions of Glinka, Moussorgsky, Rimsky-Korsakov, and Balakirev. Like these, they too to a large extent were based upon the styles of Slavic folk music, pieces of which are interwoven in their fabrics; and they also groped for the meaning of the Russian soil and Russian nature and uttered its power and wildness. They had the family characteristics: brilliance of instrumental color, conciseness of expression, pantomimic spirit, animal vitality, and episodic structure; and their special multirhythmicality and partiality to humble material, and even their relentless polytonalism, must for all their indebtedness to Strauss's example be considered direct developments of certain of Moussorgsky's innovations. Simultaneously they were the offshoots of such elements of western music as the impressionistic harmonies of Debussy, the musical irony of *Till Eulenspiegel,* and the musical primitivism of *Elektra,* and nonetheless a merger of the two traditions in highly individual, powerful, epoch-making and -marking musical forms and expressions.

Petrouchka and *Le Sacre* were not only "cubistic"; without the melting contours of the music of Debussy and Strauss, and bare of all silkiness and jewelry. Highly nervous in tension, they were robust, hard, plebeian, and struck one like hammer blows. And built up of stiff, angular phrases and often harshly harmonized melodic fragments and moving from massive block to block of color, they were above all distinguished by insistent, irregularly accented, but iterative rhythms abundantly emphasized by a percussion that kinged it over the entire orchestra. These rhythms of these frequently polytonic pieces were developed from the iterative rhythms of Russian folk songs. But they were also mechanistic, the full-grown children of the tendency to express the pulsations and spirits of mechanical things delicately begun by Beethoven in the allegretto of his Eighth Symphony and continued by Moussorgsky in the hallucination scene in *Boris Godunov*. They were primitivistic to an equal degree: wild, orgiastic, brutal. And a new, an intense experience breathed harshly through these rigid forms, one radically opposite to the majority of those which for a century had been reaching the world through music. For this young Scyth the world was bare of the exquisitely sensuous, lovely, and delicious elements that had enchanted his predecessors down to Debussy and of the ideal elements that had caused composers from Beethoven through Wagner to Scriabin to feel its plenitude of glowing possibilities; above all, bare of the Idea, and of human beings potentially noble and free. Life for him was a stark affair, a cruel affair, and a gross affair: a thing earthy and tough, all thumbs, udders, and shaggy organs; full of pain, static, entirely mechanical. The human being at best was a feeble puppet dependent upon an energy entirely without him that played him in utter ruthless indifference. The music itself was apparently a strong and stoical, occasionally bitterly humorous, adjustment to this stark and fundamentally gross reality. The bubbling of the flutes beginning *Petrouchka* introduces us immediately into this gimcrack world, with its quality of a gingerbread fair, and thorough mechanism. Human beings pervade this world, but their souls are automata: Petrouchka, the ballerina, the sumptuous Moor; and barrel organ tunes are the expression of the movement of the spheres. Prisoners and slaves of this external force, the puppets dance to music not of their making, and love and suffer and die with stiff, grotesque gestures; and in death mock their maker and owner. The entire wild and ironic score is full of the pain and the poetry of this mechanical world. The dolls and the instruments appearing upon the stage and their qualities and gestures have a counterpart in the music with its precise and iterative rhythms, its puppetlike, rigid, and angular phrases. The passage for the piano and other instruments accompanying the scene of the solitary Petrouchka in his box, for example, is a strange miniature expression, a sort of music of little things, composed of whirring, purling, creaking sonorities delicately, mordantly related to the noises of intricate mechanism, watches, meters, tickers, dolls, and other devices.

And though no automata invade the stage in *Le Sacre* and the score is bare of the clockwork music of its immediate predecessor, it, too, with its dark and ferocious coloring, adjusts us to a mechanistic order of things. It embodies another intuition of the automaton in the human being. This ballet is a representation of instinctive and unconscious action. Its subject is the vernal rite of primitive tribes, the celebration and representation of the earth and its sovereign will by pagan Russians. But its feeling is a pessimistic one that not all primitive societies have shared. Cocteau found it "a symphonic expression of wild mourning, the labor-pains of the earth, farm and encampment sounds, little melodies that come from the depths of the centuries, the groaning of cattle, profound blows: a georgic of prehistoric ages." Through the idyllically piping but brutally polyrhythmic score, with its stamping rhythms, archaic modality, and heavily moving masses of sound, we feel the weight of the earth, its dark attractiveness, its everlasting voracity of tillage and blood, its domination of man with its sightless ineluctable will, its imperious exaction of his allegiance and self-sacrifice to the end of eternal reproduction. The second part of it, especially, is another poem of pain, the pain of parturition. In an ecstasy verging upon agony it sings the suction of the earth, the goodness of Dionysiac annihilation. There is only pressure of blind instinct here, the harsh urgence of overmastering biological impulse, the mournful, voluptuous bath of slow craving. With a pistonlike iterativeness and relentlessness go the rhythms. The whole piece is full of the weight of slow-moving, dumb, irresistible mass.

Themselves progressive from cubism, these pieces in their turn influenced the whole course of music. The entire young generation of composers, under their spell, turned away from impressionism toward their kind of hard-boiled expressivity and began favoring irregular measures, demotic material, crystalline sonorities—and not only the young *composers*. One feels their influence in the "I can take it" prose of Hemingway and his school. Meanwhile, Stravinsky had succeeded these two early masterpieces with several equally genial works in the smaller forms, three of them for the stage: *Renard, Les Noces,* and *L'Histoire du Soldat,* and a piece of absolute music, *Symphonies for Wind Instruments.* Products of the war years—Stravinsky was interned with his family in Switzerland—these pieces continue powerfully to express a painful and a pessimistic vision. *Renard,* an animal fabliau, followed *Petrouchka* in presenting gross and cruel reality in the form of a grotesque. *Les Noces,* in the shape of a representation of a rustic wedding cortege and feast, embodies the relentless force that joins and sacrifices two human beings to the end of perpetuating the race. We feel it here as Schopenhauer felt it once, an unswerving dynamic urgence rushing ahead like an express train and carrying human beings ruthlessly along in its trajectory; and not a little through the painful expressions of the bride and the women bidding farewell to youth, the iron determination in the voices of the men, the ribald cries of the drunken wedding guests, and the stern, gonging conclusion, fraught with a feeling of the impenetrable mystery of marriage. *L'Histoire* mordantly expresses, in the tale of an uprooted soldier damned by militarism itself, the mortgage the devil, here the material forces of creation, has upon life; and the inevitable foreclosure of the mortgage. The score, like that of *Petrouchka,* is humble and demotic in style. For a moment, after the soldier has restored the king's daughter to health with the music of his violin, the great chorale in tones recalling Luther's famous hymn expresses the victory of faith and unity and the ideal. But the victory is temporary only. At the end the devil wins. To percussive music that utters the omnipotence of the brute creation the soldier follows him down to hell. And the *Symphonies for Wind Instruments,* dedicated to the memory of Debussy, conclude with a stark dirge that, echoing the last chorus in *Boris Godunov,* exceeds it in grim plangency.

These four pieces in many ways are Stravinsky's most perfect.

Their forms are complete, their rhythms subtle; and certain in their effects, they completely and sustainedly express intense and deep feeling. Stark as it is, his music of *Les Noces* and *L'Histoire* is full of tenderness and revelatory of the considerable sensibility that he holds in check. The bone-weary *L'Histoire* even more than *Petrouchka* shows the composer's feeling for the miniature. In other ways, too, these pieces differ from the ballets preceding them, and not only in the point of feeling or the obvious one of strict limitation of form and of material. While three of them, *Renard, Les Noces,* and the *Symphonies,* are built of material which, though stylized as in *Le Sacre,* is distinctly Russian—*Les Noces* actually contains a theme derived from the liturgy and constitutes a symphonic folk song— *L'Histoire* was anything but a nationalistic piece and represented a break with the nationalistic tradition and a redintegration in the catholic European one. The last three of the four works also exhibited a swing toward the linear principle of form. Stravinsky's early work, including *Renard,* had by and large conformed to the modified homophonic-harmonic principle of composition. From *Les Noces* onward it has conformed to the melodic-contrapuntal one. Effectively melodic, tellingly contrapuntal, swiftly moving, and firmly an entity, *Les Noces* is also distinctly less dependent on literary and mimetic associations than its predecessors, far more an absolute musical object in the mold of antiphonies of soloists and chorus. *L'Histoire* represents another step. It is extremely formally textured, cast in closed ancient and modern molds, marches, waltzes, chorales, and tangos, fox trots, and ragtime; and the music is frequently *concertante* in character. In the *Symphonies* we find Stravinsky studying his means, developing a form out of the impulse of the theme itself, and striving to discover what pure melody, harmony, and rhythm are capable of achieving. These three works are also distinguished by their novel sonorities. *Les Noces* is extremely percussive, metallic. The composer cast it for voices, four pianos, and a complex battery; and the powerful and melancholy music, almost Chinese in its melody, rings and chimes like sounded metal. *L'Histoire* ends with a virtuosic passage of percussive music; and the *Symphonies* are cast, as in stone, in the impersonal sonority of the thirteen wind pieces.

Stravinsky indeed had developed into a thoroughly neoclassic composer, and incidentally redintegrated the art of music with its great tradition. For the melodic-contrapuntal principle of composition and forms organically developed from musical ideas, the aim of the neoclassicist, themselves constitute this great line; and while the movement toward it actually was initiated by composers other than and previous to Stravinsky, it attained its goal resonantly in his compositions and through them told upon composers everywhere, from Germany and Spain to the United States and Latin America, even influencing the most eminent of his coevals, Schoenberg. And Stravinsky continued in this great tradition and continued to illustrate it: however, not altogether untroublingly. Since the *Symphonies,* his pieces had the hallmarks of a not altogether happy tendency. Stravinsky only too plainly was doubling neoclassicism with archaicism, reviving old styles and old types of pieces and mixing old material in with his own. In itself, archaicism is neither commendable nor reprehensible, the concomitant of the periodic "returns to the antique" to be found in all cultures. And the business of reviving old forms, at least that of imposing their limits upon new creations, is a kind of criticism in the medium of music, a manner of assimilating the ideas of former men and epochs. What is important is the method of this assimilation and the results. And in Stravinsky's case neither had been prime, or prime in only one instance. This was *Pulcinella,* a ballet built upon melodies of the eighteenth-century Neapolitan composer Pergolesi, and to a degree a leading cause of the revival among contemporary composers of the spry, lively, and brittle style of the Neapolitan classic *opéra bouffe.* Stravinsky had, it appeared, thoroughly felt himself into the idiom of the old master, and while introducing syncopations and rhythmic accents of his own into the adroitly composed score, maintained a unity in it. The succeeding pieces, the concerto for piano and wind and percussion orchestra, the octet for wind instruments, the Piano Sonata, and *Serenade,* however, were excessively heterogeneous in style. The material was a bewildering farrago of Bach, Handel, Johann Strauss, jazz, and the kitchen range, all served up half baked together. Stravinsky, who had quit the Russian nationalistic basis, had not arrived at a catholic style, merely at a baroque composite.

Still it was not only the heterogeneity of the material that left one unsatisfied by these pieces. It was their relative sterility. One missed the powerful impulse of the preceding works and the expression of intense feeling through vivid forms. That the elemental violence, the garish colors, and the excessive dissonateness of scheme of the early works should in the course of time have been succeeded by a more contained, controlled, calm spirit, and more consonant harmony, seemed natural: one did not ask for continuous repetitions of *Le Sacre* and *Les Noces* in that sense, or repine that for Stravinsky every composition evidently exhausted the interest of its mold; and that his energy consistently redintegrated itself after every piece on a level other than the last and in connection with another form. What one did demand, however, was music that was fresh, the testimony of a convincing creative impulse: and what one got was dryly, elegantly percussive, and soberly colored music that was frequently twice-told, and entirely without sovereignly poetic passages like those that occurred in the cell scene in *Petrouchka,* in the beginning of the second part of *Le Sacre,* in the close of the scene in *Les Noces* where the guests depart for the church and in the whole of the wedding feast, in the Little Concert of *L'Histoire,* and in the finale of the *Symphonies for Wind Instruments.* That there were striking pages in these archaicizing works was not to be denied. The second movement of the concerto, with its Bach succeeded by a Russian-style melody, was lyrical. The first two little movements of the *Serenade* were stark and mobile. The octet even as a whole was fairly diverting. The little one-act opera *Mavra,* composed during the postwar years in which Stravinsky was producing this almost sterile music, had a distinct charm and classic smoothness. But all in all, these pieces seemed perverse, the products of what appeared to be something persistently driven in a direction contrary to its natural one. The neoclassic discipline which Stravinsky was imposing upon himself, the objective architectural plasticity to which he aspired, all seemed willed.

It was this disappointment that the performance of *Oedipus Rex* finally crystallized. The opera oratorio was Stravinsky's first composition in the large forms since *Le Sacre,* for those of *Les Noces,* while bulky, are relatively limited both in scope and in material. In this work Stravinsky had sought to recreate the type of the Handelian oratorio: he had adopted its mold of numbers for chorus interspersed with solo pieces and striven for its grandeur and monumentality of style. He had had Cocteau's lines translated into Latin, to the further end of making his expression stonelike, severe, formal, archaic. In spots the score realized his aim. The ominous stoical drum beats, the square choruses and stark accents, all this virile expression of fatal knowledge, had archaic asperity and power. The arias were dramatically contrasted. Each was a portrait, executed with melodic lines often large and flowing, and strongly idiosyncratic and definitive of the character of the protagonist. The expressions of Oedipus were noble and revelatory of deep uncertainty; those of Creon, military, forthright, brusque. Teresias spoke in a priestly, evasive, mysterious manner, Jocasta in a sensuous and chromatic style. The changes of mood were definite; Oedipus' growing insecurity was marked during the suite of his arias, Jocasta's final terror expressed with all the vehemence of Italian opera. The chorus glorifying the queen at the moment of her appearance was strong, hard, barbaric, and terribly ironical. But while the dramatic tension was sustained, the total effect was not a happy one. The score, to begin with, lacks unity. The better part of the choral music has a severe ominous quality, Russian in essence, while Creon's diatonic aria is Handelian in its bravura, Teresias' Wagnerian in its exaltation and refinement, and Jocasta's has vulgar touches of Bizet and

Verdi. The light Russian melody and rhythm of the shepherd and the messenger come like something out of *Petrouchka* or *Renard*. And it remains a medley, from which the various kinds of material, especially the echoes of Italian opera, protrude, so many anfractuosities. And besides being eccentric, the music is oftentimes commonplace in quality. Next to the final outcry of the chorus, the most distinguished page of the score is Teresias' aria, with its melody overleaping intervals of sevenths and ninths. But the rest, including Jocasta's chromatic *da capo* aria, is curiously stale: and it is probable that not even Rossini or Donizetti would have been proud of the dreadful organ-grinder triolets of her second song. And music sung by the chorus and messenger before the recapitulation of the majestic initial chords and drum theme seemed a little absurd; it had apparently been lifted directly from the grandstands during a rousing intercollegiate match. In any case, for all its technical merits, the piece could not be compared with *Le Sacre,* or only to the elder work's advantage.

Stravinsky's own darkest expression of pessimistic feeling thus had become the source of dark and pessimistic feelings about Stravinsky; had become so before the night of the performance at the Metropolitan. Still an extraordinarily able musician, he seemed to have lost the better part of the genius and elemental power that had once thrilled us, and to have become something of a crank to boot. The evening on Thirty-ninth Street had merely showed one the reason for one's disaffection.

II

SINCE THAT HOUR this disappointment has nonetheless considerably been modified. *Oedipus Rex* has not proved Stravinsky's final word.

The very piece immediately successive to it, the ballet score *Apollon Musagète* for string ensemble, revived the hope of further benefits from the composer who, already superior in station to Berlioz, nearer that of the great innovators including

Liszt, and only below the level of the major composers, had temporarily appeared to be threatened with a sterility quite as lamentable as that which finally overtook his noble French predecessor. *Apollon* is cast in the form of the classic ballet of Versailles, as *Oedipus* is cast in the mold of the Handelian oratorio. It includes several *pas de deux,* variations, and a coda, and the material suggests Lully, Rameau, and Delibes: and essentially Stravinskian and Russian music appears in the "Variation d'Apollon." Sometimes sweet and enervate in its French classicism, the score is redeemed by the syncopating coda and the apotheosis: the first, dance music tense with the old swell of forces; the second, a spacious concluding page impregnated with a calm and a melancholy that recall those of the majestic gardens of Versailles.

This ballet in turn was followed by another, *Le Baiser de la Fée,* "inspired by the muse of Tchaikovsky," and expressive, with a score built on melodies and themes of the Russian symphonist's and confined within their harmonic limits, of the unfortunate's tragedy. In this work, the muse of Tchaikovsky made another low in Stravinsky's work. While the score infuses the Tchaikovskian material with a characteristic Stravinskian stiffness, it approaches bathos, especially when at the climax it thunders forth the theme of the song "Nur wer die Sehnsucht kennt Weiss was ich leide."* Intended as a criticism of a Russian composer to whom Stravinsky feels himself akin, and one whom he regards as misunderstood and neglected by the present generation, it actually brings to expression nothing that Tchaikovsky himself did not, and remains a curious but unnecessary gesture. But immediately after this redundant score, Stravinsky produced two others with distinct—one of them with great—formal and aesthetic interest. The old bole was evidently putting forth green shoots again, and the concert at which the Boston Symphony under Koussevitzky presented the two for the

* "None But the Lonely Heart," Tchaikovsky's syrupy setting of Goethe's poem.

first time to an American audience was as joyful as any reconciliation with a temporarily estranged friend.

These pieces were the *Capriccio* for piano and orchestra and
the *Symphonie des Psaumes.* The first represents the type of the
Weberian *Konzertstück.* Essentially a *divertissement,* brilliant,
whimsical, staccato, ornamented, basically consonant but typically Stravinskian in its crystalline sonority, it puts one again
amid the lusters and the *décolletages* of an early Victorian
drawing room and again permits one to savor the charm and
sparkle of pre-bourgeois manners. Possibly the piece is not much
more than a grandiose parlor ornament: it certainly is without
high specific gravity and merely aims at a social effect and pretends to nothing further. But it is easily the happiest of Stravinsky's eclectic compositions. While the material ranges from
Bach to jazz and includes, in the middle movements, melismas
in the manner of Liszt and *à l'hongroise,* these heterogeneous
stuffs are fused in a form that actually combines the capriciousness and sparkle of the old brilliant salon music with the
scintillance of jazz. It is indeed far superior to the piece with
which one inevitably compares it, the Piano Concerto; for here
the form and the moods are sustained. The first, exquisite in
detail, works up gradually to the enchanting jazzy dancing finale
which comes off with éclat: and the moods slowly progress from
the sardonic initial one—in which one sees the face and the
postures of a tragic harlequin—up to the climactic one, sparkling with malice and zest and, *mirabile dictu,* with genuine
kindness and gaiety. It is as if Stravinsky had discovered the
unseriousness, the joke of life, and were irradiating his audience with humor.

The second of the pieces, the *Symphonie des Psaumes,* is of
sterner and stonier stuff. It is in the grand style, severe, architectural, lean and spare in sonority, and frequently abrupt and
stark in attack. Its orchestra has been stripped of violins, violas,
and clarinets, and the choral passages are bare of chromaticism
and occasionally exploit the voices in unison. The three movements, connected by instrumental interludes, are rugged,

simple, and somberly colored: only in the final Alleluia does a kind of soft golden glow that recalls that of the mosaics in a Byzantine church suffuse the music; and even then the score is curiously rigid and hieratic. The mood is extremely elevated: the verses Stravinsky has set are taken from Psalms XXVIII, XXXIX, and CL in the version of the Vulgate; and the subject, beginning as a supplication to the Lord that he save his worshiper from the black pit—"I am a stranger with thee and a sojourner, as all my fathers were"—becomes a cry that "the Lord has put a new song into my bones," and ends in a solemn song of praise. The work assuredly is the strongest Stravinsky had produced since the *Symphonies for Wind Instruments*. Possibly it is a little less distinguished than the great ballets that towered like red girders against the melting impressionistic sky. The second movement, the fugue, with its modern counterpoint, is curiously indeterminate: Stravinsky, as if he could not achieve his original plan, lets it end somewhat lamely with a reaffirmation of the original subject in the bass. The main theme of the last movement, despite its loveliness, is a trifle commonplace: and all in all, the work is another illustration of the truth that Stravinsky's pieces in the large forms are less impeccable than those in the smaller. Yet it has much of the old feeling and power of expression. The feeling is stark and characteristically painful; while it is intensely that of the spiritual life, the raucous first movement seems haunted by the figure of the prodigal son in his degradation; and even if at the end the presence and the blessing of the Lord have become manifest, the composer does not seem to find himself in a world gladdened and saved by His presence. The Lord and His realm would seem to transcend it entirely and remain visible only through the gate of death: and the final mood, not entirely bare of agony, would seem to be that of patient expectation for release. To the world of *Oedipus* there has merely been added another in which peace reigns. This experience, however, is expressed with something of the old abrupt and elemental power: and in the third section, wild entries of barbaric music recall the early "primitivist." The first and last movements certainly have a grave beauty and the last a veritable splendor.

Was the experience a personal one or merely the result of some reference to the form of "sacred music"? It would seem to be the former, and not only because rumor has it that at some time previous to the creation of the *Symphonie* Stravinsky was converted to Catholicism, largely through the efforts of no less conspicuous a saint than Jacques Maritain.* For the music itself is a gush of waters in a wasteland, the end of a barren period; and as such the sign of some redintegration of the personality that might of itself have sent the composer to the solemn verses he has set.

And from this time forward, Stravinsky's career has appeared not entirely to conform to the order of the three prehistoric ages which used to be attributed to humanity. For in his case it had been the age of iron that followed the age of gold, while the age of silver was following the age of iron. Silver doubtless is the little Violin Concerto, the piece that followed on the heels of the *Symphonie* and was presented early in 1932 in New York by Samuel Dushkin at a concert of the Philadelphia Orchestra. It is modest in its proportions, but not at all the bad piece the New York critics found it: in fact it is as complete in its way as the *Capriccio.* Its two arias are austerely expressive of emotion. Their final measures are exquisitely musical, and the capricious finale sparkles and charms with its elfish sonorities. What appears to have happened is that some of the composer's remarks about his new piece, carried by the newspapers and the program notes and cast in the form of a comparison of his little concerto with Mozart's, lent themselves to misunderstanding. Stravinsky was quoted as saying:

> For Mozart the invention of the theme or themes represented the maximum effort: all the rest was made up

* Stravinsky tells us in *Stravinsky in Conversation with Robert Craft* (London: Pelican Books, 1962), p. 276: "I had returned to the Orthodox Church in 1926 (I became a Communicant then for the first time since 1910 . . .)."

of a certain formalism . . . and with the developments
of the theme, the repetitions, refrains and necessary "ca-
denze," the half-hour was soon reached. . . . But now
that this development of the theme in a scholastic sense
no longer exists, and still less repetitions (I am speaking,
of course, of my own work) ; now that every measure
is the result of an enormous condensation of thought
(sometimes in a whole day's work I just manage to write
one or two measures), proportions have changed, and a
concerto of fifteen minutes is already a monumental
work.

Now, Stravinsky's comment upon the conventional in
Mozart's concertos and the comparison of their forms with
his own is far from erroneous. But at the same time, the brief
toccata that begins his own little concerto contains a forty-bar
recapitulation; and the second aria repeats its initial figure
unaltered: hence the statement appeared a bit arrogant and
sophistical. Thus, the exacerbation of the critical fraternity,
who came to the performance spoiling for a fight, and the volley
of Irish confetti which expressed their greetings to the poor
victim.

Silver, too, is the latest of Stravinsky's major scores that have
been presented to the public, the "melodrama" *Perséphone*,
upon a text by André Gide, performed in concert form by the
Boston Symphony under Stravinsky himself in March, 1935.

The deeply moving Gide-Stravinsky creation itself is a sort of
Eleusinian mystery.—The mysteries yearly performed at Eleusis
in ancient times in connection with the nine-day worship of
"the Mother" and "the Maiden," Demeter and Persephone,
were dramatic representations, resembling the medieval mysteries, of the events in the stories of the two "holy" and "pure"
savior goddesses. Developments of the primitive worship of the
spiritual forms of the earth and of the seed, these representations and some of the other exercises of the festival came, under
the presidency of the Eumolpidae and members of other sacer-

dotal families, to express certain of the deepest and most consoling conceptions of the Greek religion. Men like Pindar and Sophocles derived from them immutable convictions of their eternal welfare in this world and the next. Like the bas-relief of Demophoön or Triptolemus between Demeter and Persephone now in the museum at Athens, the mysteries conveyed these goddesses' loyal guardianship of their human nurseling and the inalienable blessing laid by them upon him.

And the new Franco-Russian "melodrama" imparts in the form of a mystery of Persephone, freely conceived in the manner of the Eleusinia, modern intuitions similar to those allied in the minds of the ancients with the myths of the Mother and the Maiden. The Persephone of Gide and Stravinsky is a divine person, at once the spirit of the spring and the seed and the unfailing human Lover: "She who if men go down into hell, is there too." She is also the human heart, the creative spirit that—periodically drawn by pity into the realm of death and dreams and "the shades of men outworn," temporarily held there and eventually reborn like the springtide, in love and greater consciousness to the earth and breathing men—lives not unto itself.

The poet and the composer have intended their work—a "melodrama" in so far as it associates the speaking voice with choral and instrumental music, but one that partakes of the nature of the ballet and of the oratorio—for the stage. The part of Persephone is written for a chanting mime—actually Ida Rubinstein; that of the Eumolpidus—simultaneously the interpreter of the mystery and the counselor and companion of Persephone—for a singing actor. The chorus participates in the action. And the first performance of the work was dramatic, forming part of Mme. Rubinstein's season at the Paris Opéra.

The representation, like one of the evident guides of Gide's conception, the Homeric hymn to Demeter, begins with the scene of the rape. The stage represents the precincts of a temple. It is "the first morning of the world," and the great heart of Persephone, who is playing among the nymphs to whom her mother has confided her, is moved to love. As in the hymn, the rape is precipitated by her discovery of the sweet and deathly narcissus. But in *Perséphone* there is no Aïdoneus with his chariot and black steeds. The motive of the descent is the compassion aroused in Persephone by the flower's odor. Eumolpus and the nymphs tell her that whoever looks into the narcissus sees the unknown underworld, and, gazing, Persephone views "a people wandering hopelessly, sad, restless, discolored." Advised by Eumolpus that "her youth will lighten their distress, her spring charm their endless winter," and already "married to Pluto by her compassion," she bids the nymphs farewell and takes the springtime with her from the earth.

In the unending night of the underworld, she lies clasping the narcissus, seeing the host of those who "pursue—what dwindles and glides away" and, in a death of time, "recommence without end the incompleted motions of life." Eumolpus tells her that it is her destiny to rule; that she must forgo pity. They offer her cups of Lethe and the treasures of the earth. She rejects them. At length the gods send Mercury, who offers Persephone the pomegranate; and "finding in the darkness a relic of the light above," Persephone eats. The savor of the lost earth returns to her, and gazing once more into the narcissus, in anguish she sees the world in its winter and her mother wandering in rags among briars, sharp stones, and tangled branches. She calls to Demeter, but her voice does not carry. Then Eumolpus declares that the winter cannot remain eternally; that in the palace of Celeus in Eleusis, Demeter is nursing Demophoön who will be Triptolemus. Persephone sees the Mother leaning toward the child over a burning brand and carrying him in the salt breeze; she perceives the noble lad, "radiant with tawny health, rushing toward immortality." She greets him who will "once more teach man to plow." Reviving, she sees the day; with love, in joy, she salutes the earth, and her earthly husband, Triptolemus. A chorus, including children's voices, hails the returning queen as Persephone falters forth from the gates of the tomb. She dances; she plights her troth to the hero; and once more, of her free will, prepares to return to the unhappy underworld:

> "Je n'ai pas besoin d'ordre et me rends de plein gré
> Où non point tant la loi que mon amour me mène;
> Et je vois pas à pas descendre les degrés
> Qui conduisent au fond de la détresse humaine."*

The chorus celebrates the departing Lover, and Eumolpus delivers the precept of unselfishness derived, as at the Eleusinia, from the mystery:

> "Il faut pour qu'un printemps renaisse
> Que le grain consente à mourir sous terre
> Afin qu'il reparaisse
> En moisson d'or
> Pour l'avenir."†

But though the performance of *Perséphone* in Boston, like that in London, was in concert form, even in this partial shape the work is solid and very affecting: in Boston, for instance, critics and public were quite in accord respecting its impressiveness. The first reason for this effectiveness is that the poetic work is narrative and dramatic; the second, that Gide and Stravinsky have transmitted the idea through their mediums so clearly and fully that it touches one without the aid of the pantomime. Stravinsky in fact has transmitted the general sense and mode of the piece with extraordinary depth and warmth.

---

* " 'There is no need to command me; I give myself up willingly
  Not where the law but where my love leads me;
  And I see step by descending step the stairs
  That lead to the depths of human misery.' "
† " 'For spring to be reborn
  The seed must be willing to die under the earth
  So that it may reappear
  In a golden harvest
  For the future.' "

His method is the classical one: that is to say, he neither has described with music, nor attempted the cosmic, nor stopped to illustrate the word. He has written pure music, letting the general mood of the music, or the speech-recitative of the soprano—which resembles the arialike delivery of Racine at the Comédie Française—express his subject. But the expression is there, fully; we feel the sorrow, the suffering, the grayness of the underworld, the divine goodness of Persephone, the ecstasy of rebirth.

Indeed, the eminently religious atmosphere of the work flows chiefly from his setting. Elevated in style and mood, silvery and reserved, and with something of a starry brilliance, it is also strong and austere and even ascetic, like a Russian icon; indeed, Stravinsky's Persephone has somewhat the quality of a Byzantine Theotokos. Where Gide has apparently, as in the opening scene, given him an opportunity for graceful and voluptuous music, Stravinsky has written music (the *Ländler* of the nymphs, for example) that is willfully uncouth and banal. This is not because he cannot write a beautiful melody, for he can: one has but to hear the second eclogue in his recent *Duo Concertante* to be assured of it. The reason for these banalities is probably either a fierce contempt for the senses, or a sense of the impropriety of an appeal to them in a work of religious mood. The score contains severe and ascetic instrumental combinations: oboe and tuba; flute, tuba, and timpani. But it is also full of thrilling music, such as that expressing Persephone's new vision of the light . . . it is spiritual light for Stravinsky, the light from the sphere transcending that of the underworld that is our earthly home . . . or the gorgeous, Russian barbaric chorus hailing the reborn queen, with its festive drum beats; or the final chorus. Not a reconstitution of music, the work is nonetheless very satisfactory. The style, the diatonic one of the latter Stravinsky, containing elements ranging from the Italian operatic to the Russian primitive, is more unified than in *Oedipus Rex*. The work stands high among his best later things with the *Symphony of Psalms* and the *Duo Concertante*.

III

STRAVINSKY'S GENERAL FIGURE and position have meanwhile been growing ever plainer: it would appear as if we were commencing to see him with more than merely contemporary eyes.

He stands before us as the inventor of a new kind of music, an extremely virile kind, the healthy antithesis of the later romanticists' excessively feminine music: and the composer of work essentially religious, not only in the sense in which all art is religious, insomuch as it expresses the meaning and the value of life, but in the sense that it expresses the relations of God and man, oftentimes in forms recalling the liturgical; and, finally, the author of pieces that, high in endeavor and couched in the grand style, severe and great and classic in their orderliness, convey a great experience, and one ultimately weightier than that of any other contemporary composer. At the same time he appears to us as one who, destined to remain conspicuous among the composers of the last centuries, will never, except with a very few of his pieces, probably the very early *L'Oiseau de Feu,* and *Petrouchka* and *Le Sacre,* find widespread favor, and not because of any limitation of his art's emotional scope or of his craftsmanship. The cause of this prelimitation of appeal, which even today renders his work the possession of a relatively small section of the musical public, lies for us in the circumstance that Stravinsky is the great reactionary; and the great reactionary is never a popular spokesman.

We use the epithet "reactionary" in the sense in which it was employed in Thomas Mann's recent paraphrase of Nietzsche's characterization of the work of the romantic school of 1800 in Germany, and by inference, that of this group's western allies, De Maistre, Chateaubriand, Montalembert, and the youthful Victor Hugo. This imaginative work Nietzsche, and Mann after him, called "progressive in the form of a reaction," and its creators "powerful and infectious and at the same time anachronistic spirits, who for a last time conjured up a past epoch of humanity, as a sign that the new tendency of things against which they strove was not yet sufficiently strong victoriously to withstand them." Brilliantly expressive of the whole prescientific, medieval, Christian world-idea, it contributed to the experience of the race precisely by virtue of its illuminativeness.

And in Stravinsky we feel a spirit very like that of these poets of the early nineteenth century, challenging the feeling men have had in the last centuries and conjuring up past epochs of humanity as a sign that the new tendency is not yet sufficiently strong victoriously to withstand them. Stravinsky has not only given us a series of musical pictures of the past: that, after all, is what many artists do. He has been re-expressing past ways of feeling and world-ideas very much at variance with those of the great composers who have created our music. These great composers, as we have said, felt idealistically and found a world full of ideal elements and glorious possibilities, containing above all the Idea, and human beings potentially noble and capable of freedom. Their work expressed a grave optimism, a feeling of the real presence of God in the world, and a world all-identical with the godhead. To this idealism, Stravinsky has opposed the pessimism that informed the world-pictures of earlier societies, and societies even more primitive than the medieval one evoked by the reactionaries of 1800. The first of these world-pictures were nihilistic, expressive of a cosmos oppressively a senseless mechanism, and also troglodyte. In *Le Sacre* Stravinsky associated his musical ideas with a pagan ceremonial representing the primitive religious complex of ideas about the earth, night, the dark side of nature and the human psyche, and death: a complex of ideas very much in line with those of the German "romantic" school. And with his archaicizing works—in contradistinction to his neoclassicism, which is progressive, Stravinsky's archaicism may be explained as symbolic of his reactionary tendency—with these post-war works, he began giving us world-ideas which may even be pre-Christian, and certainly are very primitive. And while a benevolent God appears to throne over the *Symphonie des Psaumes,* the composition seems to posit him entirely removed from the bitter and painful cosmos and in a realm approachable by man only through the gate of death. In *Perséphone,* too, the underworld would appear to be the earth, or at least the earth deprived of the divine light; and this light would appear to fall into it from without, and not to be, as the great idealists would aver, an element of the creation itself, if not its very essence.

That to a degree the whole phenomenon of Stravinsky's contribution is closely connected with the phenomenon of the war and its consequences is undeniable. One recognizes in his amazing compositions the images of a world dictated by materialistic science and the feeling left by the catastrophe. Nonetheless, we do not see the relationship as one of cause and effect, rather more as one resulting from the circumstance that the war gave the genius of Stravinsky a particularly brilliant opportunity for realizing itself. The feeling of life which Stravinsky has conveyed would have materialized itself even without the war. Its idealistic antithesis had grown rhetorical in inheritors of the Beethovenian tradition such as the early Strauss, Mahler, and the Scriabin of the orchestral poems; and itself and its pessimism and feeling of a static and painful world is permanent in the race, and periodically eloquent. Precisely what its source is, we cannot say. It would appear kin to that fatalism, that feeling of oppression and contraction and of the world-cave—very different from that expansive feeling of limitlessness of the great Europeans, and periodically releasing itself in fanatical outbreaks like that of *Le Sacre*—which Frobenius* and Spengler have named and attributed the one to the Semitic and the other to the Magian worlds. Probably there was nothing fortuitous in the circumstance that the *Symphonie des Psaumes* called to our mind the mosaic-gilded interior of one of

* Leo Frobenius (1873–1938), German ethnologist and student of African culture. His theory that society develops into civilization in ways similar to the organic developments in man, animals, and plants was popular around the time of World War I. His name is often coupled with Spengler's.

the Byzantine domes that for both these critics represent this eastern world-idea: one of those domes from whose vaulting the Christ and his Mother gaze pitilessly down upon the accursed human race. What is curious is that Stravinsky is not a Semite, and thus we must attribute this fundamental primitive, pessimistic, and fatalistic feeling conveyed by his music to a source in Russian nature, itself in many respects Asiatic and oriental, an attribution made easy for us by the fact that the Russian fatalism we hear in the music, say, of Moussorgsky, would appear to be very closely related to the "kismet" of the Levantines. But that is but another way of saying that Stravinsky is one of the great, the representative, Russian composers; and one who through the power of his genius as well as circumstances will stand among the great representatives of a world-idea that has long haunted and continues to haunt the race of men.

Bartók (1923)

IN FORESTS, sometimes, a stranger sprouts among familiar plants. Migrating birds have brought a seed from distant parts, and left a foreigner to spring far from his folk in the presence of species unrelated to him. We chance upon the little pieces of Béla Bartók with a surprise identical to that roused in us by sight of one of these wandering growths. They also, *Esquisses* and *Bagatelles*, are curious and apart among the organisms mid which they push. Stalk and leaves are not perhaps the most luxuriant, the woodland sports. A dozen almost of neighbors spread an amplitude of members; and this vein of stranger music out of Hungary is not abundant and overwhelming. It gives itself most pungent and pure in smaller forms. In the larger, it flows adulterated, more. Nevertheless, the product of Béla Bartók stands distinct through the perfect novelty and unusualness of quality and scent and hue. Stravinsky-tree, Bloch-bush, Schoenberg-plant, and Ravel-flower are descendants in straightest line from the bodies which in other decades composed the musical acreage. They are not strange at all, but the conservers of tradition. Each hearing of the work of these musicians makes us approach them themselves more closely to the very march against which we fancied them rebellious. Bartók is not as readily connected. Brahmsian thicknesses, the ninths of Fauré, the cerebral fluids of Schoenberg, many derivative colors and banalities, do flash into certain of his compositions, and mar them not unoften. But only what is weak in him is capable of relation. What is personal and intense defies account. It is utterly queer-savored, and of a whimsicality and gnomishness which will not be fitted even partially into an established category. The man is an original.

It is possible the curious originality of the music is chiefly of the race. One of her recent writers, Béla Belasz, has compared Hungary to a ferry-bark plying between cultured Europe and a vast formless Asia, an Asia without traditions, and more remote and shadowy than Russia's or Judea's; and heard in each of her creations the grating of the ferry's keel upon the shore of Europe and the moment and today; and seen in all her counterrevolutions and failures and refusals the dwindling of a stern into the fog that lies upon the past's mysterious bank. And it well may be that what Bartók brings and what appeals to us so inexplicably is an expression of the racial subconscious through the instruments of the modern world; the deposit in the region of musical art of the flyer that at intervals enriches the age with the substance of Magyardom. Certainly, the little professor is the first Hungarian composer who has made an art song kindred mysteriously in accent and in spirit to the folk tunes. He is the first who has remained uncontaminated entirely of the showy orientalics and superficial emotionalism of the music of the *tziganes*; cut away the parasite and laid bare the strong sinewy limb, the true Hungarian idiom from which it sucked the life. The darkness, the acridity and mournfulness, Asiatic without being oriental, are in his musics as they are in the folk song. In the process of arranging some of the peasant tunes for the pianoforte, Bartók seems to have moved in perfect sympathy with these inherited forms; breathed in them his proper air. He seems to have within himself the men who first beat out these little patterns. For in his transcriptions, the melodic line and the supporting harmonies are not, as they are in the most of transcriptions, two separate objects artificially conjoined. They are one, miraculously; and indivisible. There is no suspicion of the mechanical in the position of the attendant chords. They are placed with utmost freedom and irregularity, with marvelous subtlety. They reinforce without emphasis the form of the melody. The multi-voiced piano sings not otherwise than men while hoeing sang, and maids hanging out linen and mothers rocking babies at their breasts.

But, whether indeed the unusual quality of the music of Bartók is of the race, tradition of the blood, or whether it is more an expression of an individual plasm, modified somewhat by the in-bearing of the folk tunes, that, we shall not know until another Magyar composes music of a depth and plangency as real as this man's, and furnishes us, in supplying us with another instance of modern Hungarian musical expression, with a point of comparison. For, prior to Bartók, civilized Hungary has had no luteman. It has had in Kodály a charming, light, and accomplished musician, a most capable and distinguished composer. But it has had in him not a perfectly free spirit, but rather one of those dwellers upon the European shore, part Gaul, part German, part Magyar, even, but cut off from the spreading Mother Asia. And dwellers on the European shore have never dredged stuff from the vitals of Hungaria, no more than those who in America dwell upon its New World shore have dredged deep from the womb of the Old. For a time, therefore, Bartók must remain a unicum. Still, although the principal question must remain temporarily unanswered, of this we can rest assured: the question has reality. Out of some subconscious realm the best of these compositions do come. They possess the vibrancy, the warmness, of matters made not in the head, but down in the darkness of the bowels and the reins; and with the intuitive man. It is the earth, black and gritty, that swims up to us in them; not shut casements and drawn portieres and the airless state of objects manufactured in the brain. They are natural things; and could have grown, seconds, sevenths, ninths, and other modern refinements notwithstanding, in fields with the corn. We know where they put us, from the first bars; and thank them, as we thank all music, with the full blood.

The movement is outside the conventional patterns. The little pieces have laws their very own. Brusquely, naïvely, gnomishly, they commence, folk song and *raffiné* at once, and go their free and whimsical way. They hang well; they are simple, thin-voiced, and solid at once; they hang by inherent and individual weights. Something determined and very sure of itself pushes them along. Whatever it may be, it remains perfectly conscious of much musical culture. It hears rich complex tone-clusters, right hand in one key, left in an unrelated other; adventures intrepidly in harmonic walks. But, withal, it pipes along with a sort of nonchalance, like a child performing a two-fingered improvisation, impish in humor oftentimes. Rhythms run free, beat and clatter and modify themselves to their heart's content. Rhythm for us is *Petrouchka* and the *Sacre,* and some of Bloch and Ornstein. And it is Bartók, too. The Hungarian's patterns are smaller and slighter. The heavy bulk of a dynamo man is not on them. Yet, his, also, belong to the sacred band. They, too, are fullest play, record of coordinated faculties, dictated by no Malipiero* and Cyril Scott† sophistication. The Pucks have it their naughty way in the scherzo of the second String Quartet. Even when he is very childish, as he is in his Sonatina, the rhythms are spontaneous and unexpected.

And, in a dozen different figures and ideas, Bartók produces and affirms and develops a consistent individual color. On the piano, in the strings, he remains darker woodwind. He grunts nasal and portly, like bassoons, over his quaint intervals. When he sings lyrically beautiful, it is with a voice whose timbre

---

* Francesco Malipiero (1882–   ) , Italian neoromantic composer.
† Cyril Scott (1879–   ) , minor English composer.

recalls the English horn and its dark, penetrating, medicinal hues. One of the memorable moments of the second quartet occurs at the close of the scherzo; and there, it is the tones of clarinets and oboes and not of violins, which rise off the instruments. Sometimes, a grotesquerie seems to dictate these sounds speaking the nether gut. As often, more often, ideal moods make use of them. Certain composers, Schumann for example, are tenors always; in the bass, in the treble. They are always high in the chest. Others, whatever the range in which they find themselves, are baritone and color of snuff. Bartók is one of these.

Immediately, too, he is in between everything. The most of the *Esquisses* and *Bagatelles* are no more than a pithy page or two in length. A line here, a line there, suffices the composer. But they are white in heat. Something broke out under dire necessity in them, and said what it had to say in the concentrated form born of passion. You cannot manufacture such subtly moving, poignant things: all essence like the third *Bagatelle* and "Elle est morte" in the *Esquisses*. Either they are cast up out of lava-like experience of grief, or not produced at all. The third movement of the second quartet is the shortest of three short movements; but in a small space, with its ferocious rasping seconds and ninths, it communicates a memorable picture of balked and nevertheless thorough-pushing force. And never is the composer more the poet than in his wistful conclusions. They are pure magic from the heart, these codas; full statements of inner questions; questions the propositions of which are in themselves answers almost; risings of inner suns of longing and wistfulness that make the human being high and inheritor. The true pieces seem only to begin where these of the Hungarian leave off. But we are satisfied completely with them for the distance they have led us. It is not for them, or any other outward substance, grave as they, or graver even, to go the rest with us. That is alone for the bird of the breast, now aloft on the wing.

How great a clarity obtains at times in Bartók may be felt from this: that no more than a couple of handfuls of small pieces give us positive sense of a perfectly new quality, of a spicy new-tinctured wanderer come up solitary among the elm trees, birches, and hemlocks of the European ground. The peppery inexplicable plant is present entirely virtuous only in the *Bagatelles,* "Bear Dances" and their like. In the Second String Quartet, unconventional as it is in form; in the one-act ballet *The Wooden Prince;* in the *Sonatine* for pianoforte, the primitive, naïve, innately graceful musician vests himself partially in the form of two beings who have no relationship whatever with the primitive, with the naïve and the inherently graceful. The delightful gaucherie and freedom of the bear is become a flat childishness; childishness of idea and childishness of harmonization. The perfect essentiality and relentlessness of the dark singer is become a sort of spurious Frenchified and Ravelesque elegance. Pages of the ballet are most banal; anybody's music. The first movement of the quartet is unpleasantly international in character, and descends, toward the close, to Chausson.

That the infant and the *précieux* should threaten continually Bartók's musicianship is, unfortunately, not unnatural. His problem lies in maintaining a very difficult balance. The Asiatic, he has to maintain himself upon the European bank; to bring a vast, chaotic, formless past within himself up to the single European moment; and with his roots earthfast in native soil become the bright hard instant today. Small wonder, then, that not unoften, and just in those forms which demand Brünnhilde-like strength of their compeller, we should find him becoming unrooted; becoming the shadow of Europe; assuming unconsciously the airs of the European *naïf,* and losing the sense of his own rude stuff in admiration for the polish of the older cultures. That is the danger threatening every child which becomes conscious, and every autochthon who encounters the immense corpus of classic art. To be sure, Siegfried compels the warrior-maid. Whether Bartók will develop eventually the power to remain true to himself and do the massive thing, or whether the Bradamante will succeed in hanging him at every attempt to the post of the bed, we do not as yet know. We have not as yet been given to hear his Violin Sonata; it may be that it contains the work we would like to have of him. If it does not; if nothing large as well as perfectly new-minted comes from his table to give us it; we shall not necessarily blame Bartók. It may very well be our age needs just such musical moments as he has already given us more than it needs the more complicated forms. But the recalcitrancy will make us painfully aware of a kind of limitation in the man, and perhaps in us; a limitation which, because of the marvelously new-colored sparks already struck out of him, we heartily wish wiped out entire.

Great sun Moussorgsky, shine down upon your progeny!

Bartók (1936)

BÉLA BARTÓK'S MUSIC has a powerful urgency, one of the most powerful that contemporary music shows. It is the urgency of the primitive, of the child and the child of the skyscraper period: a wild, intolerable tension bringing him to his instruments as to drums, and releasing itself through their beats and rhythms with fire and fury. It is like Stravinsky's: in fact, the whole of Bartók's work parallels the Russian's to an amazing degree. And as it does so honestly, in instances anticipating that body's deviations, and where it keeps pace with it, doing so in perfect independence, it provides another proof that the developments in the art of music incidental to the present generation's life are due not to individual willfulness, but to the *Zeitgeist*. For, confronted with this honest parallelism, we cannot but recognize the agency of a commonly informing spirit.

Like Stravinsky—his junior by a single year—once his academic period was over, Bartók began composing in the spirit of nationalism; for his part, as one of the musical representatives of the particularist or separatist movement in Hungary. Two immature works, *Kossuth,* a tone poem for grand orchestra, and the *Rhapsody,* Opus 1, for orchestra and piano, convey, like *The Firebird,* their junior by a few years, a sense of the national identity through more or less traditional forms. *Kossuth* and the *Rhapsody* move indeed as fully in the wake of Liszt, Brahms, Wagner, and Richard Strauss as *The Firebird* in that of Rimsky, Scriabin, Moussorgsky, and Wagner. But shortly Bartók's individuality projected itself clearly in the little piano *Bagatelles,* in 1908, much as Stravinsky's in his brilliant *Petrouchka* in 1911, both compositions constituting original nationalistic music.

Still, in Bartók's far more than in Stravinsky's case, this original nationalism was entwined with a thoroughgoing folk-lorism of which it was both the cause and the consequence. Stravinsky had used popular Russian music, as the good nationalist, the pupil of Rimsky, that he then was; and his style was modified in accordance with this material. But the folk material he had used was fairly familiar: if he had gone to the people, it was much more for the color of their music, its rhythms, instrumentation, robust spirit, than for its actual melodic substance. Bartók, however, had begun, out of nationalistic love of local Hungarian man, collecting actual Magyar folk music—not the songs and dances the musical world had hitherto considered the actual Magyar folk music; that was merely the deformed and vulgarized version of the actual thing exploited by itinerant gypsy musicians. The music Bartók found in use among the country people was a much more distinct, dignified, juicy one than the Hungarian gypsy and was based on scales that pointed to its partly Byzantine, partly Asiatic, origin. And in the course of the next two decades he helped collect many hundreds of Hungarian and Rumanian and Walachian folk songs, and recorded and published, and harmonized and even incorporated in the forms of original compositions, many of them. The *Bagatelles* indeed represent only the first of the far-reaching effects that the acquaintance with the actual musical lore of his people and the solution of the problems of the stylistically correct harmonization of its melodically and metrically subtle songs, was to produce on his imagination.

At the same time both the *Bagatelles* and *Petrouchka,* anticipating their younger brethren, contain passages frankly, unequivocally bitonal. Music in two simultaneous tonalities, like that in the *Bagatelles* and in *Petrouchka,* had probably been made not only possible but natural, according to the law of progressive evolution, by the chromaticism of the late romantics. That had broken down the walls between the various tonalities. There had been suggestions of bitonalism in Moussorgsky, in the original version of the polonaise in *Boris;* and Strauss in *Also Sprach Zarathustra*—a work that had deeply impressed the young Béla Bartók—had ended the piece in two different keys and in the finale of *Salome* had most effectively superimposed a chord in F on a chord in C. Over in America, Charles Ives had in his total solitude actually been writing polytonically since the early 1900's. But the bitonal *Bagatelles* and the extended bitonal passages in *Petrouchka* were the first of their kind to reach the public—and reached it with a vengeance, since the very unimpressionistic robustness, earthiness, and what Von der Null* calls the glassy precision of these new works, set their revolutionary methods and expressions in "the most glaring light." Meanwhile, they coincided more or less with another revolutionary step in harmony, also the consequence of the thorough chromaticism of Wagner and Rimsky and the impressionism of Debussy—the atonalism of Schoenberg.

Again, directly after their respective passages of the tonal Rubicon, Bartók and Stravinsky both developed into thoroughgoing "primitivists," the first in the little "Bear Dance" and in the "Allegro Barbaro," the second in the mighty *Sacre.*—To a degree, this "primitivism" of the two composers was also made not only possible but natural by the law of progressive evolution, through developments in the immediate past of music. It is an outcome of the "barbarism" of the late romanticists, especially that of the Liszt-born Russian Five; of their exploitation of wild and frenetic rhythms, of oriental monotony and color, and of other effects antithetical to the elegance and grace of salon music. Yet the short, rigid phrases reiterated with

* Edwin von der Null, author of a book on Bartók.

hammerlike regularity, so characteristic of "primitivism," constitute a realization of the possibilities of static music far more extreme than any attempted by the "barbarians"; indeed, they seem to have appeared in Stravinsky's music as much in consequence of intuitions of the life of mechanisms as of any others. And Bartók, too, has had his "mechanistic" fantasies, most notably in the idea of the ballet *The Wooden Prince,* although to a lesser degree than his great coeval. Both composers meanwhile have remained "primitivistic" throughout their careers, Bartók somewhat more, Stravinsky somewhat less. Primitivism ceased to dominate Stravinsky after *Les Noces* and appears only episodically in *Oedipus Rex,* in the *Symphony of Psalms,* and in *Perséphone.* But all through Bartók's music, from the early orchestral *Two Impressions** through the Second String Quartet to the very latest pieces, you will find passages in which rigid phrases are repeated with very slight variations with almost hammerlike emphasis and insistency and wild frenetic rhythms; and feel a familiar impulse, something like a wild man's and nonetheless modern, expressing itself vividly, through instruments sounded as are drums.

The parallelism has continued up to the very present hour. In complete independence of each other—unlike Picasso and Braque, the two composers have never worked together—and still as though shoulder to shoulder, they have been leading music ever further away from Wagnerism. For Bartók, representative of a small nation though he is, has none of the provinciality of outlook that is so frequently the defect of such representatives; he is as much the good European, as much in the van of life, as though he lived in one of the major capitals. And progress from Wagnerism (in the sense that Wagnerism and poetic or expressive music are synonymous) toward pure music is the achievement of the day. They have also been developing a classic-dynamic music, classic inasmuch as it is

* Rosenfeld is probably referring here to *Two Pictures* *(Images)* , which was written in 1910, or possibly to the *Two Portraits* of 1907.

conceived in the closed classic schemes of the suite, the sonata, the concerto, dynamic insomuch as it contains a continuously evolving, progressive material. They have furthermore been eschewing harmonic methods in favor of contrapuntal ones and also reviving old ecclesiastical modes and making original mixtures of major and minor keys, and latterly have reverted from bitonalism toward a new sort of diatonism—pandiatonism, in Nicholas Slonimsky's* happy nomenclature. And they have been producing music bonily structural in the spirit of the day, and both in structure and content expressive of the present hour. That hour's tempo, its nervousness, its strain, its stimulation, its lassitude, all are here; its energy without grace, its excitement without passion; its irritations. Grotesque, mordant, even scurrilous feelings come certainly very frequently to expression in both men's compositions: feelings of revolt, of exasperation, of satire, in Stravinsky with something of the irony and caricature of the clown, in Bartók with more of the wit and mischievousness of the kobold. (Or is it the child's? There are pieces of Bartók's, the second movement of the Suite, Opus 14, that recall the demonry of a child, determined to be impossible to his heart's content.)

Still, these two parallel bodies of work are perfectly distinct. We never, for instance, find Bartók archaicizing, like Stravinsky, recalling now Bach, or Handel, or some other eighteenth-century composer, now Italian opera from Pergolesi to Verdi, or forming a compost of these idioms blent with Russian primitivism and with jazz. Bartók's style feeling is more consistent than the mercurial Russian's. He has pretty faithfully continued to cast his thought in the style developed by his treatment of the old Hungarian folk music. Nor does he ever verge upon the neo- or the pseudo-classic. Besides, the piano is Bartók's medium to a degree that it is not Stravinsky's. Bartók, too, has composed for the orchestra—the *Images* and the *Dance Suite;*

---

* Nicholas Slonimsky (1894–   ), pianist, conductor, composer, and author. He pioneered in playing the works of American composers.

and for the stage, an opera, *Bluebeard's Castle,* and two ballets, *The Wooden Prince* and *The Miraculous Mandarin*—the latter one of his most significant works. And he has written five string quartets, and a violin sonata, and a number of songs. Still, it is in piano music that he has worked out most of his cardinal problems—first in the little *Bagatelles,* then in the *Nenias* or laments and in the *Rumanian Dances,* then in the Suite, Opus 14, and later in the Piano Sonata and in the great Piano Concerto. Bartók himself, incidentally, is a most distinguished pianist, a fine interpreter of Beethoven sonatas.

In fact, it would be impossible ever to confuse the works of the two composers: they are two branches that have grown close together but separately from a single bole. Bartók, to begin with, is more the miniaturist: despite the concerto and the sonatas, huge structures in the grand style like the *Sacre* or the *Symphony of Psalms* figure less frequently in the roster of his works than in that of Stravinsky's. Again, Bartók is by far the more subjective and lyrical of the two men; and his music reflects brooding states of which Stravinsky's gives little evidence. The essential quality of his music is also extremely individual: finely dry like a wine very moderately infused with liqueur and without sweetness and fruity flavor. One is tempted to say it has a nutty taste, for it is frequently dark of timbre, gritty, earthy, acrid, bassoon-colored, or silvery. All in all, Bartók's music is by far more special, like Debussy's, than Stravinsky's is—reflecting a life somewhat withdrawn, outside the forum and the market, shy, sober, aristocratic, and indifferent to the floodlights.

Bartók is also the less powerfully gifted of the two men, more restricted in his somewhat more subjective, lyrical scope of life than Stravinsky in his distinctly objective one; less varied in mood. The first movement of a work by Bartók is very likely to be an *allegro barbaro;* the second, a *nenia;* the third, one of his characteristic scherzolike dances. His mind has gone into subtlety and intricacy more than range and scope of experience. He is less evenly inspired than Stravinsky and has given fewer perfectly sustained works. Works as representative of Bartók as the Piano Sonata, the Second and the Fourth String Quartets, all contain powerful, completely distinguished and fascinating movements that exhibit his singular power of combining immobile harmonies with developing melodies, or his gift for varying rhythmic patterns or exploiting the color of the stringed instruments; and yet the *nenia* of the Sonata, for all the effective relations of the reiterated plangent E, is somewhat static; and the first movement of the Second Quartet is somewhat "out of style" and reminiscent of Scriabin; and that of the Fourth Quartet far less pointed and significant than the other, fabulously pungent movements. In matching perfect pieces like *L'Histoire du Soldat* or *Les Noces* among Bartók's compositions, one finds oneself somewhat restricted, and turning to some of the smaller piano works, particularly the Suite, Opus 14, of the mounting excitement sustained through three contrasted movements, and after a tragic fall, beautifully dissolved in the ethereal finale. But these are the negative aspects of an extremely positive achievement. Like Stravinsky again, Bartók has written powerful and subtle and solid original music, powerfully articulative of the tense, nervous feeling of the age of steel; and timeless too. One has the impression that the Piano Concerto is among the greatest of modern pieces, worthy to stand beside *Le Sacre,* and that the musician who after hearing it cried, "Grand; like a new Vittoria," was not far from the truth.

The Group of Six

TO THE RATTLE of snare drums and the crowing of toy trumpets, a new band of youthful Parisians has paraded onto the musical boards. It is called the Group of Six; and there are five composers in it, one superfine, four fine. Durey was the sixth.* But, being Ravelesque, an impressionist, and, it is not to be

---

* Louis Durey (1888–   ), least known and least important of the Six. He left the group in 1921 and retired subsequently to southern France.

doubted, essentially respectable, he found himself out of place; and, a while since, resigned. There are five of them today; five fairly distinct persons who compose, nevertheless, a compact band. They hold ideas, views, theories, techniques, processes, exhibitions, and, probably, ladyloves in common. Their work stands distinct from other work, a thing by itself. Often, the work of one member resembles the work of another. But nothing quite like this music has ever before been made. Suppose a concert of new music, a concert without names, at which, among other modern things, some of the pieces of the Six were performed. You could not fail to recognize the group-men's for their own. You might not know which of them had done the thing. You might not like it. Or, you might like it for a while, and later find yourself a trifle strained and wearied. But you could scarce mistake it, not even for Stravinsky's, or Satie's, with which it has some relations. The group has authenticity.

The music of the men is full of edge; sharp, brusque, uncompromising. It comes at you like edges of paper, rims of pressed rubber, blades of polished steel. There is no Debussian fluidity, dreamfulness, satin. There is frowning mass; jagged, square outline. The polyphonies grind upon each other like millstones; grate and protest like metal parts borne heavily upon metal; like express train wheels upon the rails down in bends of *subvia dolorosa*. The music starts suddenly and jerks, like machinery through which the brakes have been thrust. Sharpness and violence are in the acrid harmonies; the shrill and garish analine dyes of the instruments. The breath cuts into you, like ammonia.

Machinery is in the music of Stravinsky, too; and many moderns are working for severity of contour. But the Six-men's, on closer inspection shows a distinct individuality of substance. Their music is a startling mixture of archaism and hard bright modernity; of conservatism and the crassness of the streets and music halls. The Six are oftentimes simply diatonic. Whole passages of their works do not budge from the safe C major.

They cling to it with an almost eighteenth-century fidelity at times. Other times, they are to be found playing two diatonic figures in totally unrelated keys contrapuntally off against each other. One of their beloved tricks is to take a strong, rectilinear, even banal, melodic figure and envelop it and set it off in meshwork of acid, piercing polyphony. But, later, like prodigals, they return, and bask in the innocent sunshine of Mozart.

Tunes of all ages and sorts live in this element, like fish in the aquarium. Some have pastoral and eighteenth-century airs; strut like the rapid subjects of ancient symphonies; coquette like the flute tunes of antique duets. Others, might have figured in the defunct operas of Boieldieu and Adam; have a good-hearted stupidity. But, by the side of these venerable figures, there come vulgar modern ones. Banal military marches trail their tatters through the orchestra. The music is full of effects and motives borrowed from jazz; wrenching and braying of brass. These men have had their ears opened to all forms of popular music of the day; jazz, ragtime, military signals, dance tunes of Negro and South American orchestras, and even the canned and absurdly inhumanized expressions of gramophones, automatic pianos, orchestrelles, and steam calliopes. In Milhaud's ballet, *L'Homme et Son Désir,* the brass roars forth brutal Brazilian dance tunes. Sandpaper hisses, boards are beaten upon, whistles skyrocket and shrill. A rhythm of the drums imitates an exhaust. Human voices moan and sob as do those of nightmare-ridden sleepers. Milhaud has among his works a "shimmy," a "romance et rag-caprice." Auric, too, writes a brutal fox trot, "Adieu New York"; a joyous and ironic "Paris-Sport" which sounds as though his head were full of the timbres of *bals,* movies, cornet music at national fetes, carrousels, and pianolas.

This music makes its bow most unpretentiously. It seems gay, modest, discreet. Symphonies are not written for one hundred, two hundred, three hundred performers. Symphonies are not written for even sixty performers. Small bands of instrumentalists oftentimes suffice the group. Pastorales, suites, symphonies, serenades, are composed for ten, seven, sometimes even fewer players. Milhaud has a symphony for seven reeds. Brevity, also, is the soul of these men's wit. There is a general reaction from lengthiness everywhere. But none are so short as these young Parisians usually are. Their sonatas recall those of the early eighteenth century. Three brief vigorously contrasted movements can appease them: *prélude, rustique, finale,* say; each one requiring a few minutes in transit only. They seem to have learned from Stravinsky that music existed before the days of free fantasias and "développements."

It has, much of it, a sort of popular, easy, vulgar freedom, this music. Grandiloquence is not in it. Whatever flows from the stylographs of the group is as much at home in the vaudeville house and movie cavern as in the concert hall; could be played at fairs, on streetcars and ferryboats. It seems to know the tricks and turns of the music halls, the braying little bands; has seen the rectangles flicker on the silverscreen, and felt the abominable and gorgeous emotions awakened by the films. Like the music of Stravinsky, it takes us into gingerbread fairs, among carrousels, steam calliopes, scenic railways, the imbecilic and glorious exhibitionism of the military parade, jazz bands in dance halls, barmen mixing violent alcohols. Poulenc, for example, has little fanfares for fife and drum such as might appropriately be performed outside the walls of a side show at a country fair; or by itinerant musicians at some crossroad; by soldiers loafing outside their barracks; before the rising of the curtain upon some acrobatics in a vaudeville. Into Auric's song, "Les Joues en Feu," again there has somehow gotten the boldness, the exaggeration, the crass coloring of the music hall.

This music is at once charming and ill-mannered, gay and bitter, simple and scurrilous. There is much wit in it; many clever musical quotations—*Louise,* Schubert's "Marche Militaire"; and not a little sarcasm. Auric writes joyously, ironically, a little scurrilously, as if fatigued by the incredible banality and idiocy of things. His lyricism is sweet as vitriol. "Je n'aime pas les catastrophes, les tragédies, les ruines," he says, "et

je n'aime pas me promener près de l'Acropole. Ces paysages
célèbres sont aussi sots que les âmes de mes voisins célèbres—
Dada, La IXe symphonie, Debussy. Les leçons d'humilité m'as-
somment, et je suis assomé par le *Sacre du Printemps*. Préfèrons-
lui une piqûre de strychnine."* Milhaud's *Soirées de Pétrograd*
stick out the tongue at the corpses of men. Poulenc, in a
gentler vein, contributed to *Les Mariés de la Tour Eiffel*, the
ballet upon which the entire Six collaborated, a charming
malicious parody of prim little dance tunes, prim little musical
gestures; a parody of the authorities of the sort Schumann loved
to make and actually inserted in *Papillons* and *Carnaval*.
Indeed, not one of the group is above making, at times, the sign
of the thumb and nose. Even Honegger, most heavy and
conservative member of the crew, generally respectable and
serious in mood, has taken his shot at the sacred cows. His
funeral march, played in *Les Mariés*, is an amusing burlesque
of Wagnerian grandiloquence. After the limping passage of
some horribly Mahleresque triplets, jerked forth to make a
professorial holiday, his brass blares forth, quite as the *Götterdämmerung* orchestra blares forth the Wälsungen motif during
Siegfried's death train, the banal motif of a fat military march.
All in all, it is a musical generation of vipers quite worthy of
Stravinsky and of Satie, its foster fathers.

II

INDIVIDUALITIES do protrude from the pile. The shapes of men
are as apparent in the group as underneath the hide of the
elephant on the stage. There is, in the foreground, Germaine
Tailleferre, the woman of the house, *die Muse des Mont-
parnasse*. She and Arthur Honegger stand out from the group

---

*" 'I don't like catastrophes, tragedies, and ruins, and I don't like to walk
near the Acropolis. These celebrated landscapes are as stupid as the souls
of my celebrated neighbors—Dada, the Ninth Symphony, Debussy. Lessons
of humility bore me stiff. I am bored by the *Sacre du Printemps*. Let us
prefer an injection of strychnine.' "

for the reason that they fit into it a little less than the remaining three, Darius Milhaud, Francis Poulenc, and Georges Auric. There is the distinctest family resemblance between the trio. But the resemblance is far less pronounced in the features of Tailleferre and Honegger; almost as indistinct as it was in Durey's case. Tailleferre has nothing of great novelty to say. There is a certain charm and cleverness in what she writes that is feminine. She may in time prove herself a sort of Marie Laurencin of composition. But, at the present moment, the personage she resembles most is Chaminade; a vitriolic Chaminade, it is true, who prefers drinking *amer Picon* straight, musically speaking, to sipping *eau de cologne* off loaves of sugar. For *Les Mariés,* she wrote a dance of the little pneumatic blues; and it was as impudent as Offenbach and as steely as the tubes which conduct the missives. But her talent is very frail; and her inclusion in the group must be attributed chiefly to a fine enthusiasm for the sex on the part of the five male members.

Honegger is more respectable a musician than is the lady. He is also more conventional a soul than are the remaining three. The attraction of Poulenc, Auric, and Milhaud lies in the quality of openness they have. They have some contact with the flood of life, and respond to it with a certain directness which even in its exaggeration remains vivid. They, too, are more conventional than they would know; but if they err, it is on the more pardonable side of insolence, indifference, slanginess. One recognizes in their muse the unsentimentality of some of those amazing junior leaguers which the accelerated modern world is casting up. Now, Honegger has a sort of sincerity, too. He puts down what he feels, and as he feels it; and even when his music is bad, as it often is, we respond with a sort of emotion. Only, we resent the output. For we see that what he excites in us is somehow old hat; the pawing over of old stuff. His own mind is not quite modern. It persists in dwelling amid objects whose reality has passed out of them. His *Roi David* puts us in touch with a state of a sort in which one holds conversations with God as with a kind parent, which is not at all today. Our religiosity expresses itself in more realistic forms. There is something derivative in all Honegger's moods. They come not so much from life as from other music. His pieces have some worth no doubt. He achieves the nude melodic line, the simplification, the absence of impressionist scintillance, to which the Six as a man aspire. But a work like his *Pastorale* for orchestra is almost painfully pastoral in character; reminiscent of a great many other men's landscape moods. His *Roi David* suggests very plainly the fact that the composer has been steeping himself in the work of the clavecinists antecedent to Bach. The passages of tender devotion, the little fugal battle pieces, sweet and simple as they are, recall a little too much another *David and Goliath;* that of Kuhnau. And so his music, stronger than Tailleferre's although it is, brings us something, too, which is never quite fresh.

III

WITH Poulenc, Auric, and Milhaud, we penetrate more closely into the heart of the artichoke. These are the men who indeed carry the group. Without them there would be no Six. What is really vital and daring in the work of the band flows from out of them. They have the bite, the courage, the brutality. They, too, are candidates more than musicians arrived. But each one has something new to give, and in all three one senses excellent possibilities.

Of the three, Poulenc is as yet the least developed. Auric is just as young in years as he; they were both of them born in 1899, later than the rest of the band; but Poulenc rests more juvenile. His music makes one represent him to oneself as a child playing gleefully with toys; chuckling and grinning and holding up objects to show them to the elders, and throwing them exuberantly about the nursery. He is gentle, amiable, and devoid of the cruel mockery which makes its appearance in Milhaud at times, and in Auric often. He comes out of *Pe-*

trouchka; but he has added Gallic salt and coolth to the playfulness of Stravinsky. He writes sophisticatedly childish tunes for the piano; rhythms repeated over and over again as the improvisations of children sometimes are; "perpetual movements," but subtly varied, subtly prevented from becoming monotonous. There is no one so simple or so complex, so young or so old, who would not smile with pleasure at hearing Poulenc's little gamineries. High spirits, wit, and animal grace break out of the merry brass in the *Overture* composed by him for Cocteau's "Spectacle-Concert." The best of his work is still contained in the setting of the *Bestiaire* of Guillaume Apollinaire for soprano, string quartet, flute, clarinet, and bassoon. We will not pretend that the work manifests a rich or a profound musical gift. The music is thin; and witty more than moving, although a genuine poetry sound from the last song, "La Carpe." But it is exquisitely appropriate to the mood of Apollinaire's polished little epigrams; and lightly and surely executed. It is said that the newer of Poulenc's works exhibit a satisfactory development.

In Georges Auric, the Group of Six finds its purest expression. If there is one man who sums up in himself what the band as a whole represents, and who is expressed through the group, it is this young meridional, youngest of the bunch. The number of his works published is not large. By the side of that of Milhaud's it is small. He is even indebted to his elder. His overture to *Les Mariés*, "Le Quatorze Juillet," with its joyous trumpet calls, could not have been written had Milhaud's overture to *Protée* not existed; the indebtedness of Auric for certain orchestral processes found therein is evident. But Auric has a way of setting things down; a directness, a *robustezza*, a sort of perverted splendiferousness, which not one of his associates can match. Between what he feels and his form, there is least disparity. That is attested by its liveliness. The gesture of the group as a whole, its defiance, its preference of raw colors and rude sonorities, its satiric laugh, comes out of him with greatest naturalness, and most engaging in impudence. Perhaps this fact is what Satie intended to remark when he said, "Des Six, il n'y a que cinq; des cinq, il n'y a que trois; des trois, il n'y a qu'un."* Auric is the magnificent mucker. His music has the most amusing bad manners. It takes off its shoes in public. It goes along the sidewalk with a grin elbowing the pedestrians aside. In perfect good humor which nothing can shake it tells you that if you don't like it, you can lump it. *Basta!* Listen only to the first of his three pastorales for piano. It is, "I do not care a damn" in two-four time. But sardonic humors are not Auric's only vein. He can write tranquil and limpid music, too. The second pastorale has a simplicity and clearness of outline, a delicate sonority like that of some of Satie's happiest essays. There is a sort of largeness, of excitement, in the settings of three of Raymond Radiguet's poems, *Les Joues en Feu*, which is good to hear.

IV

THE BOUQUET sets Milhaud's music apart from that of the other members of his group. The wine is older; of a mellower, smoother, dryer flavor. The grapes which secreted it may not, it is possible, have grown in a soil as fat as that which nourished the fruit from which Poulenc and Auric distill. Milhaud's compositions record nothing quite as distinctive and personal as Poulenc's effortless wit and charm, and fetus-like gaiety; nothing as arresting and sharp as the directness, the relentlessness of attack which makes of Auric at once the most insolent and the most expressive of the Six. His work is more eccentric and external than theirs. Still, the grapes which gave this drink were riper when pressed. The liquor was permitted to stand sealed a longer while and exchange its violence for softness of texture. A felicity of touch which the others of the group do not as yet possess has played into the mold of many of Milhaud's fantastically various works, and given the most of them at least a

* " 'Of the Six, there are only five; of the five, only three; of the three, only one.' "

seductive shapeliness and elaboration of surface. Through all the studied vulgarity and hardness of the raw-colored, flaunting music, there breathes the subtle scent of refined old worlds.

Milhaud is indeed an older musician than are the rest. Honegger was born some months before him, it is true. But Milhaud had gained his direction before any of the others were afoot. He was up and known before the war commenced; he was the only one who brought a growing reputation and cast it into the common pot. It is probable that something of the comparative warmth and vibrancy of his music is due his larger experience. His skill is very evident. He has learned to write for orchestra in such a manner that under his treatment small bands of instruments give forth volumes and sonorities which we commonly refer to the large size of the bands themselves. The music composed by him for *L'Homme et Son Désir* has a most vigorous throat; and yet, the number of instruments demanded by the score, if we except the battery, which is fairly large, and the singing voices, does not exceed fourteen. He has acquired a freedom with the percussion pieces, which constitutes a little science. Like Satie and the rest of the Six, he has studied the noisemakers of the jazzbands for effects; and his orchestral works, the ballet and the ballade in particular, are hot and bright with color produced by tambourines, cymbals, bass drums, triangle, celesta, sandpaper, clapboards, whistles, and other profane apparatus. His music, as a whole, is well written. With what elegance and quietude and humor has he not transcribed those jazzy tangos and Brazilian music-hall tunes! He has kept the melodic lines iron and clear among the dissonances; and still softened the banalities. The conflicts of rhythms, of tonalities, are managed with the utmost economy of emphasis. The elegant little vulgarisms cross races with real success; combine the artistry and delicacy of the French with the vigorous coarseness of the Spanish and Latin American popular rhythms in most agreeable form.

Some principle older and less sharp of edge and more soaked with the sun than that of the other members of the Six must be in this composer, creating a terrain favorable to intellectual and acquired culture. Perhaps it is the rootfastness of generations; the century-long usedness to a certain condition of life, to certain series of objects, which we in America have practically nothing of, which liberates the man and harmonizes him. Suavity and voluptuousness and liqueur-like richness must be in the plasm itself. Hence, even within the limits of the intellectualized group-expression; even among externally grasped and not quite approfondized ideas, Milhaud achieves a density and a weight which distinguishes the body of his work. Auric, and Poulenc in a lesser degree, may both of them be truer to themselves and more fundamentally expressive within the limits of the common mannerisms of the group, impudence, violence, irony. Milhaud's hand remains the happier, more delicate and gratifying. It may even be that the refinement present in his personality is lodged there as something of an unwelcome guest; as something which the possessor would gladly exchange for the hardness, the lighter and tougher entrails of his two fellows. Nevertheless, the density and brownness of blood stands this one in good stead, and signals him, despite his defects as the artist.

Variety of mood further sets the work of Milhaud apart from that of the others. To be sure, he remains the faithful partisan in whatever form he attempts. The common baggage of the movement, diatonic passages, little cocky-doodle-doo's for orchestra, excruciatingly dissonant contrapuntal effects, jazz-rasps and jerks, strutting march rhythms, are carried through the range of his compositions. The hardness of edge, legacy of Berlioz, affected by him; the mordant irony; the broad grin with which much of the stuff is presented, are not his alone. But the Latin American dance-hall tunes which he utilizes extensively are his own *trouvaille*. He appears to have become familiar with them during his sojourn as attaché in Brazil and to have conceived the hope of doing with them what Chabrier and Bizet did with their Spanish forebears. And the range of forms to which he has set hand, is unusually wide. He has written for piano, for voice and piano, for violin and piano, for oboe, clarinet, flute and piano, for large and chamber orchestras. The music composed by him for the theater includes a strictly operatic setting of the *Eumenides* of Aeschylus*; incidental music for the *Choëphores* and the satyr-play of Claudel, ballet music and the accompaniment to a pantomime farce. He has made songs on fragments of the tender and anguished letters of Eugénie de Guérin and on the sneering little *Soirées de Pétrograd* of René Chalupt. The list of his compositions includes sonatas and sonatines, symphonies, and serenades classical in intention; a neurasthenic *Psalm* for men's chorus; and a "shimmy" for jazz band, a tango for the clowns of the Cirque Médrano, a "romance and rag-caprice," and a collection of Brazilian dances. And, to a certain extent, he has entered all these different subjects. The exuberant, obstreperous incidental music for *Protée* has Gallic gaiety and verve and salt. There is something of real hysterical overwroughtness in *L'Homme et Son Désir* and in the song "La Limousine." And the ballade for orchestra, and *Le Boeuf sur le Toit* and the *Saudades do Brazil* show genuine feeling for the full-blooded character of the popular musical expressions of the day.

But although the ground plan of Milhaud's work is vaster than Poulenc and Auric's, the building seems somewhat shaky. His compositions exhibit musicianly tact of a superior sort, and marvelously alert sensibilities; they also exhibit power in a state of dissipation. It is seldom one of them thoroughly compels the interest on second hearing. What they have in them of reality, the smell of the crowd, the millstone-like grinding of steely polyphonies, the iron contours, nervous sudden unprepared contrasts of louds and softs, bright color and brisk movement, freedom from romantic exaltation and the jewelry of the impressionists, evaporates too quickly. The garish hue of the instruments has too little body. The pungency and high spirits grow thin. On first acquaintance, *L'Homme et Son Désir* was

---

* The setting for the *Eumenides* was actually incidental music, not opera.

poisonous and terrible. The human voices crying as they cry out of nightmares; the savage banging of the percussion; whistles and wan monotonous flutes and brutal blaring of the horns, seemed to be carrying the enervation of fierce tropical nights, the states of utter dejection when the whole force of nature seems bent on dissolving the character in slime, and no doorway offers escape, the mad dance of inhuman rejected instincts, the depleted morning hours. One felt the music miasmal and suffocating as dead August nights and stagnant green; the instrumentation the very edge of today. But on second acquaintance, the baleful potency was out of it. The score was wearing sheer. It seemed the scratching of a surface, not the penetration of the subject matter. The nerves only had been touched. The music wanted suspense and cumulative effect. A third hearing intensified the impression given by the second. The flute-gurgling music which accompanied the gyrations of the two women about the helplessly winding man; and the music of final exhaustion seemed a trifle insipid. Indeed, the interpolated Brazilian tunes set in the score began to appear the most vital substance in the work.

V

THE WEAKNESSES of Milhaud's music; the weaknesses of the work of the entire Six; lie in the unclarity of the motive which drives them all.

The impulse in them begins as a vital, necessary movement. Somewhere in the Six, there is the push that is evolving the art of music. Behind them, one feels Moussorgsky sitting and writing his unpretentious, popular, miraculous little things; humorous, ironic, stripped of everything not to his purpose. Behind them, there is the gay scandal of Stravinsky; the free, Dionysiac polyrhythms of *Petrouchka* and the *Sacre,* unrhetoric polyharmonics, the taste of cool, crude earth; and Satie, uneager to be the savior of the universe, putting down his modest, delicate designs for his own pleasure. They, too, these young

Frenchmen, are carried forward by the movement in life which is seeking to make man discard the sense of his importance, his centrality in the scheme of the universe, and is actually tending to make him more self-reliant and human. Absolute truths, immutable systems, fixed concepts, C-major scales, equal temperament, they are no longer in the center of the arena. What has come to stand there is the need of rendering as exact an image of the thing which exists; the need, irrespective of tradition, irrespective of what the past has handed down, of approximating the machinery of music, the tones of instruments, to what is quivering and sounding and starting in men this very day. And to this need, the Six commence a response.

They, too, in answer to the modern sense, are moving to recapture the balance which the eighteenth century began to have and the nineteenth came near losing; the capacity of seeing in everything, great and little, one thing; of being light without being trivial; of not forgetting amid the tragic and solemn aspects of life, the sly winking joke of it all. It was with this balance, this sense of the universal, in minuet or catastrophe, game of blindman's buff or symphony, that Mozart and Haydn brushed their tears away, and remained the sovereign, sane, and healthful minds. Beethoven and Wagner had it far less. In them began a kind of heaviness, a gesture of grandeur, which threatened at moments to become pompousness; and did end in the Titanism of Mahler and Strauss. What one heard was—sixteen horns. With Moussorgsky, a reaction commenced. He had a way of writing for the orchestra and the entire operatic machine so that folk songs, little dances, childish scenes, jokes, even, fitted perfectly into the atmosphere of tragedy and suffering. He had a sense of life fresher and directer than any of his contemporaries; a closeness to the realities that comes like the cold good air.

The understanding of the beauty of the modern freshness of will is in the Six, also. They hear in Bizet's direct speech what Nietzsche heard there, too, the free acceptance of one's fate, the resolution to perform the thing which one has to do; and hold it high like him, above the division in the will of Wagner and

Brahms and the other cultured North Europeans. That is what repels the Six from Debussy, with his irresolution, his tendency to evasion, his preference of the solitary dream. They feel the necessity of making a music more grim, more on the earth, more sharp and sudden in its decisions; a music fuller of the hardness and athleticism and *robustezza* of men who choose, who dare to cut and act and go, who face the grim reality of human life and nevertheless accept it and live themselves through. Like Bloch, like Bartók, like Stravinsky, they are almost unconsciously being impelled to move toward the solidity, the violence and maleness which Cézanne added onto impressionism; and which music, still too impressionistic in quality, requires lest it lose its power.

What is watery, savorless, stale, in the Six comes from an untruthfulness to this modern movement, a deflection of its natural course. The Six have by no means generally the courage of themselves and to themselves; if they think they have, then their right hand is unaware of what their left hand is doing. Satie has said of Ravel that while his mouth rejects the ribbon of the Legion of Honor, his music demands it. Far truer is it that the Six, while outwardly rejecting the attitude of self-importance, the look of responsibility, dignity, and grandeur, inwardly persist in the sort of self-conceit which their lips deny. We have already seen a good old-fashioned feeling of the omnipotence of his thoughts revealed by Honegger in the God-conversations of his *Roi David*. The old infantile egoism persists in the others, too, in other forms. It is very patent in Milhaud. He affects the self-forgetfulness, the humility, and warm human feeling of the eighteenth-century men. But he does not really understand it. He is attracted by it; but, instead of taking courage from it, and going his own way, he falls to imitating its outward forms. He, too, has erected K. P. E. Bach and Mozart and Mendelssohn into a sort of absolute truth. We find him hiding in the shadow of the rock of his absolute; proclaiming a sort of apostolic succession and laying-on of hands in music; asserting that he and his band are the sole conservors of the classic proportions of Mozart and Mendelssohn amid the machinery and jazz of the advancing century. He will have it that his serenade has the proportions of those of Mozart; we find him using Mozartean tunes and Mozartean rhythms. But, as in all cases in which reverence for the past cloaks mere desire for disinfection and sanctification, the traditionalism of Milhaud has resulted only in dead children. His classical stretches are without form, empty and sterile. For his own spirit, and, therefore, the spirit of the classic masters, has remained shut to him.

In running from self-determination, the Six run from their subject matter, too. Their gesture says, "Look, we dare do the light, the little things, like Rameau, like Mozart! We dare be popular, be playful, like Bizet and Chabrier! We are not saving the world!" But the urbanity, the lightness of touch, reveals itself oftentimes a sort of slapdash impotence, an impudent disregard of the subject matter, of the dignity of the craft, and of the rights of the public. They begin with the modern feeling, the desire to acquit themselves of as exact a representation of the existent matter as they can achieve with their technique. But the most of them, Milhaud, for instance, cannot completely carry through; cannot lose themselves in their subjects; cannot make the thing round and vital in itself. Milhaud's work seems at times a perpetual glancing-off from states of incandescence. He cannot give himself completely to any work. The glare and labor and self-obliteration of creation seem to affright him. He is finished too quickly with each of his compositions; overready to chase off and attack a new subject before he has really mastered the old; overeager to have his work printed and out in the world proclaiming his name. It is as something of a Don Juan among the music staves that he appears to us. The fish is not more prolific than he; but of the eggs he scatters upon the flood few hatch completely free-swimming organisms. The person who declared that each composition of Milhaud contains at least one interesting idea spoke an almost final word.

In the relation of the Six to the popular expressions of the day, there is visible the result of a third great deflection of impulse. They have misunderstood the promptings in them beaconing toward a great decisiveness, ruthlessness, directness of musical attack. They feel its beauty in Bizet and Chabrier. They thrill when Nietzsche demands of music "the salt and fire and the great compelling logic, the light feet of the south, the dance of stars, the quivering dayshine of the Mediterranean." But once again, they run away from the act they have to perform. What the German wanted of musicians was the sign, the breath, the reality of the state in man that loves its fate; that does not evade the necessary choice; that measures itself always against the impossible thing, lives dangerously, makes the selection of the higher, further, more perilous, more exacting; leaps out of itself and beyond itself. And what the Six have done, is to make heroes of Bizet and Chabrier, just as they have made heroes of Mozart and K. P. E. Bach; and, at the same time, to run away from the doorway through which their heroes started to go. Instead of becoming choice-men, they have nourished a perverse desire to revert to the type of men who have no serious choices to make. Instead of dreaming of becoming aristocrats of the spirit, they have dreamt of becoming like to the common man, whose acts come easy because they are half reflex; whose responses no preconception, no inner elegance and refinement limits and conditions a priori; for whom no individual woman but only the sex exists. Hence, the peculiar fascination exercised on them by the musical expressions of the proletariat and of America, in which the choicelessness lives; jazz, ragtime, mechanical music of all sorts; and their curious fashion of handling it. For their adapted motives are not really synthesized and essentialiciced by them. These men are not Stravinskys and Sandburgs. What they find they scarcely alter. Their jazzing, their fox trots, shimmies, rag-caprices, are imitative, largely. And for all its surface brightness, this music bores us almost as quickly as the jazz without the wrong notes.

Small wonder, though, that the Six are none of them really more than half and half; none of them as yet fully foaled and free! They are young men; and the current of life bears against them. Their France, too, is trying to dodge the necessity of having to go through a certain door. She, too, is seeking not to make the choice she has to make, the choice of the new European cooperation, perilous, higher, further; and trying to revert to the habits of times gone by, to the manners of celebrated thugs, Richelieu, the Sun King, Napoleon; trying to avoid throwing her Heart of Wallace into the welter and finding it there again in triumph.

They will have to learn to stand alone, to fare alone, these group-men. They will have to find chart and compass within themselves; forget Cocteau and his aestheticism and the man who named them Group of Six; forget the proportions of Mozart and the Latin Genius and what other musicians are doing. The artist is ever a man who walks alone. Self-sufficiency, self-determination, carelessness of what men say or do or understand, trust in what is pushing and urging and speaking deep within him, all the antisocial virtues; they are what give him his value. The more he is the tramp, unrespectable, resident of a world proper to himself, the more he serves. Today, the Group of Six may still have the reality it had a few years since. It came out of a common experience in a number of individuals. It was formed probably for purposes of self-protection in the hostile environment which is outside and inside the men of every new generation. There had to be a wedge for the attack on the fortress of the established ideas. Tomorrow, it may be, the reality will withdraw itself from the group. The men are known, respected, granted a hearing. In persisting, it may defeat its own purpose. They are a danger, groups. They make it far too easy for the members to avoid becoming their own justificators; substitute the law of the herd, always inferior, for the law of the individual. The tendency to evade is already too strong in the Six. Only by showing itself an instrumentality whereby some young ones have gotten themselves the rich courage to their own thoughts, will the Group of 1919 prove itself of worth, and create its own past. And that proof can be given only by men who leave their fathers' houses indeed, leave all the caves and shelters of the tribe, and go their own and solitary ways.

Satie and Impressionism

SOCRATE has made grave the figure of Erik Satie. The tiny symphonic drama, based on fragments of the *Symposium,* the *Phaedrus,* and the *Phaedo,* has given it something of the dignity of those of the composers who have felt life simply and generously. Before the nude, unpretentious little score was published, one conceived the good man first the clown of music. The tragedian one saw in him second always. Debussy, Rimsky, Strauss, Ravel; all the musicians of the time who were intrigued by the mysterious presence of the other senses, sight, smell, touch, as overtones in the sense of hearing, and who dreamt of stirring all five senses at once, of composing perfumes, lights, textures—these appeared the serious performers. Satie, like the sly zanies of the circus, waltzed in at the conclusion of the acrobatics to burlesque them. All hampering, impeding magnificence and ineffectual beauty and color misplaced; he came to humiliate the excessive pride and complacency of the exhibitors by reminding the audience and them of the complete indifference of the universe to such human accomplishments and prowesses. He, too, in the region of music, lost his brilliant trousers while parading, and stumbled over his own feet just as he had succeeded in getting all six oranges revolving in air.

Indeed, so delicious and biting was the clown-play that it is possible Satie has already, or will shortly, put a close for the present to impressionistic music-making. The partisans of absolute music found in him a champion, perhaps not of the sort they preferred, but one very serviceable, nevertheless. The bladder he wielded struck double blows always, one to the theory of program music, the other to the practice of its votaries. The first he made ridiculous by forcing it to logically illogical extremes. There can be no doubt, of course, of the fact that tones, phrases, timbres, excite visual images in composer and auditor. And still, it is equally sure that the images evoked are by no means inevitably identical. The verdict of the lady who held that Beethoven's Piano Sonata, Opus 27, No. 2 is called the *Moonlight* for the reason that the second movement resembles so much the shine of the moon on Lake Lucerne, amply instances the rule. Music is too idealistic a thing to permit itself to be bound to concrete references. You cannot have a white horse in music. It was precisely the white horse that Satie mischievously pretended to make his music represent. In a series of burlesque "program" compositions for piano, "Descriptions Automatiques," "Embryons Desséchés," "Croquis et Agaceries d'un Gros Bonhomme en Bois,"* and others, he joined some sophisticatedly banal and childishly absurd music to very detailed and concrete arguments. Several of these parodies, "Sur un Vaisseau," "Tyrolienne Turque,"† "Españaña," pretend to atmospheres much in favor with Debussy, Ravel, and Albéniz. In each, the program is made ludicrous through the perfect meaninglessness of the music. One is reminded continuously of the powerlessness of music to be concretely narrative and pictorial. The idiotic figures of "Embryons Desséchés" are supposed to describe minutely the habits of sea slugs and other crustaceans. A sort of hunting theme of the kind that is given hapless infants to play in the first year of their pianism is supposed to describe the manner in which the Podophthalmia pursues its prey. The mock-nautical figures of "Sur un Vaisseau" have attached to them words that inform the performer that the music is to represent, among other things, a breath of wind, maritime melancholy, the captain's remark, "Très beau voyage," a distant landscape, waves, and the landing stage. The allegedly "Spanish" music of "Españaña" illustrates "La belle Carmen et le peluquero," the Puerta Maillot, the good Rodriguez, the remark, "Isn't that the *Alcade*?" the Plaza Clichy, and the rue de Madrid.

Besides these particular slaps at the theory of program music,

---

* "Automatic Descriptions," "Dehydrated Embryos," "Sketches and Provocations of a Wooden Dummy."
† "A Boat Ride," "Turkish Yodeling."

Satie, in all his pieces, mocks the descriptive, definitive music with burlesque and impossible directions to the performer. Even in his delicate lissome dances, *Gnossiennes, Gymnopédies,* as he entitles them, one reads continually suggestions such as "Arm yourself with clairvoyance," "Counsel yourself meticulously," "Carry this sound further off," and "Open the head." Otherwheres, one reads "In the manner of a nightingale with a toothache," "Epotus, Corpulentus, Caeremoniosus, Paedogogus," "From the end of the eyes and withheld in advance," "A little bloodily," "Without blushing a finger," "On yellow plush," "Dry as a cuckoo." The "Prélude de la Porte Héroïque du Ciel,"* that wicked, amusing parody on the prelude to *The Blessed Damozel* by Debussy, is interlined with directions to the performer to play, "superstitiously, with deference, very sincerely silent, without pride, and obligingly." One is reminded a little of some of Percy Grainger's directions. The chief difference between the two types, however, is that these of the Frenchmen are funny without being vulgar.

But if Satie hit the theory of program music smartly in his "tone poems" he buffeted the impressionistic musicians themselves even more stingingly. For if his parodies adumbrate the cardinal disability of music, they declare very plainly the fact that the program had helped those who used it to make things fairly easy for themselves. The suggestions of titles and arguments had made it a simple matter to obtain effects with music without really making the music do all the work. Strauss, for example, had come to rely more and more upon elaborate programs to give point to a good deal of uninteresting music, and make foolish titterings of the violin appear to say something profound about the capriciousness of women. Debussy, too, had suggested by means of his jeweled and precious titles moods which the music either did not need or did not justify. And as we play over the music of "Españaña" and "Sur un Vaisseau," and contrast it with the mock local color of the

---

* "Prelude to the Heroic Gate of Heaven."

interpolations, Puerta Maillot, Plaza Clichy, it comes to us that we have been lending our imaginations a little too cheaply to the impressionists. At the command of titles and programs, we have set an elaborate stage in our minds for the musician; seen some sort of literesque Spain when he has spoken "Soirée dans Granade" or *Ibéria* or *Rapsodie Espagnole;* some sort of romantic sea when the word was "Une Barque sur l'Océan" or "La Mer"; and been ready to lend out our imaginations cheaply. No matter what the intrinsic value of the music of Debussy and Ravel and Albéniz is, and we do not for a moment wish to belittle its loveliness, it still seems to us that the attribution of romantic titles to compositions is an unfairness committed to the auditor. A sort of violence is done his imagination. One should be permitted to hear music as music, and create one's own images, if images one must create. Titles like those which Debussy strewed about so freely constitute a sort of assault; even when they do not assist the composer to gain illegitimate effects with his work. And one turns with relief to the humorous, modest, unpretending names, *Trois Morceaux en Forme de Poire,* "Airs à Faire Fuir," *Véritables Préludes Flasques,* "Danses de Travers,"* which Satie has given to some of his most diaphanous compositions. These little jokes, at least, make no pretense. They leave one be in one's voyage through the musical pages marked by them. And the voyage often leads one to the very soul of music.

For Satie, like his brethren of the circus, is a good acrobat. The clowning and parody of the zanies oftentimes conceal an art as delicate as that of the legitimate performers. And if Satie's talent is not a very rich or very powerful one, it is nevertheless exquisite and original and real. Even in his broadest pieces of fun, his horsiest horsing of Debussy and Ravel, a real musical wit points the satire. Debussy's complacent *tristezza,* his softly wailing arpeggios and consecutive minor

---

* *Three Pieces in the Form of a Pear,* "Airs to Make One Run Away," *Genuine Flabby Preludes,* "Sideways Dances."

triads, are very slyly taken off, reduced with no little artfulness to a comic banality; and though the song on the words beginning *Dis-moi, Daphénéo, quel est donc cet arbre dont les fruits sont des oiseaux qui pleurent?** burlesques the lachrymosity, yearnfulness, and pleasure-painfulness of Ravel's lyrics, a very limpid and gossamer-like music accompanies the fun. And Satie's less ironic work, his delicate, curiously simple, whole-tone-scale pieces for piano, are both poetic and interesting in form. Never, perhaps, has an atom of the living Apollo been incarnated in more unprepossessing matter. The gift of Satie, the power of momentary genial play with tone, is a bit of purity thrown into a heap of rubble. Neither variety nor extended form are latent in it. It is a vein of sudden visitations only, sudden genial movements of music with the capacity for pricking and exciting the ear with novelties of line and rhythm; and it does not trickle often. Were Satie not as cute as he is; were he without his healthy humility, his good-natured perspective on himself, it might easily have been abused, spoilt in the forcing-process to which so many a slight and real talent has been subjected by an unwise possessor. The man has the capacity for producing trash; an occasional potboiler demonstrates the fact only too plainly; and, were his balance a little less sure, he might have spent his life adding terrible grand opera upon terrible grand opera to the number of terrible grand operas already in existence. Fortunately, he has not needed to see himself writing "great" music. He has been able to listen for his diminutive vein; to let it murmur its few measures when it will; and then to set them down for what they may be worth.

His output is not large, although want of facilities for publication has probably made it seem smaller than it is indeed. Now that the charm of his music is being recognized, it can be seen that he has been steadily working on his little things through the years. What he has written for the piano has the charm of objects born in a medium. As one traces the gentle

---

* "Tell me, Daphne, what then is that tree whose fruit is crying birds?"

arabesques of his *moments musicaux* over the keys, one hears again the piano. One is really, once again, "playing the piano" for the sake of the play. His little suite, *Trois Morceaux en Forme de Poire,* even makes four-hand music a delight both for auditor and performer, so pianistically and subtly are the movements written. It is particularly in his excessively simple and yet wavering gliding melodic lines that he has been most successful. Less fecund in harmonic and coloristic invention than some of his contemporaries, Satie has nevertheless created for himself a personal idiom through his inventions in melodic form. It is his theory that we have reached an end of harmonic invention; and that the avenue of development open to music leads through "form," through the process of contrasting and playing against each other rhythms and masses. And, in practice, we find him achieving curious, intriguing balances and pricking melodic patterns, by contrasting and opposing to each other set periods, and phrases of unequal lengths and different characters. An irregular form is established; we are always catching our breaths in surprise at the unsuspected turnings which his music takes. There is a sort of charm in the nocturnes, the pieces in which this curious sense of form has been most successfully produced; a charm which one does not seem able quite to surmount and rationalize. Nor is one ever irritated, as one sometimes is by a fellow-adventurer of Satie's, Milhaud, by the breath of an arbitrary will, a purely perverse desire to be surprising and disconcerting in his melodic line. Satie remains the musician. He has always had the rare gift of being utterly simple, tender and direct. The second of the three *Véritables Préludes Flasques* catches the attentiveness and sadness of the waiting dog with delicious sureness, and with an utter simplicity of means. The little piece is no more than a two-voice invention. One must go to Chopin's mazurkas to find piano music as nude in line, as simple in means and yet as graceful and charming and satisfying as Satie's nocturnes, his *Morceaux* and *Gnossiennes*. A sort of white and agreeably monotonous beauty pulses through these utterly unpretentious things, and calls to mind the impersonality and slowness and sleepiness of certain oriental dancers. Only, there one sees in the mind, if a momentary relapse be permitted one, a severe Greek temple-yard, and the athletic limbs of Dorian maidens.

That one perceived first, however, the more destructive side of Satie's criticism of musical impressionism, the clowning; and second, always the more constructive, is due chiefly to the fact that although the good man's talent was always a very real and exquisite one, it is recently only, roundly since Satie's fiftieth birthday, that it has attained maturity. It was within very sharply defined limits that he was able to work. Although he was younger than Debussy by very few years, and although he taught the Parisian magician much, the use of consecutive ninths, the use of certain church modes, and other refinements; he was always most successful in the smaller forms. His invention was far too thin to permit him to essay the long curve, the complicated pattern. There are even pure and limpid sketches of his that make us merely to feel that the composer deserves the name of artist chiefly because he knows when to stop; another few bars, and we might commence to grow a little weary.

It may be that a course of study undertaken at the Schola Cantorum during the year 1911 helped Satie in his development; although the immediate result, a prelude, chorale, and fugue entitled *Aperçus Désagréables** does not suggest that its author found much to delight him in the post-Franckian discipline. What probably proved itself more decisive was the sympathy which came to him, during the years of the war, from some of the younger musicians and critics. In Jean Cocteau, Satie found both a prophet and a stimulating collaborator. With him he composed the ballet *Parade*. The members of the Group of Six brought him aesthetic corroboration. A few intelligent amateurs commenced to recognize the genuineness of his gift; and the Princess Edmond de Polignac ordered

* *Disagreeable Impressions.* Rosenfeld is in error about the year. This work was written in 1908.

Socrate of him. In the two works produced under the direct stimulation of his friends, Satie has given himself at his largest. Both works very decisively reveal his particular orientation to musical art. The ballet shows him very deliberately rejecting all grandiosity of material; all grandiloquence of style; holding to a nude, unemphatic elegance. He is content to take the material, the tone of his work, from off the streets. The imitation of the sounds of revolvers and typewriting machines in the orchestra is symbolic of a general effort to capture something characteristic in color, in timbre, of the ordinariness of life; to play the circus, too. *La petite fille Américaine* dances to a sort of essentialized ragtime. The Chinaman's little fugato has the unpretentious quality, the slightly down-at-the-heel animality of the vaudeville turn. And the music is innocent of scene painting, of illustration in the impressionistic sense. It is straight design: delicate, frivolous, sophisticated; *un peu de musique* which dances its way as self-consistent as a movement of a Haydn quartet, and breaks off and ends without ceremony.

Perhaps even more definitively than *Parade*, *Socrate* is both the logical continuation of what Satie has been about in his music during the thirty years of his career, and the most solid of the forms he has created. Under the star of the anti-impressionistic aesthetic he has been following, he has managed to communicate a sincere feeling of the depth of life. There is no attempt at description, no attempt at fixing local color, in his setting of the lines from Cousin's elegant Plato. In all three fragments he has left it to the words to realize the pathos and beauty of the incidents immortalized, and striven only to sustain with infinite reserve the emotion of the poet himself.

Where Debussy would have outdone himself in depicting the tranquil scene of the cold brook and plane-tree shade that opened itself to the senses of Socrates and Phaedrus during their unforgettable stroll without the walls of Athens, Satie has modestly contented himself with supplying a tender, swinging piano accompaniment that merely intensifies the effect of the language itself, and does no more. The verbal portrait of

Socrates sketched by the drunken Alcibiades during the ban-quet is supported by a lightly moving rhythm in two-four time, broken at rare intervals by some rich brusque chords. The music of the third fragment, the narration of the incidents of the death of Socrates, does no more, with its piercing and simple and sad tones, than help communicate the grief of the beloved disciple over the end of the most sage and just of men.

But very rarely since the hour of "La Mort de Mélisande" has music more touching been produced. The deep pure sense of life that guided Satie in the selection of the three fragments for setting, remained with him when he penned his music. Those rhythms and chords and melodic figures that stir us so effort-lessly stem from a clear, simple, humble feeling of what the beauty and tragedy of human life, what the grandeurs and sweetnesses of character really are. They interpret Plato for us indeed. They place us, without grandiloquence or sentimen-tality, in some place a little above, a little removed, from the flow of life; and even in the broken contemptible world of after-war, make us to feel again the love of the *ascesis,* serenity, reserve, selflessness, undogmatism, playfulness, which the old Greek knew alone made good again the cruelties of human society. Indeed, one must go to Moussorgsky almost to find a simpler and truer statement of one who has eaten his bread in tears and knows the sad beauty of human life on this planet. Only, in the fine nude designs of *Socrate* one feels not so much the product of religious feeling, as of the wisdom of the philosophers, born again in the modesty and sanity and hum-bleness of a musician.

So it is no longer the clown of music we perceive first when we think of Erik Satie. Life does strange and wondrous things to men at times. It takes from them for long years some faith and sweetness with which they came into the world; lets them wander disinherited of the strongest powers of their being; then suddenly brings them back again that which it stole, and grants them full play and enjoyment of their souls. So, in a way, has it done with Satie. The old diablerie, the old wit and spiritual

bohemianism is still in him. But another side of him has waxed
serenely and beautifully. And, when we gaze with the mind's
eye out toward Arceuil, we see something that harmonizes
entirely with Cocteau's epithet of *bon maître*. We go richer for
knowing that the world contains one more poet.

III

American Music

Jazz and Music: Music in America

AMERICAN MUSIC is not jazz. Jazz is not music. Jazz remains a striking indigenous product, a small, sounding folk-chaos, counterpart of other national developments. What we call *music*, however, is a force, adjusted to the stream of the world in which materials float and elements play, and active like them upon the human situation; and, bold and debonair as it is, seductive with woodwind in minor thirds and fuller of bells than a bayadere, our characteristic "dance music" is cheerfully quiescent. Fox trot and Charleston, its special figures, have supplied several ultramodern composers with happy motives—Milhaud, Copland, Hindemith, Chavez, Auric, among others. So, too, its novel instrumental effects; since jazz composers have been ingenious in combining timbres savorsomely. It may, conceivably, contain a spirit in embryo, the palpitancy, the peculiar giddy, half-erotic bobbing, possibly announcing a state of levity bound to make much of our old solemnity seem impotence. Yet, in itself, jazz, or rather more what the great run of our commercial musicians continue to produce with their material, their themes and instruments, has changed nothing in the human environment. On the contrary, it has let everything sit.

Beneath its superficial irregularity, snap and go, the best of jazz stands inert. Rhythm is precluded, not permitted to develop itself in its hard-boiled sphere. In place of truly rhythmic, periodical, unpredictable displacement of volumes and accents intrinsic to phrases and freely flowing periods capable of organic extension and development, the typical jazz composition offers mere beat; mechanic iteration, duplication, conformation to pre-established pattern. Its alternation of bars of three and four and five units, the so-called jazz polyrhythm, is sheer willful contrast and change. The chief excitement in it proceeds from a series of jerks, systematic anticipations and retardations of the arbitrary, regular, unfailing beat.

For jazz heartily and consistently violates the identity of its medium: the sonority of instruments. Rhythm, manner of being and of moving, is as intrinsic to the material of the artist, whether that of tone or of color, language or granite, as it is to the artist himself; to be produced only through the free sympathetic relationship of man and thing, craftsman and medium. But in jazz, there is no penetration of the subject stuff, no empathy, no union of the man and the matter, no tension. Tremendously dolled up, the core of jazz is prearrangement, repetition, succession. Metric schemes inflexible as all preconceptions, are arbitrarily imposed on the means and the artist; and to dictate is to exploit. As for the jazz melodies, they are largely synthetic, either inappropriate arrangements of old, tried matter dredged up from the more sentimental European romantics, or not too dangerously novel recombinations of phrases of jazz and other popular compositions.

This sharp denial of the stream of things and the conditions under which materials exist and forces move, is not only symbolical. Jazz's first blare revives the lure of ready-made Elysiums. Sparkling as a soda fountain, the blissful region rises amid its pebbly beats, luxurious, immediate as the dance floor, apparently no less easily accessible than some smart clothes and a complacent embrace. Merely to let go and to pass in is to attain apotheosis. The saxophone says so, insinuative and enveloping; and reserve and ponderation, discrimination of the identity of things and the conditions shaping us, all indeed making for tensity, discomfort, and pathos, suddenly become the folly of the living dead. Smoothness of enamel, gaiety of flowery dresses, airiness of speed are there for the mere taking, or the inconsiderable price of a little willingness, a little cash and snap. The "not impossible she," or he, is at hand in a thousand persons. There are myriads of persons, each one the one—here where existence is canoeing down flowing blue and sailing on ocean breezes and throbbing in the pink of a perpetual spasm: hard, assured, winning people, decided and smart as the cut of straight limbs, youthful with earth's sweetest bloom; and at night (the urgent trumpet swears it) the cars are sapient glowworms transporting rapturous pairs through moving spaces.

Precisely that is the function of jazz, its great *raison d'être*. Jazz is an "entertainment"; and an entertainment, in very simplest Boeotian, is something which temporarily removes people from contact with the realities. Perhaps it is a little ungracious of us, to analyze what, like an entertainment, pretends merely to please? But we have here to do with an extraordinarily popular drug-like use of the materials of sound; and it is certainly not for mere purposes of disparagement that we seek to explain its prevalency by reminding ourselves that the great number of men are incapacitated for either a large or consistent acceptation of the world, the stream of things, the conditions of existence. Yearning for a new life potential between them and the world appears too weak or too nonexistent to reconcile them with conditions making life possible. Unable to grant a satisfactory embrace, reality seems merely cruel, merely treacherous, merely tragically hazardous; and satisfaction to lie only in security from its caprices. This is sought in the ostrichlike act of disorientation and disarticulation by which man withdraws from contact with materials and people into himself. The illusion of an established, waiting, easily accessible apotheosis is consequent of it. For how could retreat, and the revivification of past experiences, the repetition of familiar ideas and habitual gestures following it, be attended by anything but feelings of a dissolving sweetness? They weaken the lure of the actual, so baleful to weak passions, do they not? and dissipate tension? In other days, this sort of exercise was amply given by religious practices. At present, particularly in America, it is provided by "politics," "all the news that's fit to print," Florida, Hollywood, the rest of Southern California, "the education of our children," "sophisticated" fiction, and above all, by jazz. The heaven our exercises offer, has merely become a little more sensual, a little more earthly than that of the middle ages, something like the Mohammedans'. That is because in many ways it is merely the intensification of the

fictitious world in which most people consistently dwell. No
doubt, the American exercises focussing it possess much of the
snappiness of the civilization to which they bring relief. Jazz,
for example, embodies a knack with materials. It is smart;
superficially alert, good-humored, and cynical. Essentially, nonetheless, it is just another means of escape.

What we term music, the representative work, say, of Bach
and Beethoven, Mozart, Wagner, and Brahms, primarily is
what jazz from the beginning is not: the product of a sympathetic treatment of the sonorous medium. *Music* is a chain of
temporal volumes released by sensitive manipulation of an
instrument. Music has rhythm, indeed, each piece of it has its
own way of flowing, its own logic of temporal volumes not to
any degree mechanical, or identical with the motion of another
thing, even one of its own species. In works like the last sonatas
and quartets of Beethoven, the fantasies and fugues of Bach,
Tristan und Isolde of Wagner, the logic is so universal that we
have the impression these pieces existed since the beginning of
the world, and must persist till doomsday. Still, no matter how
special it may be, the piece of music is never stationary or
disintegral. You cannot arrest a composition midways without
disturbing a balance. Moreover, the accents are intrinsic to the
phrases; and the phrases themselves develop from the initial
idea, theme, or quality of sonority, freely; in conformity with a
law which we can recognize after the piece is done, but cannot
predict. For pieces of music, when they do not involve literature
and try to tell stories, are compositions *for* the violin, *for* the
piano, *for* the orchestra, reverend of these identities; born of a
sort of auscultation or penetration of the means and themes, of
a sympathy between the man and the instrument or material, a
subtly following adjustment of his will to that of things. They
are never the product of preconceived schemes or mechanical
beats or mathematical formulae arbitrarily imposed. What if
they do bear the names of fugue and lied, sonata and fantasy?
These names are little besides rough significations of genera
and species. Musical art is spontaneous and original, the reverend adjustment of sonorous means to new conditions, new

states of being, new experiences. Not only are no two fugues of Bach, no two sonatas of Beethoven, no two fantasies of Chopin or Schumann identical as wholes, or, for the overwhelming part, in their phrases. In many cases, they radically vary the type to which they belong. Many musicians have indeed established their own forms, their own types: Haydn the binary form, Beethoven the scherzo, Schubert the dramatic lied, Wagner the structural opera or music drama. But, whether radical in norm or not, they are each autonomous, showing evidence of a spontaneous and original, uncalculated and uninduced approach to the medium. No doubt, there are compositions, the clavier and organ works of Handel, for example, whose interest is slight for the reason that they are little besides talented manipulations of a means. And there are others, the piano pieces of Brahms, perhaps, whose interest is large in the face of a none too sympathetic approach to the keyboard. Still, penetration of the medium and its individual nature and way of being and moving, in the spirit of the moment and mood, is prerequisite.

And music cuts away the foundations of ready-made Elysiums. Music is expressive, carrying us out of ourselves and beyond ourselves, into impersonal regions, into the stream of things; permitting us to feel the conditions under which objects exist, the forces playing upon human life. In conformity to the terms of materials, each piece of music has not only thing-ness, continuity of texture, and "a beginning and a middle and an end." To some degree, consequent to the state of the composer at the time of composition, it contains and communicates a rich pathos. Musical art's fundamental acceptance of the identity and limitations of its medium is not, by any means, consent in the conditions of a mere fragment of the world. The medium is the microcosm, the splinter of Yggdrasill* shot with the grain of the all; and the embrace of it, the consent in its identity, the acceptance of its law of motion, the recognition of the whole in

---

* In Scandinavian mythology, the great tree whose roots and branches span and support the universe. If it were to be uprooted, the world would collapse.

the fragment, involves adjustment to the great rolling universe. Hence, we are *moved* by music, find it expressive and full of feeling. For to live, to merge with the stream and become part of forces larger than ourselves, is to feel, to know something about the entire world; and the music lets us share in a great man's absorption: at least to the degree to which we are capable of being lost to ourselves. Indeed, musical literature embodies a tremendous gamut of intuitions, from deepest sorrow to highest joy, in combinations as individual as its combinations of the tones of the scale. Graver feelings preponderate in the work of certain composers, Bach and Brahms for example, and lighter feelings in that of Haydn and Mozart. Still, without exception, the representative pieces of the chief composers present irreproducible harmonies of the pathetic palette, opposing, balancing, and conciliating the elementary intuitions much as great experience of life itself does.

To call Bach's music the soul of Protestantism, Beethoven's the affirmation of man's nature, Wagner's the gospel of a religion of love, and Debussy's the sensuous embrace of the cosmos, is very roughly to indicate the immense effect music has exercised on our environment. Together with painting and the novel, perhaps even more grandly than either of its sister arts, music has recently been tending to supplant formal religion. It is not without profound reason that Martin Luther, himself more of an adaptator than a composer of original music, figures perennially in musical histories. The art he cultivated in his leisure has proven more active in his profounder intention than the dogma he laboriously established; mediating between the individual and the universe. Indeed, with her immense flexibility, her semi-materialism, her direct address to feeling, *Frau Musica* has been more subtly, immediately revelatory of the ever-moving, unpredictable something at the core of life than a fixed dogma could ever be. Her immense responsiveness to the curve, the way, the law of things, has actually sustained the individuals capable of larger, subtler, more sensitive harmony with the invisible forces. (One could scarcely imagine modern idealism deprived of Mozart and Beethoven and Wagner.) For, like all art, music itself is an act, an offspring, of potency, of pregnancy with fresh spirit and life; therefore the director and ally of all that is able to adjust to things and move beyond itself in new embodiments. The musician's acceptance of the conditions of existence, of inevitable tragedy and extinction, so abhorrent to the jazz artist and the jazz public; his very delight in a "Creation" almost indifferent to man: what is that but the act of the creature strongly impelled, strongly loaded with the seeds of life, full of yearning for the thing imminent between him and the world; bound to find his cosmic partner, his instrument, satisfactory—mortality, failure, and final extinction notwithstanding; and everything for the best, in what may even prove the worst of possible worlds?

Not only the effects of music are loud in their testimony of its origin. The personal developments that have accompanied its appearance declare it plainly. The great composers were no less victorious as men than as musicians. The world has not frequently seen a human clarity as intense, a capacity for receiving, digesting, and giving life as uncompromised, as that of Johann Sebastian Bach; or a loveliness as warm as Mozart's; or a majesty as simple as Beethoven's; or experienced a lifelong increase in wisdom and power as steady as Wagner's, with its culmination in the death mask of a Buddha. And for two hundred years, a succession of great musicians had the power to receive and move a technique onward: Karl Philipp Emanuel Bach receiving it from his great father; Haydn from K. P. E. Bach, and Beethoven from Haydn; Wagner from Beethoven; and the newest men from the old demiurge of Bayreuth.

And today a force related to theirs is at work in America. This is one of the most significant aspects of the national situation. We have an American music: there existing a body of sonorous work, not jazz, made by persons associated with the American community, to be grouped without impertinence with classic European works. Jazz may continue to bulk large and remain the most striking product of our direction toward the instruments of music. Still, side by side with it, and side by side with other products of energy directed toward the means of art, there continue to appear with an accelerating speed, compositions rooted in the American "soil"; exploiting the material of sound in characteristic ways, and releasing a typical pathos. Possibly, the product is still small in worth. The creative talents are, assuredly, few and not mature. As a whole, the musical movement is still slighter and of less importance than either the pictorial or the literary, in proportion to its comparative recency. But it exists; it swells. New creative talents appear with every year; and while they may yet seem uncertain and anything but overwhelming, they have added a new interest and excitement to life, filling it with the vibrance of gathering powers. How many revelatory experiences do we not owe to the work of Varèse, of Chavez, and Copland? How much of the intensity of American life does not come from the burgeoning of the talents of Harris and Sessions and Ruggles? It is of course too early to make prognostication of the final intensity and importance of the movement as anything but idle amusement. Nonetheless, it is by no means too early to estimate the initial force. Considering the seriousness of the accomplishments, the fact that some of the most important living composers are Americans by nationality and by culture, such an estimation indeed becomes one of the tasks most incumbent on criticism. It has long been one of the most attractive adventures offered by present American life.

Beginnings of American Music

IN VIEW of the body of alleged American folk song, the contention that an American music is very young must appear fantastic. It is in fact anything but absurd. The belief that the Negro spirituals and the songs of the Appalachian mountaineers constitute an authentic folk music, like the English, the Russian, and the Magyar, flatters our vanities. But there is little realism in it.

Of the charm of many of the spirituals and Kentucky mountain ballads, there is no question. They are to be cherished, whatever their origin. Still, by what right are we to claim them for our own? "Folk songs," says the dictionary, "are marked by certain peculiarities of rhythm, form, and melody, which are traceable, more or less clearly, to racial or national temperament, mode of life, climatic and political conditions, geographical environment, and language." Neither the spirituals nor the ballads fit this definition. The bare fact that both are found in use in the western hemisphere is certainly no argument for their originality. The peculiarities of each are traceable to extra-American conditions. As we know it, the Negro spiritual is an obviously sophisticated arrangement of some more primitive song. Its harmonizations are, unquestionably, the results of the contact of an inferior with a superior musical culture. We can merely guess at the basic tunes. Whatever they were, there is every reason to suppose them, too, arrangements rather more than native compositions. The characteristic syncopation, the short note on a strong beat followed immediately by a longer note on a weak beat, is found throughout the folk music of the West African Negroes and the Hottentots. Again, the characteristic intervals of the fourth and fifth are significantly those of the Scotch folk song, are even called the Scotch intervals. In view of these facts, we can scarcely hold them autochthonous. They are perhaps adaptations of the folk songs of other nations to American conditions, perhaps even superior to their originals. But, purely American they most certainly are not.

Evidences of derivation come even thicker in the music of the Appalachian mountaineers. To find people living hundreds of miles inland singing ballads on subjects born of sea life and filled with allusions to details familiar to sailors, is in itself sufficient to make us pause for reflection. It was scarcely necessary for Cecil Sharp and the other musical anthropologists to collate the old Scotch and English originals of many of the ballads with their American variants, to convince us that the number of mountain songs actually born of the new situation and original to this country is relatively too small to count. No doubt, the mountaineers have produced a number of variations of the old originals; but they frequently constitute deteriorations of the primal ideas, not improvements on them. The Old World folk tunes have a sad habit of deteriorating in the New World, a fact that must be familiar to all who, on a vocal summer's evening near the high school steps, have recognized in "The Bear Went Over the Mountain," the coarsened features of "Malbrough s'en Va-t-en Guerre."*

A degree of originality must be allowed some of the early American hymn tunes. But even these follow English models. No; American music, the body of music rooted in the American soil, begins with Edward MacDowell and is of our times. The circumstance is not at all mysterious. America was settled by people developed beyond the stage of civilization that is productive of folk songs. Americans have never lived a strictly communal life attached to the soil; and while such an attachment may appear in the near future, it will scarcely restore the form of primitive society. Straitened as their circumstances in the New World were, the settlers could not and did not recapitulate stages of growth already behind them. The culture of Europe was their tradition, their past experience; forgotten and unconscious perhaps, but nonetheless active and inevitable. Growth of their own was necessarily an evolution of the tradition, the development in some direction of what was already experienced and accomplished. The fact that for a while no growth was apparent is no proof of reversion to earlier stages; the world knows seeds that after thirty centuries in Egyptian tombs, come up again as wheat. (It is noteworthy that primitive as the idiom and characteristic as the spirit of many of our most original composers, Copland, Harris, Chavez, Ruggles, are, their work implies as little of a denial of the European past as that of Stravinsky, Bartók, Milhaud, or any other radical European modern.)

But an American development along musical lines was

* A French nursery song of the seventeenth or eighteenth century.

obliged to wait on the event of a transnational America; at the very least, on the event of the latter nineteenth century with its improved communications and increased advantages. Musical culture, sympathetic familiarity with the instrumental technique and musical developments appropriate to their station in civilization, was at an extremely low point among the Anglo-Saxon settlers of the continent. England had a musical orientation up to the Revolution of 1688. After Tudor days, nonetheless it was pretty thoroughly confined to the upper circles; and the majority of the settlers, in the southern as well as the northern colonies, were drawn from the more Puritan, less musical classes. What culture they had was mainly ideological, literary, and dry. Painting, for example, was practiced among them merely for personal record; and while hymns and folk songs did come across the Atlantic in the many little Mayflowers, not many fanatics of Gibbons, of Purcell, or even of Handel, accompanied them. Had the early colonists possessed an instrumental technique and musical culture, it is quite possible that American music might not have had to wait on the last decade of the nineteenth century, and that in the time in which creative energy first came to the community, a part of what went into literature might have gone into composition. Something which exists in tone would have made men want to compose. Symphonies based on old American hymn tunes, like the recent one of Virgil Thomson, can easily be envisaged paralleling the poems of Emerson; and a development of the Anglo-Irish folk song like the melodies of Roy Harris might very conceivably have answered the Homeric yawp of the man of Manhattan. Is it entirely fantastic to believe that, had music-making been as widespread in the America of 1820 as in that of 1920, Poe would have turned to instrumental sonority rather than to words and verse for expression, and paralleled Chopin not in poetry but in music itself? Or that Lanier would have become a sort of American Robert Franz?* Certainly, both

* Robert Franz (1815–1892), German organist, conductor, composer, editor of Bach and Handel. A minor song writer.

these poets sought to make words do something much more directly to the power of tone. Besides, the number of artists from Michelangelo and William Blake, to John Marin and Marsden Hartley, who have successfully treated more than one medium, sustains the assumption with the lesson that force, to a degree, remains independent of means; and very possibly may precede material determination.

As it was, abortive efforts to imitate Bellini and Donizetti were made in the forties. But it was only toward the middle of the nineteenth century, that Boston and New York grew familiar with the technique of instrumental music; and only during the last decades of the century, coincident with the heavy immigrations from Central Europe, that a musical life, at least a concert and opera-going habit, established itself in the great centers. Even then, the seeds of an original music were slow in sprouting. There are various good reasons for this continued tardiness. For some unknown cause, music is invariably slow in developing; by no means only in America. It was the last of the arts to attain rebirth in Italy during the great Renaissance; Palestrina, Vittoria, and Monteverdi working in the latter half of the sixteenth century, almost after the main burst of creative energy in the plastic arts was past. Indeed, the history of art is prolific in instances in which forces manifest themselves in poetry and painting an half century before they show themselves in music. The spiritual relationship of Wagner to the romantic idealists Tieck and Novalis is very close, but the music of *Tristan* was written almost fifty years later than Novalis' darkly voluptuous *Hymns to the Night* and *Heinrich von Öfterdingen*.* Debussy's impressionism, blood brother of the symbolism of Verlaine and Mallarmé and the pointillism of Pissarro and Seurat, is distinctly the junior of the late nineteenth-century Parisian poetry and painting. However, the chief obstruction to the early birth of an American music appears to have been not so much the native slowness of musical art, as the

* An unfinished lyrical novel by Novalis.

fact that the first familiarity with the technique and developments of musical art appropriate to the stage of evolution
reached by American civilization fell upon bad times and
insensitive ears. No time, we know, is entirely bad (i.e. impotent) for all men. The fantasy of the Wasteland, recently
popularized by the poetry of T. S. Eliot, and the criticism of
several young Americans, is not to be taken seriously. There
may be wastelands. Many such cursed phases of existence
doubtless do exist. But we know that a nation or a time bare of
energy and thus prohibitive of the artist, such as the one
implied by the generalization in the title of T. S. Eliot's poem,
remains the phantom of some inexcusably limited feeling; and
the perpetuation of a condition at the worst largely relative.
Someone is always managing to work and to produce in every
age. Someone is always finding his age propitious to his form of
artistic activity; the world and someone's idea are always managing to harmonize. Even the weary soil on which European
music fell in America, the period after the Civil War, saw the
rise of Henry James, certainly as pure and disinterested an
artist as ever lived, the flowering of Emily Dickinson, the
appearance of the painter-poet Albert P. Ryder, and of the
lesser but nonetheless unusually gifted Homer Martin, Winslow
Homer, Mark Twain, and William James. Still, the period, like
that following every great modern war, was an exhausted one.
Weak in forces, it was not prolific of expressive individuals. Not
that the American environment was "hostile," as certain recent
critics would have us believe, thwarting and condemning to
sterility great unknown geniuses, and reducing a potential Cervantes or Rabelais to the scale of Mark Twain, a potential
Dostoevski or Tolstoi to that of Henry James, and a potential
Dante to the size of a T. S. Eliot. What we call a favorable
environment, and what we call creative ability, are actually but
two aspects of a single force, basically at one with itself, and
productive in its two-part play. Of these parts, one is the "not-
I," the other the "I"; but essentially they are lovers; and in
which one the divine spark arises is known to God alone. No, it

was not the indifference of "society" to the artist that delayed the birth of an American music. It was the fact that after the Civil War there were few potencies in any field. There was little "doing" in the strata of being close to the collection, itself close to the supporting earth. Perhaps the "soil" was weary. Certainly, the race was so. The determined musicians, men like Paine and Lowell Mason, were forceless; weak personalities.

And, when at length music did sprout in the United States, it had neither the freshness and the power of the great mid-century prose and poetry, nor the intensity of the new American painting. It was "winter on earth"; and the impulse was weak or convalescent. The music of Edward MacDowell, the first American to deserve the name of composer, amounts more to an assimilation of European motives, figures, and ideas than to an original expression. In any case, the original elements are small and of minor importance. Trained in Germany under Raff, MacDowell continued for the first and longer part of his career, and as late as the *Tragic* and *Heroic Sonatas,* a mere sectary of the grandiose German romantics. His conceptions followed theirs in falling into heroic, impassioned mold, and "Ercles' vein." His aim remained a massive homophonic music, diatonic in feeling, and harmonized with the rich close solemn chords characteristic of Chopin and Wagner, and developed not only by MacDowell himself, but by Franck, d'Indy, and Richard Strauss. The ideas of the main romantic composers, particularly Wagner, continued to haunt MacDowell even in his later, more personal phase. We cannot avoid hearing a reminiscence of the pompous *Meistersinger* march in the slow movement of the *Celtic Sonata;* and of the diminished minor chords commencing the last scene of *Götterdämmerung* in the *Fireside Tale* entitled "By Smouldering Embers." The echoes are not only Wagnerian; the theme of the finale of the *Celtic Sonata* has a strong resemblance to that of "The Hall of the Mountain King" in Grieg's *Peer Gynt Suite.* And to the end, MacDowell shared his school's narrowness of artistic vision, embracing little outside the confines of homophonic music. He was badly equipped in polyphonic technique; and where, as in a passage of the last movement of the *Norse Sonata,* he attempted canonic imitation, we find him essaying it clumsily, and with all the obsessive rapture of a child in possession of a new and dazzling toy.

Nor did MacDowell ever sustain a direct and untrammelled contact with his sonorous medium. The closest parallels to his art are to be found in the works of Grieg and Rachmaninoff; like his, wanting the intensity that makes artistic work a new phenomenon; and contributing only slight and unimportant experiences. True, MacDowell had more talent for music and was always more natively lyrical and addressed to the instruments of his art, than any other member of his American group, Chadwick, Converse, Kelley, and the rest whose careers in several particulars coincided with his. But while his themes, musical sensations, and colorings finally grew less derivative, more original; and his style personal, readily distinguishable and of some intrinsic charm, he never attained real facility in moving his ideas, or in moving himself through them. Even where he is most individual, even in the very personal, characteristically dainty and tender little piano pieces, he frequently appears fixed and rigid in invention. The quaint little melodic idea in *Woodland Sketches,* the sort of sweetly harmonized secular hymn tune which he there calls "At an Old Trysting Place," meets one at every turn; whether we wander in the Guinevere section of the *Sonata Eroica,* or in the "Old-Fashioned Garden" of the *New England Idylls,* we are never far from the little old rendezvous. Nor did he finally become abundantly able to do something of interest with his themes and go on adventures with them. The typical MacDowell piece wants rhythm and swing almost as much as jazz does. Even a number of the fairly individual smaller later pieces have a strange iterativeness, monotony, staticity in combination with frantic Wagnerian *Steigerungen,** which in this case do not

* "Climaxes."

produce movement. The idea itself has not been extended. There is mere beat, as in jazz; and we are again and again left with the baffled feeling that the King of France has marched his men up the hill and straightway marched them down again. "Of Br'er Rabbit" is one of the few of the shorter bits that moves of itself; and the little piece has not much weight or quality.

The case is not hard to point. We have in MacDowell's music the manifestation of a force directed toward the medium of music, and still not strong enough, at least not frequently strong enough to grasp the subject material robustly, and play in the stream of things. Talented and refined as he was, the composer remained always half the jazzman, with his chronic aversion to reality, and wish to retire into his private paradise. This interior conflict and secret sentimentality, this tendency to accept the established and shrink from discovery and adventure, was not proper only to MacDowell. It seems to have run through the whole group of musicians of which he was the most eminent member. One is struck, in noting their careers, with the continual and fatal flirtation of the entire set with polite and academic circles, and with the currency of the desire to fit into powerful, established, authoritarian quarters. Not that any of these men are to be accused of the spiritual servility to be found, say, in Paul Elmer More.* All possessed some spontaneous, uncompromised delight in creation. Still, they were at cross purposes. It is impossible to doubt that Chadwick cared as much for his social position on the Charles as for the reality to which his art ostensibly was addressed. Little concerts of "American" works conducted by Walter Damrosch had a habit of getting themselves arranged for members of the American Academy. Even poor MacDowell, most independent and bohemian of the lot, finally gravitated to Columbia University,

---

* Paul Elmer More (1864–1937), American literary critic, best known for his multivolume series, *Shelburne Essays*. He was an opponent, with Irving Babbitt, of modern scientific rationalism and liberalism.

where to his sorrow he encountered the impenetrably hided rhinoceros whose park it is. Were it not for MacDowell's Celtic descent, one might almost be tempted to attribute this group-wide weakness for the odors of sanctity to a racial strain, so many instances arising in which Saxondom and snobbery (desire to stand in with the powerful, and readiness to be persuaded of the value of whatever is highly thought of in high quarters) seem almost synonymous. MacDowell, however, was not Saxon, and the earlier explanation of the general timidity remains the more reasonable. In music, this weakness took the form of sentimentality. The feelings entertained about life by him seem to have remained uncertain; and while fumbling for them he seems regularly to have succumbed to "nice" and "respectable" emotions, conventional, accepted by and welcome to, the best people. It is shocking to find how full of vague poesy he is. Where his great romantic brethren, Brahms, Wagner, and Debussy, are direct and sensitive, clearly and tellingly expressive, MacDowell minces and simpers, maidenly, and ruffled. He is nothing if not a daughter of the American Revolution. He hymns "America" thinking of the Mayflower and its lovely load. His mind fondly dwells on old-fashioned New England gardens, old lavender, smoldering logs, sunsets, "a fairy sail with a fairy boat," little log cabins of dreams, the romance of German forests, and the sexual sternness of Puritan days. This sentimentality is not only a matter of titles and mottoes. The music is drenched of it; and not alone the music of the little program pieces, confessedly poetic in content and atmospheric in intention. The more abstractly treated sonatas are equally saturated, with their themes that triumph like absolute pure heroes in golden mail; their amorous sentiments wearing whitest gauze like Elsa in the first act; and their Tennysonian ardors and valors, raptures and sorrows perfectly "as advertised."

And still, MacDowell brought something into the world not hitherto present in it; not, at least, as music. Impure in style and weak in spirit though they are; indeed, of anything but the first water, a group of his compositions, particularly the ballade-like *Norse Sonata*, certain of the more vigorous *Sea Pieces*, and the atmospheric "Legend" and "Dirge" of the *Indian Suite for Orchestra*, actually have musical value. What is musical in ourselves recognizes the genuineness and the relative vividness; and close inspection corroborates the impression. These pieces are really independent of the literary ideas associated with them. "Poetic" music though they are, they do not lean upon literature for their meanings, as do so many of the compositions of Chadwick, certainly more expert a technician than Mac-Dowell. The passion of the former's *Aphrodite*, for example, resides chiefly in its title, which must be held in mind listening to the tone poem. Failing, one might easily mistake the intention of the music, and suppose it an affectionate meditation on the fine old virtues of the composer's aunt. The spirits and recklessness of his *Tam O'Shanter* are equally a matter of convention: forget them, and the "cutty sarks" are gone, not to be coaxed to return for many an hour. Kelley's amiable *New England Symphony*, too, essentially partakes of the literary: our pleasure in it being entirely dependent on our ability to keep certain pious representations of the Puritan fathers before us while it plays, and all consciousness of Rimsky and Tchaikovsky as far from us as possible. MacDowell's best pieces, however, stand on their own feet. The *Norse Sonata* has a veritable *élan*. Romantically overpitched and pronunciatory though it is, this work; and, for that matter, the good bits of the *Sea Pieces* and the *Indian Suite*, contain authentic exploitations of the medium of tone, uniquely expressive. There is a MacDowell-esque accent, facileness and sentimentality notwithstanding; some glamour or tone added by him to the world's horizon. Perhaps it is merely a faint note of sweetness, a helpless sweetness, childlike and impotent in the world, and unbalanced by robust qualities other than voluptuousness. But in all Wagner and Grieg and Chopin there is nothing quite like it, with its queer romance.

What folly, the talk of a Celtic atavism! Even the voluptuousness, the rich, heavy harmonization, has a justification from American life, with its hot suns and fertile soils, its luxury, bursting, sudden as a summer's day in March, on the crude urban civilization of the eighties and nineties. And parallels to MacDowell's queer tenderness abound in American literature. Hawthorne, Whitman, Howells, and other more recent prosemen and poets are full of it. For it has been given the American to be strong without brutality; and with a gentleness, which the riper, rounder, far more brightly polished European has not got. No, being music, MacDowell's best work could not but carry like blood in its veins, the spirit of the civilization in which it rose. One is of course at liberty to regret that representative pieces are not more richly and robustly significant, more characteristic, and abidingly interesting to those embarked on the adventure of life. Still, they are sensitive; they are a personal assimilation of European elements suffused with the cast of originality no genuine assimilation ever lacks. They constitute a beginning. And nature does nothing by bounds.

Charles Ives

THE EARLIEST of his compositions Charles E. Ives has chosen to preserve for us are a couple of quicksteps, one of them an arrangement for "kazoo" orchestra of "The Son of a Gambolier." Dating from his undergraduate days at Yale, juvenile, and pretty thoroughly in the conventions of the brass band and college glee club music of the period, they nonetheless stand prophetic of the composer's highly individual, mature, important works.

They are the expressions of the experiences of a callow American youth of the period through forms scarcely distinguishable from the simple, limited ones habitual in the composer's native Danbury and New England of the seventies and the eighties, with its little church choirs, town bands, dance and theater orchestras. And the later works by Ives, the glorious

Concord Sonata, the *Three Places in New England,* the *Suite for Theatre Orchestra,** and the happy rest, are expressions of an almost national experience, the relations between the essences affinitive to the American people past and present through forms in some instances partially, and in others almost wholly, evolved from those of the American tradition.

Nearly all Ives's characteristic work abounds in minor forms derived directly from this store. In the second number of the orchestral suite *Three Places in New England,* we hear "The British Grenadiers"—actually one of the marching songs of the American revolutionary army, which sang it in superb indifference to its text. In the first movement of the Fourth Symphony, "Old Hundred" sounds; and favorite Virginia reels and other old fiddler tunes in the second number of the theater suite, "In the Inn," and in "Barn Dance"; and "Are You Wash'd in the Blood of the Lamb" in the little cantata *General Booth Enters Heaven,* to Vachel Lindsay's words; and "Good Night, Ladies" in *Washington's Birthday;* and various patriotic tunes in the song "In Flanders Fields," etc. Their function is always a thematic one, sometimes a symbolical and an ironical one, too. But in many of these compositions—curiously abrupt in their contrasts, full of lines finely drawn, and despite their frequent brevity large in their scales of values and deeply expressive of essences and ideas clearly, boldly felt—the grand forms themselves are plainly developments and enrichments of the rudimentary musical forms favored by American society. *Putnam's Camp* is first a waltz, then a fox trot, and last—horridly polytonically and polyrhythmically enough—a military march. "In the Inn" and "Barn Dance" partake of both the jig and the reel—indeed may be said to be jigs and reels; in these instances wonderfully shrill, jagged, and rich of substance. The song "Charlie Rutlage" is an expanded frontier ballad; the adagio of

* Rosenfeld is referring to the set for theater or chamber orchestra, or *Theatre Orchestra Set,* 1904–1911. See Henry and Sidney Cowell, *Charles Ives and His Music* (New York, 1955), p. 222. The Cowells provide a chronological list of Ives's compositions.

the Fourth Symphony a hymn tune developed in fugal form. The Hawthorne movement of the *Concord Sonata* has nicely been called "proto-jazz" by John Kirkpatrick.*

It is even possible that Ives's complex harmonies and rhythms are the development of germs latent in those rudimentary forms. We refer to the clashing harmonies and polyrhythm of his entirely characteristic pieces. . . . Ives in fact is not only one of the most advanced but one of the earliest polytonalists and polyrhythmicalists. Aesthetic radicalism was in the air of his home. His father, his first teacher, experimented continuously with acoustics in the conviction that only a fraction of the means of musical expression was being used by musical art; and even invented a quarter-tone instrument; and during his own undergraduate days Ives, it seems, was already experimenting with new chord structures. Ten years in advance of the publication of the score of *Salomé,* he began a composition for the organ with a chord in D minor superimposed on one in C major. These experiments, not only with chord structures but with exotic scales and harmonic rhythms, too, met with the disfavor of his professor in music, Horatio Parker; still, Ives persisted in them, and is said to have tried out his innovations with the help of the orchestra of the old Hyperion Theatre in New Haven. And in 1903, the year of the inception of the sketches for certain of his very personal orchestral pieces, he was already writing completely atonally, thus anticipating similar European innovations; for the atonal passages in Mahler's symphonies are of later date, and the famous *Three Pieces for Pianoforte,* Opus 11, by Schoenberg, the first European pieces completely beyond the tonal system, were published only in 1911. And he has persisted upon his course. The close of *Putnam's Camp,* for example, combines contrapuntally two march tempi in different keys: the one 25 per cent, too, faster than the other. The third and wonderfully fresh section of

---

* John Kirkpatrick (1905–   ), American pianist who promoted American music. He gave the first performance of the *Concord Sonata* in New York in 1939.

Three Places in New England entitled "The Housatonic at
Stockbridge"—a sonorous cataract, easily the jewel of the suite
and one of the thrilling American orchestral compositions—
includes a rhythm for a solo violin quite independent of that of
the rest of the orchestra, and atonal and polytonal figures that
clash with the tonic harmonies of the brass and the woodwind.
The third of the three pieces comprised in the *Suite for Theatre
Orchestra,* the magical, sensuous "In the Night," exhibits another instance of Ives's extreme polyrhythmicality in its combination of a definite rhythm played by horn, bells, and celesta
with an extremely indefinite, almost unnumbered one carried
by strings and other instruments, and seems to call for the
installation in the conductor's stand of a mechanical robot able
simultaneously to beat the two extremely distinct and varied
measures. Well, these revolutionary forms of Ives's were actually
adumbrated by the practice if not by the theory of traditional
music. The American composer very early began observing that
the melodic, harmonic, and rhythmic distortions of traditional
music—frequently of English origin—produced under the stress
of excitement by church organists, village bands, country
fiddlers, frequently initiated forms truer to their feelings and to
the essences and ideas they apprehend than the more regular
performances. The untuned organ, the choir soulfully soaring
"off key," an organist excitedly striking "false" notes in his
musical *élan,* the members of a rural orchestra embroidering
individually on the rhythms and wildly playing simultaneously
in different tonalities, the clashing bands at Fourth of July
celebrations, were actually initiating living forms certainly
possessive of a freedom the cut and dried originals did not have,
and of a truth of their own. And they actually were, in spite of
the fact that the descriptive terms had not as yet been coined,
polytonic and polyrhythmical. And in many of Ives's complexly
tonic and rhythmical pieces, notably *Putnam's Camp,* "In the
Inn," and "Barn Dance," we seem to find not only realizations
of these types of forms quite unconsciously suggested by the
excited musicians, but of certain of those they shrilly initiated.

This peculiar form of Ives's, and its idiosyncrasies, would appear to be the direct consequence of the nationalistic bent of his mind. We have defined the nationalist as the emergent individual who, in becoming conscious of his own essence, simultaneously becomes conscious of the essences of his nation and its soil, and, put in touch with national ideas by his experience, invests them with worth and realizes them with love. In most instances the musical nationalist apprehends these forces in part through the traditional musical forms of his nation, often the folk music; and often spontaneously expresses his idea with a form inclusive in warp and woof of these traditional bits for the reason that he has long since absorbed them, and that the idea to which they are related calls them forth again. Now Ives is nothing if not a nationalistic American composer. The forces conveyed by his music are deeply, typically American. They are the essences of a practical people, abrupt and nervous and ecstatic in their movements and manifestations—brought into play with a certain reluctance and difficulty, but when finally loosed, jaggedly, abruptly, almost painfully released, with something of an hysteric urgency; manifested sometimes in a bucolic irony and burlesque and sometimes in a religious and mystical elevation, but almost invariably in patterns that have a paroxysmal suddenness and abruptness and violence. We recognize their kin in American humor, in political and revival meetings, whenever and wherever a wholeness has existed in Americans. We have seen their likes through much American literature; one frequently thinks of Twain and Anderson in connection with Ives, as well as of the New England writers whose ideas his music has interpreted. They are curiously like the forces of the abrupt, fierce American Nature herself, who is vernal overnight and summery two weeks after winter has passed away; like the moods of her spring freshets and the floods that pour from the porous soil; and the moods of the vaguely, confusedly, voluptuously sonorous, suddenly swelling night over the towns. Ives has indeed felt the spiritual and moral forces of America past and present not only through American folk music, but through literary and other artistic expressions, too. Perhaps the richest, most inclusive, most beautifully formed and drawn of all his pieces, the sonata, *Concord, Mass.: 1840–60,* apparently flows from an experience including a discovery of the spirit of transcendentalism as it was contained in the prophetic Emerson, the fantastic Hawthorne, the sturdily sentimental Alcotts, the deeply earth-conscious and lovingly submissive Thoreau. Another piece, the scherzo of the Fourth Symphony, flows from an experience inclusive of another sense of Hawthorne, derived in particular from *The Celestial Railroad;* while the cantata *Lincoln,* on Edwin Markham's words, indicates a creative comprehension quite as much of the figure of the great commoner as of the spirit of the Swan of Staten Island; and the many songs on the words of American poets from Whitman down to Louis Untermeyer and Fenimore Cooper, Jr., and prose men including President Hadley and even obscure newspapermen, the connection of experiences with their verse and prose. And further works demonstrate a stimulation through still other media than musical or literary ones. There is the first of the *Three Places in New England;* called "The Shaw Monument in Boston Common," it conveys a feeling partially crystallized by the Saint-Gaudens. And there is the third of them, "The Housatonic at Stockbridge"; and it refers to a crystallizing object neither artistic nor human: the sweep of the vernal river.

Thus, musically gifted, Ives has been put in the way of the sonorous expression of American life, paralleling—possibly because of the circumstance that he was used, from boyhood up, to expressing himself in terms of the traditional forms—the Russian music of Moussorgsky, the Magyar of Bartók, the Spanish of De Falla. His characteristically American, jaggedly ecstatic, variously electric and rapturous, almost invariably spasmodic sonorous forms are criticisms, like theirs, of the folk music and the folk itself. Humorous to the paroxysmal point in the cast of "Barn Dance," "In the Inn," and the scherzo of the Fourth Symphony; traversed by an acute sensuousness and voluptuousness in the case of "In the Night"; cataclysmically passionate as in "The Housatonic at Stockbridge"; or rapturous with the quality of slowly groping, reaching intellectual processes ("The Shaw Monument") or with those of religious, prophetic, mystically intuitive moments and their ingredients of insight, faith in the human impulse to perfection, knowledge of the breath of earth ("General Booth Enters Heaven," "Emerson," "The Alcotts," "Thoreau") —his whole so very American expression puts us in touch and harmony, like prose by Twain and Anderson, Cummings or Thoreau and all who have conveyed American essences with fullness and love and beauty, with forces constant in our fellows, selves, soil, and thus with the whole American idea. We feel its parts and their connections, and the breath of the whole.

And the fates have been very generous. They have not even preconfined Ives to a single medium of expression. He has been able to represent his feelings of American life in a prose that, manly as it is racily American, conveys them if not as broadly, nonetheless as truly as the musical medium does. *Essays before a Sonata,* reading-matter intended primarily as a preface or apology for his second piano sonata, the *Concord,* but isolated in a small companion volume for the reason that inclusion with the notes would have made the musical volume as cumbersome as baroque, contributes, together with the composer's very interesting assertion of and generalization about sound's muchquestioned ability to convey material, moral, intellectual, or spiritual values, four most poetically penetrating criticisms for the "subjects" of the four movements of the work. Another juicy essay of Ives's is suffixed to the volume in which he has collected a hundred and fourteen of his two hundred-odd songs. Like *Essays before a Sonata,* it also is a sort of smaller twin to the work it is intended to illuminate. This particular one, privately printed too, and now, also, the lucky windfall of secondhand music shops, is one of *the* American books: not only for the reason that it contains most of Ives's first-rate lyrics, among them "Evening" (Milton), "The New River," "Charlie

Rutlage," "Like a Sick Eagle" (Keats), "Walt Whitman," and others, but equally for the reason that its very form expresses a distinctly American mode of feeling. That form is extremely miscellaneous. It juxtaposes within a narrow compass—indeed, the volume is a sort of record of Ives's entire development—one hundred and fourteen songs very heterogeneous in point of size, since some are but a few measures long and others cover pages; very heterogeneous in point of idiom and style, for some are based on borrowed and others on original material, and some are diatonic and others impressionistic and others atonal; very heterogeneous too in point of spirit, since certain are homely, certain racy, certain humorous, and others delicate, or intimate, or spiritual; and in point of value, too, since certain are crudely or lightly drawn, and others finely, poignantly, and powerfully. But out of that miscellaneousness, extreme for all the visibility of the personal thread in the intensely disparate fabrics, an idea greets us: the idea that all things possessing breath of their own, no matter how dissimilarly and to what differing degrees, are ultimately consonant. That is good Americanism, and the post-script but re-expresses that feeling and that idea in the maxim, "Everything from a mule to an oak, which nature has given life, has a right to that life; whether they [its values] be approved by a human mind or seen with a human eye, is no concern of that right." And when the prose runs: "I have not written a book for money, for fame, for love, for kindlings. I have merely cleaned house. All that is left is on the clotheslines," we merely recognize anew the American speaking with the spirit of the Artist.

That is Ives: the American as an artist, as a composer, and the foremost of the Americans who have expressed their feeling of life in musical forms; for even Parker's substance is not as mature as some of Ives's, itself unexcelled as yet in point of maturity of substance and richness of feeling by that of any of the younger men. The *Concord Sonata* indeed remains the solidest piece of piano music composed by an American. Its beauty and its significance still surprise us; they still are one of the wonders of the last years, which have revealed them. For

Ives had been forced to create in a complete solitude, without external support or recognition. Though individuals able to appreciate the works of literary and pictorial artists as fresh and as significant as his musical ones were not lacking during the first quarter of this century, the musically highly cultured individual was still extremely rare in the American ranks. Lucky for the composer that he was the manager of an insurance company! What porridge he would have had had he been a professional musician can be discerned from the fact that only yesterday one of the white-headed boys of American music, a voice of the official musicality and its conventional criteria, publicly affirmed that those composers who wrote atonically or polytonically did so merely because they were too untalented to compose in the old tonal schemes. But with the multiple appearance of the musically highly cultured individual—composer, performer, or amateur—in the United States a phenomenon one of the most happy of all of those of the last decades, the raising of the curtain on Ives's long-obscured works became almost inevitable. Some intelligence seems to lead the individual almost somnambulistically toward the food he requires for his existence and to bring it toward him, and what comes into the world as an idea does not go lost. In any case, up the curtain went on this good "business man's" music. Henry Bellamann* wrote about it and called it to the attention of the Pro-Musica. The Pro-Musica and later Nicholas Slonimsky, the Pan-Americans, and Copland had some of his pieces performed at their concerts. Henry Cowell began publishing and recording others. The discovery is still an esoteric one. No conductor of a major orchestra has still either seen fit or been able to perform Ives's orchestral pieces.† The Second Sonata has never yet been

---

* Henry Bellamann (1882–1945), American author and pianist. Bellamann wrote the first serious study of Ives, "Charles Ives, The Man and the Music," *Musical Quarterly*, January, 1933. He was also the author of the best-selling novel *King's Row*.

† The Third Symphony was finally performed on May 12, 1946. It won a Pulitzer Prize in 1947.

heard in its entirety. And only a few of the songs have as yet figured in song recitals. Still, the curtain *is* up. The music is beginning to be accessible not only in printed but in record form, to the benefit of a world larger than the narrowly musical one.

For artists such as Ives can help enormously to create a democratic society in America. In investing American essences with worth and presenting them with beauty, they help to convey the national idea as it actually relates these warring and still cognate forces: thus providing a matchlessly practical basis for mutual adjustment.

Aaron Copland

MEANWHILE, an even intenser force is at work, adjusting men vigorously to a rapidly changing environment. Compositions of a marked individuality have recently begun appearing in America at the hands of Americans; and individuality, we know, is the sign and condition of the strong natural impulse. Great freedom is not, of course, to be found in the works of Copland, Chavez, and Varèse, the members of this recent, most advanced class. Like so much American life, American music is still in bonds. We have no "great composers." But a certain warm integrity of style and independence in the release of form is current. New experiences in the sonorous field are forthcoming. Most important of all, music is commencing to represent the forces of American life and interpret them in a large way; to place us in what might have been a "shrieking wilderness of steel," but is now an intelligible world. To be sure, a certain amount of integrity, novelty, and vision are present in the examples of both the preceding classes of music, the eclectic no less than the traditional. But among the eclectics, the immersion in the stream of things is not direct: "protected"; and among the traditionalists, it is conservative, along racial lines. Only among the "moderns" is the contact quite spontaneous, in response to new, originally authoritative promptings; hence, it is only in their work that the elements of music appear entirely refreshed from the bath of life.

We meet this latest, most advanced sort of product, at first in American music, in the compositions of Aaron Copland. For while Copland's work is plainly that of a young man, wanting mellowness, wide inclusivity, and the warmest intensity, it is indubitably autonomous; and symbolic of the New World on every hard green page of it. We do not know where it came from. We merely know that we have not met it before; at least, not in the guise of sonority; for it has a certain likeness to other things encountered in other spheres of life; and that it places us immensely alertly in the stream of metallic, modern American things.

The earmark of Copland's music is leanness, slenderness of sound, sharpened by the fact that it is found in connection with a strain of grandiosity. For we associate grandiosity with a Wagnerian fatness, thickness, and heaviness; and Copland's concerto, and the finale of his symphony,* perhaps the two most elevated of his compositions, give us the pleasant shock of finding it both lithe and imponderous. The jarring piano and strings of the recent severe little trio, sound hard, like stone or metal things. Part of this general astringency flows from Copland's preference for shrill, cock-crowing, naked effects, and part from a predilection for staccato themes, with wide intervals and defiant flourishes. No doubt, it is to be connected with the style of the later Stravinsky, indubitably influential on the young composer. It is quite possible that, had Stravinsky not recently taken to writing archaic series of major triads, we might not find Copland using them as extensively as he has done in his sober recent piece for string quartet (later rewritten for full string orchestra). And it is a fact that, like Copland, several contemporary composers, notably Hindemith, affect an archaic severity and asperity of style; preferring the harsher,

* Rosenfeld is referring to Copland's Symphony No. 1 (1928).

sharper, more grinding and nasal tones to the softer, more mellifluous and vibrant string sounds loved by Wagner and the impressionists. Still, Copland's general slenderness is distinct and eminently individual. It is wiry. If he is a purist, he is an American one.

The whole of Copland's music, slow movements as well as rapid, are originally lively. A factor in this liveliness is the decided motoriness. By this, one means something more than mere rhythmicality, for the concept of rhythmicality is included in the concept of music: there being no music without continuity of texture, logical succession and flow, unity and variety. What one means by this motoriness of Copland's, is its strong kinesis, its taut, instinctive "go." Wistful or burlesque, slow or fast, his pieces have enormous snap. Many of his rhythmic schemes are of the greatest originality. Even though certain of his favorite polyrhythms, the slow three-eighths plus five-eighths of the intermezzo of the suite *Music for the Theatre,* and the fast three-eighths plus five-eighths of the body of the concerto, are synthesized from jazz, Copland's method of piling them up is his own. The commercial music, of course, does not sustain these polyrhythms, sandwiching them in between customary measures, and shorting them. Copland however lets them have their will, sustaining them for long, thrilling, dizzy stretches. Other of his lively rhythms are equally personal, the hiccoughing beat of the scherzo of the symphony, for example; iterated with a mad mechanic joy. And, whether careering over roofs or slowly balancing itself, this music remains a thing of abrupt, still logical changes, under high speed.

Another characteristic is the presence of control. Copland's music strikingly corroborates the theory that of all futilities, that of preaching about the necessity of discipline is the most futile, since discipline inheres in strength itself; and no strength comes unaccompanied by a direction to material, and a guiding sense of the extent of its own effectuality. Copland is one of the most critical of those at work today in the field of music. In fineness his sense of his materials is scarcely second to that of any contemporary musician; and we find him selecting ideas and discerning the potentialities of his subjects with an ever increasing acumen. It is only his earliest pieces that occasionally suffer from prolixity and rhythmical rigidity: in particular, certain dances of his ballet, *Grogh*. The mass of his compositions, even the more jazzy, relatively inconsequential recent ones, the violin pieces, say, are made of finely appreciated material well put together. Copland seems to have a developed capacity for conceiving music coolly in terms of the technical problem. The distinct architecturality of his best pieces reveals it. The concertos, the recent pieces for strings, are primarily structures of interplaying forms, volumes, movements. Not that they are not largely expressive. The first part of the concerto especially has a penetrating lyricism, something of passionate extension; and the string piece, representative of Copland's leanly grand style, is elevated like the prelude to *Lohengrin*. Nor are these architectural pieces invariably severe. Copland has a taste for hot colors and garish jazziness, perhaps a happy consequence of his oriental-American psyche; and his work is exciting with all sorts of percussive brazen brilliance. Nonetheless, the great interest of his music remains the architectural one, the interest of the independent, projected, self-sufficient object. And in their structurality, their faithfulness to the line of strength, his tonal edifices resemble nothing so much as steel cranes, bridges, and the frames of skyscrapers before the masons smear them with their stonework.

Of course, this musicianship of Copland's is still in its nubile stage. His gift is decidedly proficient but small, as yet so immature that it makes the impression not so much of something human, as of something coltlike: all legs, head, and frisking hide; cantering past on long uncertain stilts, the body oddly small in proportion to the motor power, the head huge and as wooden and devilish as that of a rocking horse. It's an amusing affair, in the incompletude of organs, limbs, and skin; charming with the awkwardness of the large young thing not long from the mother. Impressive, too: since it's so conspicuously the colt of American brass and momentum, of all that's swift and daring, aggressive, and unconstrained in our life; blood brother of the new architecture and the other constructive flights of the bold temperaments. And still, it is a colt. With all his grandiosity and *élan*, Copland has not yet found a largely symbolic and inclusive form for his gift; or achieved, symphony and concerto notwithstanding, an expression of prime importance. A certain meagerness of experience, a uniformity in his moods is not to be overlooked. Indeed, and in spite of his recent sallies in string and piano trio music, he may almost be said to have only two tempers, and to swing regularly from one to the other. The first, a rather wistful pastoral mood, a mood of lonely beginnings, early April afternoons, gray clouds, gurgling frogs, and perhaps a single, always single, blackbird, has contributed the first movement of the symphony, the third movement of *Music for the Theatre*, the violin nocturne, the introduction to the concerto, and the flute and clarinet song, *As It Fell Upon a Day*. The other, a wild, extravagant, cackling state, full of motor-madness, the old cat and fiddlesticks and the lunatic moon, is the progenitor of the early piece for string quartet, the second movement of the symphony, the second and fourth sections of *Music for the Theatre*, the violin serenade, the choral setting of Ezra Pound's "An Immortality," and the body of the concerto. Of course, other moods do register in Copland's music. Neither the finale of the symphony, the recent piece for strings, or the reflections on a Jewish theme for piano trio, fit into either of the dominant categories. Nor are the realizations of the two states ever monotonous or unprogressive. Indeed, they have become impressively stronger with the passing of the few years in which Copland's career has run. One has merely to compare the little song after Barnefield with the massive opening of the concerto, and the early piece for string quartet with the body of the work for piano and orchestra, to gauge the wide extent of his growth. By and large, nonetheless, Copland's work is contained in them; the more the pity since both moods are fundamentally incomplete; twin eccentric halves of the deeply swung state of feeling. The one is nostalgic; the other ironical.

To a certain degree, their almost absolute monarchy over the composer is to be ascribed to the fact that he found both of them, or at least their idiom, in jazz; the nostalgic one proceeding more from the blues, the ironical one more from jazz proper. Copland is one of the composers who have laid hold of the norms of our popular music, and utilized them for artistic purposes. But the mere fact that both are adumbrated by jazz, does not entirely account for their grip on him. That must be subjectively conditioned; for if Copland has helped himself to jazz effects, he has always done so independently, and inventively; anything but slavishly. A great difference exists between his use of them, and that of the great number of his contemporaries who have dug in the new mine. The European experimenters, for example, have done very little with what they have found. The music they have made with jazz rhythms and effects is of small actual value. The ragtime section of *Parade,* the ballet of Satie's that started the movement to convert rag into musical values, is scarcely more than a quotation, without considerable ingenuity or distinction. Hindemith's brutal jazz pages lack wit and smartness; the score of Krenek's *Jonny Spielt Auf* is an hastily clapped-together affair, of little intrinsic interest. The most successful European jazz music is undoubtedly to be found in Milhaud's ballet, *La Création du Monde,* with its lengthy section based on a fox-trot measure. But while this work is one of the best sustained and most charming of the prolific Frenchman's innumerable compositions, the jazz section is characteristically soft and homesick; almost timid in comparison with the body of Copland's concerto and its exuberantly piled-up polyrhythms.

The American parallels of these experiments are equally indifferent. Gershwin's *Rhapsody in Blue,* Piano Concerto, and *An American in Paris* have found a good deal of popular favor; and Gershwin himself is assuredly a gifted composer of the lower, unpretentious order; yet there is some question whether his vision permits him an association with the artists. He seems to have little feeling for reality. His compositions drowse one in a pink world of received ideas and sentiments. The *Rhapsody in Blue* is circus music, pre-eminent in the sphere of tinsel and fustian. In daylight, nonetheless, it stands vaporous with its secondhand ideas and ecstasies; its old-fashioned Lisztian ornament and brutal, calculated effects, not so much music, as jazz dolled up. Gershwin's concerto has an equal merit. The opening of the second movement, the blues section, is charming and atmospheric; but the work is utterly bare of the impulsion toward a style which every living thing exhibits; and, like the *Rhapsody*, scarcely transcends the level of things made to please an undiscriminating public. *An American in Paris* is poorer in themes than either of its predecessors; and when, after losing its way, the music suddenly turns into the lively somewhat meaningless sort of flourish usually supplied the dramatic finales of musical comedy first-acts, we seem to hear Gershwin's instrument, like Balaam's ass, reproving the false prophet; directing him to the sphere congenial to his gift.

The experiments of William Grant Still with jazz and the blues compare favorably with those of Gershwin; but the difference between his jazz music and Copland's is still huge. For Copland has actually absorbed jazz motives and correlated them with the developments of the past. Hence, the difference between his music and that of the other experimenters. For while they have taken jazz much as they found it, that is, impregnated with a superficial spirit, Copland has driven it far beyond its current uses, and substituted the expression of an almost Rabelaisian irony for its customary parody and blandishment.

For this reason, then, we find ourselves unwilling to believe that, if Copland's still dominant two moods are fragmentary and eccentric, they are so because he was constrained by their origins. No; if they are still slightly unsatisfactory to what in ourselves demands a maturer experience, it is undoubtedly because in Copland we have the youth of an original musicianship itself. What indeed is more specifically boyish than the ambivalence of feelings of exception, separation, and reckless power and affirmation bordering upon the satiric and the unconcerned; of the sense of being outside and under things, and the sense of dancing on top of them in sheer mechanical exuberance?

A development, with its consequent amplification of meaning, and extension of the number of patterns in his art casts its shadow before it; in the string music, in the etching-like trio (so much dryer than Bloch's opulent Hebraicisms) ; particularly in the last movement of the symphony. By no means his most successful page, this movement is extremely suggestive of the larger personality, the more earthfast, inclusive form, potential in the man and his musicianship. It was written, significantly, to gather and resolve the contradictory moods of the preceding introduction and scherzo, characteristically nostalgic and mechanical, and it embodies a feeling of things neither beneath them nor above them, but powerfully one with them and released through them; reconciling the two warring halves of a personality and clearing the way for its growth. True, the form of this finale is stiff; wanting the elegance and logic of the tender plaintive introduction and hiccoughing, jerking, machinery-mad scherzo; and leaving the brilliant little symphony half suspended in the air. Nonetheless, for all its abrupt transitions and lumbering volumes, the movement touches deep stratas. It is both grandiose and ardent, holding some state of being that is of our swift mechanical day and yet superior to it, in control of it; and converting man's new obstreperous, mechanical arms into agents of beatitude. And it gives us a new sense of what is working around in Copland, and what his music is about. That control of the new environment, that attempt to humanize it, to be one with it and make it express human values—is it not strangely analogous to something in which the whole administrative, thinking, executive community is engaged? Is Copland, struggling to handle mechanical, impersonal rhythms in a deep, exalted spirit, anything but an integral part of a movement attempting the same in practical fields? For us, he most indisputably is not. But then his position is merely that of any independent musician, any important artist. The psyche of the artist is an integral part of the battlefield of life; perhaps the battlefield made apparent. Its conflicts, its defeats and victories are those of the community essentialized, objectified. It is the cross section. To know what is going on in the life of a civilization, to measure its force and direction, you have but to examine its art.

George Gershwin

GEORGE GERSHWIN'S RHAPSODIES and other pieces in the symphonic forms have inspired certain critics to classify him as a good "vulgar" composer. They mean to indicate that he is a composer of the class represented by Chabrier: that, like the exuberant author of the *España* rhapsody and the *Suite Pastorale,* he organizes musical motives popular in origin or in character and infused with the lighter essences, in light symphonic molds, and while conserving the original salt and earthy charm of the material expresses all the common man's humorous, ironical, buoyantly erotic, and sentimental feelings of life with it. "Notre Chabrier à nous,"* one critic, adapting d'Indy's epithet for Debussy, affectionately called him.

This judgment is extremely uncritical, exhibiting a defective vision of good "vulgar" music and of Gershwin's ambitious product and the difference between them. That many of the expressions found in our Broadway paladin's two rhapsodies and his Piano Concerto, his *An American in Paris* and his *Cuban Overture,* formerly the *Rumba,* are popular and American, is certain. Not the earliest symphonic works merging or attempting to merge the expressions of Broadway with traditional and personal expressions—for Satie's *Parade* and a number of the pieces of the Parisian Six represented this tendency

* " 'Our own Chabrier.' "

before the *Rhapsody in Blue*—Gershwin's absolute and programmatic compositions are distinguished by their frequent,
sometimes vivacious and adroit, at other times coarse and
brutal, exploitations of the jazz idioms, rhythms, and colors.
That the result is representative of a certain kind of American
is also certain; their immense popular success is one proof of it.
Yet to qualify as a vulgar composer and rank with Chabrier,
Albéniz, Glinka, and even with Milhaud and Auric at their
best, a musician has to "compose" his material, to sustain and
evolve and organize it to a degree sufficient to bring its essences,
their relationships, their ideas, to expression. And that Gershwin has accomplished to no satisfactory degree, at least not in
any of the larger forms he has up to the present time given the
public.

Take any one of his ambitious products. It is only very
superficially a whole, actually a heap of extremely heterogeneous minor forms and expressions. Individually these minor
forms and expressions, themes, melodies, rhythms, harmonies,
figures, ornaments, are frequently piquant and striking, and
richly dissonant, and brilliantly colored. But they are extremely
disparate, first of all in point of freshness. Some are the raciest
of rhythmic and coloristic neologisms, effective exploitations of
various elements of the jazz idiom or original material. Others
are very worn and banal. Again, they remain equally disparate
in point of style, some of them being popularly American in
essence or gaily, brightly Yiddish, and others impressionistic, or
vaguely grand-operatic, or reminiscent of the melodramatic
emphasis and *fioritura* of Liszt, or Chopinesque. And they also
remain disparate in point of quality, since a number of them
have sharpness, jauntiness, dash, indicating a perhaps shallow
but distinct vitality, while others are weak, soft, cheap, representing a vitality duller and lower than that at which interest
commences—so soft and cheap indeed that in comparison with
them the best of Gershwin's ideas, mauger the fact that very few
of them have the delicacy and power of first-rate stuff and that
his treatment of jazz is by no means highly sensitive, appear
almost the expression of another man.

Too, these expressions, for the most part, are insufficiently extended and frequently fizzle out. By and large, the Gershwin symphonic piece is a lot of preluding, a succession of fairly unrelated advances toward a whole that, if at times it appears to come into being, never sustains its existence very long. The composer introduces subjects upon subjects, mostly short ones. But rarely does he do anything with them, rarely relating them to one another so that they complete each other and advance the interest of the whole piece. Most of them remain static, mere phrases, which he either ornaments with Lisztian *fioritura*, or repeats with ever greater dynamics, or sets soaring in a series of sequences that, ascending by half-tones, recall the worst of Wagnerian *Steigerungen*. Long rhythms rarely appear. Gershwin at best has what might be termed merely "local" rhythm, due to his keen ear for irregular popular dance measures, especially the Charleston beat. But of actual movement, actual organization, his compositions are pretty bare. Whether this is due to the extreme heterogeneity of his material, so extreme as to prevent coordination, we cannot say. It must suffice us to remark that no integrating principle has borne on them, bringing them into relationship with one another, establishing with them a moving, developing form made up of emotionally related parts. Upswells of creative energy momentarily manifest themselves, it is true. Yet they seldom break over and flow into new developments, variations, ideas. Sometimes, for periods, wholes with some direction, some determination, make as if to appear. But they never sustain themselves.

Take the juiciest and most entertaining of Gershwin's concert works, the F-major Piano Concerto. It commences with a number of disconnected flourishes. At length the composer comes to grips with his material: the first original theme enters, syncopated, impassioned, on the piano. It is repeated by the saxophone in a low register and by the piano, and after short divertissements, twice by the *tutti*, the last time with decided dash. A certain tension has been created, impelling one to look forward to some sort of contrast and development. What now follows, however, is an irrelevant theme, very popular, and in a

Charleston measure. For a period the music flows. Sometimes lyrical, sometimes merely rhetorical, the page is one of Gershwin's most sustained and charmingly orchestrated expressions. But it, too, stops short of completion. And after a brief polyphonic passage the first theme is restated with inflations recalling some of the grandiose effects of the Capitol Theatre, and the movement ends inconsequentially with more irrelevant flourishes, leaving one with the feeling that something which started to happen has not come off. Still, tension sufficient to make one look forward to the second movement hangs over from the composition's beginning. Again, for a minute, one is engaged. The second movement begins with an interesting, muted, atmospheric treatment of a blues theme; but after the melody has been stated and we have been led to look forward to some inevitable development, the composer introduces some more material which one would call similar to the original blues theme were it not so very much more inferior to that original theme in quality. All tension has disappeared. The impulse of the beginning is entirely let down. The weak material grows pathetic amid strains of the Liebestod. And the movement is concluded with a nostalgic little coda made from the "blues" theme. Hope that the composer is going to get somewhere or can get somewhere has entirely dwindled, and though the last movement begins vigorously with a good scherzando theme for the xylophone, one is not surprised to find the movement largely a recapitulation of old material, leading up to a restatement of the original theme more grandiosely inflated even than any of the preceding ones and concluding inconsequentially with further flourishes.

While the succeeding composition, the tripartite *An American in Paris,* starts somewhat more energetically, it, too, has no real movement. Somewhere during the second section the composition stops advancing, and it too concludes with mere meaningless recapitulations; and with the exception of the amusing passage imitative of French motor horns, the material itself is less attractive than that of the ritzy concerto.

Thus, deficiently expressive of essences and of ideas, even the lighter, saltier, more comic ones that are the vulgar American composer's objects, these strings of melodies and rhythms put one in touch with little that is real. Momentarily we feel the forces of ambition and desire: imperious, unmitigated appetites, yearnings for tenderness, intoxications flowing from the stimulation of novel, luxurious surroundings, Parisian, Cuban, Floridian, from the joy of feeling oneself an American—Americanism apparently conceived as a naïve, smart, inept, good-natured form of being, happily and humorously shared by other good fellows like oneself—and from a gaminlike eroticism. But neither they nor their relations are explicit or steady. True, at moments in the Piano Concerto and *An American in Paris,* an idea, curiously enough a tragic one, of an inevitable chaos, a predestinately incomplete and unsuccessful connection between complementary forces, feebly glimmers on one. But its glimmer is fickle and disappears as the form itself loses its impulse and falls into idle repetitions and meaningless flourishes. The whole, if it points to anything, points to a creative energy too feeble and unenduring to afford sustained contact with reality and a mind that, lacking creative power, remains the prisoner of by no means idealistic dreams. It is impossible to hear Gershwin's symphonic music without being from time to time moved by its grandiloquences to conceive—with the aspect of things having some immensely flattering, glorifying bearing upon ourselves—of towers of fine gold rising amid Florida palms, splendiferous hotel foyers crowded with important people and gorgeous women *décolletées jusqu'à là,* and immediately contingent upon paradise; or rosy banks of nymphs amorously swooning amid bells of rose-pink tulle. A tawny oriental city acknowledges us as its conqueror in the sundown, and the superb naked woman who stands above the city gate, starred with the diamond in her tresses, descends and advances toward us with exalted words and gestures, hailing our peerlessness while we ourselves recognize in her the one we have always sought and loved. Are these atrocious dreams our own? Possibly, but they have grown articulate through this music.

That these pieces are characteristic American productions is not to be doubted. Their spirit unfortunately makes them so, since weakness of spirit, possibly as a consequence of the circumstance that the New World attracted the less stable human types, remains an American condition. It makes of the American business man often a poor organizer and the American artist frequently an advertising man. With spirit, both types would create a material and a spiritual order, based upon human relationships, the one with practical, the other with aesthetic, means. For spirit apprehends actual forces and their ideas and creates a human relationship, a society, with them. But materialism sees nothing but its personal objects, and investing them with bogus glamours and glitters, perpetuates the disorder, the waste, the anarchy, the solitude, that are favorable to its limitless expansion and gratification. Thus, most American art is advertising, glorifying the material objects and fanning up the appetite directed upon them; and this category of aesthetic products is dangerously close to that of George Gershwin. Indeed, we are tempted to call Gershwin the laureate of musical advertisers, perhaps the most genial of them all, but the head of their company: the musician of the materialistic age that saw the bloom of the worst business and best advertising America has ever endured, the jazz age. True, one of that materialistic period's most poetic representatives, the mercurial Zelda Fitzgerald, has with indubitable authority declared in *Save Me the Waltz:* "Vincent Youmans wrote the music for those twilights just after the war. They were wonderful. . . . They lay above the streets like a white fog off a swamp. Through the gloom, the whole world went to tea." Nevertheless we still dare call Gershwin the typical jazz musician.

Of course it is possible that the idea of the musicians who called him our vulgar composer was entirely prophetic and that Gershwin is not yet but will be the musical interpreter of what the ordinary American feels in his genuine living moments. The event is certainly not without the bounds of possibility.

Gershwin is still a relatively young man. There is no question of his talent. The musical language is natively his own: one can see he was not introduced to it yesterday, that he knows it and feels and likes it, and has a decided knack with it. He has spontaneity, an ear for complex rhythms, a feeling for luscious, wistful, dissonantly harmonized melodies. Above all, he has a distinct warmth; and if the main honors for the symphonic exploitation and idealization of jazz have gone to Milhaud for *La Création du Monde,* to Honegger for his Piano Concertino, and to Copland for his Piano Concerto, rather more than to himself, he at least stands almost gigantically among the other sons of Tin-Pan Alley, Bennett, Levant, Grofé,* who have grappled with more or less symphonic forms. At least he has a veritable urgence and a spirit of endeavor that commands sympathy.

Only, we remain unconvinced that he has sufficient of the feeling of the artist. The artist's remoteness from material objects, his suspended, selfless, aesthetic touch of them, his tension and experience of order, and his impulse to organize his material in conformity with that experience—we have not as yet caught more than a fleeting glance of them in Gershwin's products.

We remain obliged to him mostly for *Funny Face* and his other smart musical shows. His talent burgeons in them.

Porgy and Bess, produced since this book passed into the hands of its publishers, but fortifies one's conviction of Gershwin's shortness of the artist's feeling. The score is a loose aggregation of somewhat heavily instrumented numbers in many instances conforming to the style of American Negro music, especially the blues, and in others to that of the Puccini grand opera. Some of these pieces, for example the entire thunderstorm music, are very bad and empty; others—one thinks particularly of the lullaby and the fugue in Scene I, the antiphonies of chorus and solos in the scene of the wake, the street calls in Act II, and certain popular numbers like Porgy's

* Robert Russell Bennett, Oscar Levant, Ferde Grofé.

song, "I Got Plenty o' Nuttin'," embody musical, melodic, or rhythmical ideas, and have a quality and sensuous charm and flavor. An aggrandized musical show, the opera contains triple the music of the ordinary one, even the ordinary one of Gershwin's make, and in some spots music of triple the interest of the best of the species. But the score sustains no mood. There is neither a progressive nor an enduring tension in it. The individual numbers spurt from a flat level, and ending, leave one largely where they picked one up. Nor do they communicate a reality, either the rich, authentic quality of the Negro or the experience of Porgy the pathetic cripple who unexpectedly gets his woman and rejoices and suffers with her and then at last loses her, or of Bess, the weak victim of the flesh and the devil. It would seem as if Gershwin knew chiefly stage Negroes and that he very incompletely felt the drama of the two protagonists. At moments there is a warmth and emotion in the expression that indicates some sense of the experience. Ultimately, nonetheless, the expression lies in conventional patterns, as if the feeling of the composer had been too timid to mold musical forms in accord with itself and had succumbed to conventional and, alas, sure-fire gestures of the musical theater. Long before the conclusion one feels the music has got one nowhere new and true. What endures is largely the splendid sense of the artistic spirit of the Negro singers and dancers, who give themselves 100 per cent.

Roger Sessions

ROGER SESSIONS follows Rudhyar; and allays an uncertainty inevitable in view of the fact that Loeffler,* Ornstein, and Rudhyar are all three deracinated men, transplanted from the Old World to the New. This is the doubt whether the eclecticism of much American music may not flow from the early and

---

* Charles Martin Loeffler (1861–1935), a violinist and composer, frequently identified with impressionism. His best-known work is *A Pagan Poem.*

therefore strong European associations of many of its authors? Rudhyar was a youth, Loeffler a full-grown man when they arrived in the States. While Ornstein was only nine in the year of his hegira, he was a small boy bristling with experience not merely of the Russian Pale, but of the St. Petersburg conservatory sphere as well. Where then is the illogicality, one hears oneself arguing, if these individuals are divided and their music hybrid? What indeed would be more *natural* than that their work should constitute a variation of contemporary European music rather more than an independent and American thing? During formative years they were in contact with the Old World soil; and might it not be possible to declare that integrity of impulse and purity of style are inextricably connected in America with American birth, perhaps with descent from long acclimatized stocks; in any case with adolescence in an environment superficially, linguistically, germane to the growing artist?

This argument falls flat before the phenomenon of Roger Sessions. Sessions comes of the oldest Puritan New England stock; and still neither Loeffler nor Ornstein nor Rudhyar is essentially more eclectic in his ideas and forms than he. (Later, Copland, Chavez, and Varèse will supply other disproofs of the contention of those tempted to identify integrity with hundred percentism, or pretend that America is not the native soil of anyone who *feels* it to be his.) Meanwhile, it is important to observe how frankly Roger Sessions has done his recent severely simple, perhaps most valuable work in the shadow of the later Stravinsky. Indeed Loeffler is not a bit more the sectary of the Wagnerizing Frenchmen, or Ornstein the sectary of the earlier Stravinsky, or Rudhyar of Scriabin, than Sessions of the composer of the *Symphonies for Wind Instruments,* the *Octuor,* and *Oedipus Rex.* Not that this young old New Englander has duplicated Stravinsky, or made literature of him. In these respects he is sharply to be distinguished from several other young men, among them one George Antheil, a great composer in Parisian literary circles. Antheil's well-advertised *Ballet*

Mécanique is a skyscraper built of girders synthesized from *Les Noces, Le Sacre,* and *Petrouchka,* and dependent for support on associated ideas. At best it is a clumsy musical illustration; a simile for factories, downtown New York streets, the beat of American life or the experience of *subvia dolorosa;* devoid of the freshness of impulse or the structurality that gives such humble musical illustrations as the tone poems of Smetana their charm. And though a certain musicianliness is evident at many turns of his work, the creative force of the *signor* Antheil remains as yet too embryonic to be clearly discerned. No, Sessions has not had to call on flashy literary associations to give his helpless efforts significance and cohesion. His symphony,* for example, is an independent, self-definite structure, working as music and not as a little auxiliary powerhouse or subway train. Indeed, there is reason for holding the second movement of this composition superior to any of the instrumental pieces of Stravinsky that so largely helped determine its form and manner. There is more warmth and necessity in it than in the *Octuor* or the concerto or any other of the experiments of the archaizing Russian. Only, we cannot help feeling that while Sessions at present figures conspicuously in the field of music, he nevertheless does so as a winsome young pachyderm shambling in the lee of its parent.

The influence of Stravinsky on Sessions is two-fold. One part of it bears on general aesthetics, and is anti-religious in tendency. All attempts to continue in the exalted and ecstatic style begun by Beethoven, developed by Wagner, and perhaps abused by Strauss, Mahler, Scriabin, and the twentieth-century romanticists, are condemned by it as bad, at least as unrealistic. To such elevated, excited expressions it instinctively prefers the humbler, dryer, and more disabused manner of much eighteenth-century music. There has always been a strongly eighteenth-century cast on the music of Stravinsky, ever since *Petrouchka:* something of clarity, pertness, and levity; but the ascendancy

* The Sessions symphony Rosenfeld mentions is the First (1927).

which the anti-religious, hard-boiled aesthetic has recently and most sensationally gained over him is to be attributed to the strongly collective trend of present society under the leadership of the U.S.S.R. and the U.S.A. The hard-boiled aesthetic is essentially an expression of collectivism. Feelings of humility, anonymity, and helplessness bring man out of his conceit and into sympathy with and understanding of his fellows; hence collectivism's abhorrence of all grandiosity, exaltation, and sumptuousness of style. Like all radical tendencies, this aesthetic of Stravinsky's had been gathering momentum long before its assumption of power in our day. Its father, at least its parent as far as the present is concerned, is Moussorgsky, himself roughly contemporary with Wagner. The style of *Boris Godunov* is as humble and popular as that of *Tristan* is exalted and emphatic; and characteristically gives the conspicuous role not to beplumed and clanking heroes and heroines, but to the great anonymous chorus. Already in the 1890's, coincident with the rise of Richard Strauss and the titanism of *Ein Heldenleben,* this abhorrence of the heroic and unreserved, and preference of the unemphatic and unpretentious, was exerting its influence on Debussy in Paris. A stage of its progress indubitably is to be found in the simplicity and relative taciturnity of *Pelléas et Mélisande,* mixed though it is with ultraromantic jewelry, dreaminess, and feeling of rarity and aloofness.

Then it triumphed in Stravinsky, in all his uncertainty one of the most uncompromisingly determined musicians of our time. (While the effect of Satie must be allowed, it cannot be aligned with that of Stravinsky, for the reason that while Satie was a very charming musician, he had neither the Russian's freshness nor strength.) Beginning as the most promising pupil of Rimsky-Korsakov—Stravinsky is spiritually the descendant of Moussorgsky's group—and as a composer of somewhat religious leanings, Stravinsky steadily evolved in the hard-boiled direction. *Petrouchka* is significantly popular and humble in style; *Le Sacre du Printemps* expresses the strata of man where he is still the unindividuated herd-being; and in the uncompromisingly polytonic *Renard, Les Noces,* and *L'Histoire du Soldat,* the disabused, dry aesthetic dominates. In the more recent concerto, Sonata, *Octuor,* Serenade, and the cantata *Oedipus Rex,* an archaicizing tendency, often the companion of an anti-religious one, puts in its appearance.

It is precisely these later works of Stravinsky that have so profoundly impressed Roger Sessions. Sessions' symphony, to date his largest, most affecting and engaging work, is eminently "music for every day" in the spirit of *Renard* and *L'Histoire du Soldat;* and as such distinguished from all preceding pieces of American music, predominantly exalted and grandiose in their conceptions. One doesn't feel the temple dome over it. It seems to live in the atmosphere of weekdays, serious, sober, but never ritualistic. There are no hot clashing colors, no heavy emphasis, no Wagnerian intensifications and ardors and exaltations in this symphony. The material is stark and the outline strong. Sessions' polytonality and polyphony are uncompromising, and sometimes harsh; his whole manner is abrupt and somewhat uncouth.

Certainly, the bare fact that Sessions has written a piece of music eminently dry in spirit does not mark him as a follower of Stravinsky. Aesthetics are everybody's; and hard-boiledism is probably the most appropriate to American life. What does couple Sessions with Stravinsky, is the fact that his little symphony pays homage not only to Stravinsky the prophet but to Stravinsky the technician. We have called the Russian's influence on Sessions two-fold; and if one part bears on general aesthetic matters, the other bears on methods of composition. Several of Sessions' typical processes resemble tactics personal to Stravinsky. Now, a tendency to eschew chromaticism and orientalism in melody; and a practice of letting counterpoint bear the brunt of composition, are not in themselves sufficiently exclusive to Stravinsky, characteristic of him though they are, to warrant our calling all other composers exhibiting them partisans of his. But when they appear in company with the very Stravinskian strategy of using unit groups of eighth-notes irregularly divided, we cannot help feeling that the musician combining them has more than gone to school to the classicizing Russ. Besides, eclecticism is an attitude familiar in Sessions. He began under the wing of his master Ernest Bloch. The work which won him his first renown, the incidental music to Andreyev's *Black Maskers,* was full of the warm passion, vehemence, and sardonic grimaces characteristic of the composer of *Schelomo.* This homage was not at all remarkable since nearly all composers begin as scholars of some older man: Bach as Buxtehude's, Beethoven as Mozart's and Haydn's, Wagner as Weber's and Meyerbeer's. What nonetheless *was* singular, was the circumstance that when Sessions broke away from the dominance of Bloch, and should, by rule, have gone his own and solitary way, he merely exchanged one influence for another, substituting the overlordship of Stravinsky for that of the vehement late romanticist. His eclecticism embraces not only contemporary musical forms. If the symphony shows the presence of Stravinsky, the *Three Choral Preludes for Organ* and the Piano Sonata have a decided archaistic cast: the former pointing back to Bach and verging on the scholastic; the first and third movements of the latter bearing a disquieting resemblance to the nocturne-style of Chopin. And while a pervasive passion might conceivably make one overlook the eclecticism of these pieces, none is present to any satisfactory measure.

Still, if Sessions is an eclectic composer, he is also an admirable one. All his pieces have some personal imprint. Even where he is closest to Stravinsky, he has more robustness than ever comes the way of the somewhat chlorotic Russian. There is a certain "sitting on the notes" that is very characteristic of everything Sessions writes. *The Black Maskers* had a grim mournfulness and morbidity characteristic of a race, recalling the fact that the most celebrated scene of British drama is that of Hamlet with the skull of Yorick, and that the favorite poem of eighteenth-century England was the "Elegy Written in a Country Churchyard." Besides, Sessions is a very able musician. The twenty-eight or twenty-nine instruments for which the

Andreyev music was cast were handled with a skill remarkable in an American; and all the *Three Choral Preludes*, the sonata, and the symphony have an elegant structurality, an honest bareness and logic, that command respect, however unintegrated the pervading spirit may appear. As for Sessions' symphony, it is not only the sturdiest, most forceful and intricate of his compositions, it is rounder, more inevitable and texturally continuous than any other symphony written by an American, the brilliant one by Aaron Copland not excepted. While the second movement, with its antiphonal string choirs is perhaps the most spontaneously fluid of all three, as a whole the work represents an integrity certainly as great as Ornstein's and perhaps even greater (the line is cleaner). And in giving Sessions his place in the advance of American music, it suggests the course a development of his powers might take. Sufficiently fortunate, it could scarcely fail of producing an American Brahms. To be sure, the distance between a merely eclectic composer, no matter how sturdy a one, and one who, like Brahms (while scarcely enlarging the medium, and developing no new methods), nonetheless strikes traditional material with his own effigy, is indeed a large one. But it is not unnegotiable; and the "sitting on the notes" of Sessions is suggestive enough of Brahmsian robustness to make the possibility of the progress seem not at all remote.

Edgar Varèse

BUT THE GREATEST FULLNESS of power and of prophecy yet come to music in America, lodges in the orchestral composition of Edgar Varèse. While they, too, like the works of Copland and of Chavez, are minor underneath the stars, relatively unvaried and circumscribed; they nonetheless, as products of a dogged, developed personality, and of large and original exceptions, display a considerable degree of freedom.

Following a first hearing of these pieces, the streets are full of jangly echoes. The taxi squeaking to a halt at the crossroad recalls a theme. Timbres and motives are sounded by police whistles, bark and moan of motor horns and fire sirens, mooing of great sea-cows steering through harbor and river, chatter of drills in the garishly lit fifty-foot excavations. You walk, ride, fly through a world of steel and glass and concrete, by rasping, blasting, threatening machinery become strangely humanized and fraternal; yourself freshly receptive and good-humored. A thousand insignificant sensations have suddenly become interesting, full of character and meaning; gathered in out of isolation and disharmony and remoteness; revealed integral parts of some homogeneous organism breathing, roaring, and flowing about.

For the concert hall just quit, overtones and timbres and rhythms corresponding to the blasts and calls of the monster town had formed part of a clear, hard musical composition; a strange symphony of new sounds, new stridencies, new abrupt accents, new acrid opulencies of harmony. Varèse has done with the auditory sensations of the giant cities and the industrial phantasmagoria, their distillation of strange tones and timbres much what Picasso has done with the corresponding visual ones. He has formed his style on them. Or, rather, they have transformed musical style in him by their effect on his ears and his imagination; much as Picasso's city walls, billboards, newspapers, and chimney pots have helped the Parisian magician to his original and intensely personal idiom. Like Picasso, Varèse has used his new sonorous medium in interests other than those of descriptivity. He has never imitated city sounds, as he is sometimes supposed to have done. He is not to be classed with the Marinetti–Pratella* group of new instrumentalists. The members of that group did have the imitative idea. They argued that modern life could be expressed only through the noises of its practical, mechanical, unconscious activities; and built instruments to convey them. Varèse, however, did not

* Italian Futurist composers.

begin with a theory, or a literary idea of representation and expression. He is a musician; and if the auditory sensations of modern life have developed the musical medium under his hands, it is merely because they have sought him out. It appears that he has always been extremely susceptible to acute, high, strident sounds. He will tell you that as a boy, while reading the *Leatherstocking Tales,* the feeling of the prairies became associated in his mind with the sound of a piercing, bitter-high whistle. This image has persisted in his imagination, although he has never heard its actual replica anywhere in nature. Apparently, he receives impressions of mechanical sounds part consciously, part unconsciously. In *Hyperprism,* one of his most daring compositions, a very shrill high C-sharp is reiterated several times; and during the first performance of the work, this tone produced convulsive laughter in the audience. But when the composer returned to his home that evening, and sat working into the night, he heard from somewhere over the city, a very familiar sound, a siren; and realized that he had been hearing it for many nights, over six months; and that the tone was exactly a very shrill high C-sharp.

Nor, for that matter, has Varèse added new sounds, new timbres, new combinations to the musical palette for the mere sake of enlarging the musician's instrument. He is sharply to be distinguished from his amiable confrere, Henry Cowell, a musician until very recently chiefly interested in the production of novel sounds on the pianoforte. (Not that Cowell is entirely devoid of musical gifts. Still, if he figures at all in the company of the musicians, it is primarily in the role of the skilled mechanic. Some of his innovations are not even effective: the introduction of the thunderstick of the Hopi Indians, for example. The thunderstick has a very charming sonority, resembling that of a wind machine capable of subtlest modulations. No doubt, it's a dead ringer for the voice of God the Father. But it's an uneconomical device, requiring so great an effort to manipulate it, that one feels Cowell might with far greater profit have turned his energies into experimentation with small electric fans, and sought for an equivalent of the soaring sound through regulation of the little mechanisms.) No, if his artistic medium has developed and spread under Varèse's hands, it is only because his entire activity is directed toward encompassing the reality of our swift prodigious world in its terms.

That is to say, that Edgar Varèse follows in the steps of Wagner, of Debussy, of the younger Stravinsky and of all the modern musicians not so much interested in the creation of beautiful objects as in the penetration and registration of the extant. He, too, is a kind of philosopher or sacred doctor, hearing the logic of things, the way the world is put together as other logicians may see or feel it; and his art is a sort of revelation, made through the manipulation of the musical medium. All works of art are such; but Varèse's is one of the conscious truth-seekers; and his music is a genuine declaration of things as they are; not the mere illustration of a system, in the manner of Richard Strauss, for Varèse thinks in the terms of his medium; while Strauss's ideas appear to be literary, extra-musical. Varèse, no doubt, has learned considerably from Strauss, in the way of dense instrumentation; just as he has learned from Mahler, whose development of the orchestral role of percussive instruments foreshadows his own prodigious one. Still, Varèse is to be placed entirely in the company of the composers who have actually philosophized in music.

What if his music sounds crasser, profaner than theirs; with its sirens and rattles, and all that gives it affinity with the ground bass of the city? His high tension and elevated pitch, excessive velocity, telegraph-style compression, shrill and subtle coloration, new sonorities and metallic and eerie effects are merely the result of his development of the search-and-discovery principle in the twentieth-century world. Indeed Varèse has not a little of the synoptic gift of mind that made Wagner so sweepingly big. Only, in the case of Varèse's music, the synthesis of the industrial, mathematical, and scientific perspectives has been made in a mood more germane to America than to

Europe. The conviction, the sense of direction responsive in Varèse to the fast-moving, high-pitched, nervous, excited reality surrounding us, as inventions, research, new proximities, new means of communication, new intuitions have shaped it; the feeling of pitch and beat making its multitudinous disorderly details simple, and setting him moving in harmony with it toward a common goal, indeed are not to be distinguished from the vivacity and unconstraint, speed and daring of the pioneer spirit of our best American life. His music significantly orientates us to a kind of world to which America is closer than Europe is, a new world not only of the new scientific and mathematical perspectives but of the latent, the immanent, free of prejudice and habit and dogma: the whole glittering region of the unrealized. Besides, he is the poet of the tall New Yorks; his music showing a relation with the "nature" of the monster-towns paralleling that of the elder music to the "country," and revealing the new nature to man.

Characteristically, the first of Varèse's compositions to utter and signify and declare this newest world and newest world-feeling, is called *Amériques*. It is also, excepting the charming little "Deux Offrandes," the first of his personal pieces. The preceding ones, written before the hegira of the young composer in 1916, appear to have been apprentice works. At least, their titles, "La Chanson des Jeunes Hommes" (1905), "La Rapsodie Romane" (1906), "Prélude à la Fin d'un Jour" (1908), "Mehr Licht" (1911), and "Le Cycle du Nord" (1912), suggest as much; though one of them at least, "Mehr Licht," has a typical cast. *Amériques* itself is something of a transitional expression, exhibiting the peculiarities of such pieces. Its inner coherency is weaker than that of its successors: there is a somewhat too arbitrary opposition of volumes of sonority in it, a somewhat too regular alternation of monstrous *tutti* with more thinly scored passages. Echoes of the *Sacre* momentarily obtrude, in the initial theme for low flute and bassoon, and in certain elephantine rhythms. The feeling of abnormality too, is a trifle Berlioz-like, and obviously expressed. The raucous sluggish symphony, with its immense metallic sonorities, sharply appreciated vulgarities, and overdelicate contrasts, actually borders on the caricatural. Still, by and large, the sonority of *Amériques* is extraordinarily novel and happy. The title, eternal symbol of new worlds awaiting discovery, is beautifully justified by it; had Varèse no other scores, this would nonetheless proclaim him a virtuosic genius with the full, complex, dense-sounding modern orchestra in his veins. There is a distinct quality about it; the style being both metallic and strident, and aerial and delicate, like the reflection of a prairie sunset on steel rails. *Amériques* contains Varèse's first realization of percussive music; the battery, daringly augmented, constitutes an independent family and in several passages plays alone. The bars with the triangle *pianissimo* amid the full percussion are especially bewitching. So too are the effects gotten from the suspended cymbal struck with the triangle's metal rod. Perhaps the most original writing appears halfway through the piece, where the violins die away in the very high minor ninths over the pedal of the horns and basses.

Immediately after *Amériques* come *Hyperprism* and *Octandre;* and both are the work of an artist in control of his forces. The slightly arbitrary sequences and oppositions constraining us in *Amériques* no longer obtrude. *Hyperprism,* for example, is notable for its sympathetic treatment of the musical medium, its great naturalness of movement. Sounds come in waves, a single sound advancing; then, as it fades, another rising to take its place: the sequence corresponding curiously to that in which the unconscious ear synthesizes the vibrations of objective nature. We hear somewhat as Varèse writes. The movement of this fantastic little symphony, with its quality of percussive sound conjuring up fragments and vistas of the port and the industrial landscape invested with new magic, is actually extremely relaxed, quiet, gay, even a little jazzy. *Hyperprism* is in fact the scherzo among Varèse's compositions; for while the thematic material is subject to continual emotional modifications, no single experience being allowed to repeat itself; and while the score is built up of telegraphically sharp and concise phrases; and the form is a counterpoint of rhythms, the tension is less fierce and dramatic than it is in the later *Intégrales* and *Arcana*. *Hyperprism* is also notable for its extremely artistic and discreet use of an astounding battery of anvils, slapsticks, Chinese blocks, lion roars, rattles, sleighbells, and sirens; and for such magnificences as the introduction of the sleighbells in the sudden *calmato a tempo,* and the full brass in the last overpowering measures. *Octandre,* too, represents an advance; recapturing the tense impulse of *Amériques* and finding a happy form for it. The sounds of the eight instruments: flute alternating with piccolo, oboe, clarinet, bassoon, French horn, trumpet, trombone, and double-bass, are uttered with held-in, stubbornly emitted power, that seems to shape and twist not only brass notes but brazen and steely objects in its ejaculations. The three tiny movements stand solid as metal objects, hard of surface, machine-sharp of edge, deeply colorful at moments, and beautiful with economicality and concentration. The idea is continually developed. There is no doubling of parts. The instruments play in extreme independence, and in a very terse and concentrated counterpoint. Apparent slight reminiscences of Wagner (the "solitude" of *Tristan,* Act III, in the opening recitative; the reiterated E-flat, which commences the scene between Siegfried and Wotan, in the close of the second section with its marvelously stammering clarinet) disappear during a second hearing.

In *Intégrales,* we have a kind of cubical music. This piece, one of Varèse's most representative compositions, exhibits his polyphonic art in all its opposition to that of Stravinsky, now so favored abroad. While Stravinsky's polyphony is fundamentally linear (most polyphony is, no doubt), Varèse's is somehow more vertical (you must ask the professors); in fact, his music moves in solid masses of sound, and he holds it very rigorously in them. Marianne Moore abhors connectives no more energetically than he. Even the climaxes do not break the essential cubism of Varèse's form. The more powerful emphases merely

force sound into the air with sudden violence, like the masses of
two impenetrable bodies brought into collision. The severity of
edge and impersonality of the sonorities themselves (there are
no strings in the orchestra of *Intégrales*), the peculiar balance
of brass, percussion, and woodwind, the piercing golden
screams, sudden stops, and lacunae, extremely rapid *crescendi*
and *diminuendi*, contribute to the squareness. The memorable
evening of its baptism, *Intégrales* resembled nothing so strongly
as shining cubes of freshest, brightest brass and steel set in
abrupt pulsing motion. And for one impressionable assistant,
they were strangely symbolic. They were not merely sounds like
metals. They were sounds strangely related to the massive
feeling of American life, with its crowds, city piles, colossal
organizations, mass production, forces and interests intricately
welded; sounds that for a moment revealed them throbbing,
moving, swinging, glowing with clean, daring, audacious life. A
new power exulted in them. Majestic skyscraper chords, grandly
resisting and progressing volumes, ruddy sonorities, and mastered ferocious outbursts, sung it forth. For the first time in
modern music, more fully even than in the first section of *Le
Sacre,* there sounded an equivalent of Wotan's spear music. But
in this case, the feeling of German power had something to do
with the life forms of the democratic, collectivist new world.

The most definitive piece of Varèse's, nonetheless, is *Arcana,*
the latest of them to be presented. *Arcana* is of course the best
example of his method of composition; and revelation of the
tendency of the forces playing through him. In form, it is an
"immense and liberal" development of the passacaglia pattern,
and an exposition, scherzo, and recapitulation. A basic idea, the
banging eleven-note phrase which commences the work *fortis-
simo,* is subjected to a series of expansions and contractions, cast
for a grand orchestra heavily reinforced by percussion. The
treatment yields a series of metallic tone-complexes compulsive
of extraordinary space-projection. Bristling with overtones as a
castle with turrets and a dinosaur with warts, the almost
unbearably straining chords shoot feeling tall into distances.

Varèse's method creates a number of air pockets, suspensions of sound between various thematic metamorphoses; and the volumnear accentuation resulting from them augments the excitement of the relationship between the strangely towering, reaching, bursts of sound. And, as the high-tensioned piece proceeds, feelings seem to find cold interstellar space; material volumes to signal and respond to each other; and a fantastic habituation to the gloomy valleys and arches of the nonhuman universe obtain. We have previously had music born of biologistic world-feeling—*Le Sacre du Printemps* is the dance of the human bacillus, certainly—and before that both *Das Rheingold* and *Tristan und Isolde* exhibited music corresponding with evolutionary theories—but *Arcana* apparently is the first piece of music harmonious with the *Weltanschauung* of modern mathematical physics, and corresponding with science's newest sensations about matter. The final variation of a subsidiary theme, given to contrabass-clarinet, bassoon, clarinet, and muted trumpets and trombones, came like a long-awaited answer to intuitive searches in some unexplored portion of the cosmos, or sudden vision of a new constellation hanging jewellike before the telescope's eye.

On the title page of this amazing score stands a quotation from the Hermetic philosophy of the "Monarch of Arcana," Paracelsus the Great:

> One star exists higher than all the rest. This is the Apocalyptic star. The second star is that of the ascendant. The third is that of the elements and of these there are four: so that six stars are established. Besides these, there is still another star, Imagination, which begets a new star and a new heaven.

As appropriately as this fragment of scientific poetry, *Arcana* might have borne Leonardo da Vinci's wondrous phrase, "The greater the consciousness, the greater the love." For its impulse is not only *Bemächtigungstrieb,* desire to control and dominate an environment as it is found in scientists, technicians, and engineers; strongly as that sublimation may have influenced it. (Varèse originally studied engineering, his father's profession.) The impulse is one of unity, or perfection, borne of a wholeness in the psyche and moving toward a condition satisfactory to the entire man. The large, smoky, and metallic sonorities; the gorgeous explosive violence, its brutal surges so singularly mixed with the feeling of thought and cerebral processes; the dry nervous vibration of the Chinese blocks; the high erotic tension controlled with a rare sensitivity, embody the spirit of many experimental groups, artistic, scientific, moral and plumb their common bourne. Deep within, one feels the force which thrusts up towers of steel and stone to scrape the clouds, and creates new instruments and combinations, and forms new field theories, seeking, on many fronts, here, there, again and again, to break through the hopelessly dirty crust of life into new clean regions. Balked, it persistently returns to the breach; till at last a new light, a new constellation, a new god, answers its wild penetrations from afar. That is the emotional aesthetic man of today no less than the technical scientific one; that is every Columbus directed to every America; that is the spirit of the new western life; and the revelation of this single frustrate, battling, finding impulse finds us, here in the New World and its century, in the middle of our way again.

Ionization

IN THIS, one of his most recent compositions, Edgar Varèse has given us a complete piece of music for the "nonmelodic" components of the battery. The feat indubitably is marvelous, and still no bolt from the blue. Varèse has always, to a singular degree, thought in terms of the percussion instruments and leaned toward expression through them. His scores have usually called for unusually complex and active batteries: in composing *Hyperprism* in 1923 he even set up an orchestra in which the percussion predominates over the melodic band in the proportion of seventeen to nine.

Besides, as it is now constituted, the pulsatile and frictive choir is perfectly capable of functioning as a sonorous unit. The newer composers have not only immensely augmented and diversified it; they have included in it instruments corresponding to the high and low string and woodwind pieces. The slightly enlarged normal battery which composes the orchestra of *Ionization* contains definite soprano, alto, tenor, and bass groups, susceptible of combination in four-part harmonies. It also contains two sirens—instruments which are capable of running continuous ascending and descending scales.

Thus the production of a piece such as *Ionization* was indubitably in the evolutionary order of things, predestined both by the direction of Varèse's own development and by the development of musical feeling and musical resources during the last century and a half. Since Mozart, indeed, composers have almost steadily been exhibiting an increasing sensitivity toward and an increasing appreciation of the musical possibilities of percussion and exploiting them ever more frequently and weightily. The romanticists laid ever larger quantities of pulsatile instruments under contribution. They associated snare and bass drums with the regular tympani and introduced xylophones, tom-toms, gongs, and bells of various kinds into the classic orchestra, steadily augmenting the once minute percussion choir in a ratio greater than the choirs of strings, woodwinds, and brasses, till at last it became the equal of the other three. The motive of this exploitation was first of all a desire for color. It was the desire for oriental and barbaric color that impelled some of the French and Russian composers to multiply the number of drums in their orchestra. It was also the desire for realistic effects: for this reason, Mahler introduced cowbells into his Sixth Symphony and Strauss whips into the orchestra of *Elektra*. Again, the motive for the augmentation of the percussion choir was the desire for dynamic expansion that culminated in the titanic ensembles of Mahler and Strauss,

Holst, the younger Schoenberg, and Varèse. Still, almost from the beginning, the composers of the last century were tending to use nonmelodic pulsatiles as the means of producing something more than coloristic effects or accentuating rhythms: and by nonmelodic pulsatiles we mean instruments of percussion other than pianos, xylophones, celestas, bells, and other pieces usually considered capable of playing tunes. They began introducing their sonorities into the melodic line: first Beethoven in the Fifth and Ninth Symphonies, later Wagner in *Das Rheingold* and *Die Walküre*, then the rest. The moderns but capped the entire tendency and made the pulsatiles play not only melodic but, episodically, solistic roles as well: actually for the first time in Stravinsky's *Petrouchka*, with its celebrated interlude for snare drums alone, later in some of the interludes of Milhaud's setting of *The Libation Bearers,** and still more recently in some of Shostakovich's movie music and in the interludes and stage music of his incidental pieces for Gogol's *The Nose*. And the battery as a whole began to king it, as it were, over the other instrumental choirs, and to function ever more independently and absolutely. Events of this sort took place, probably for the first time, in the largely noise-making bands of Pratella and the rest of the Futurists. But as the compositions of this Italian group were purely brain-spun and empty, they do not concern us here. What does concern us is the fact that in 1917 Stravinsky gave the instrumental portion of his score of *The Wedding* with telling effect to an orchestra composed entirely of pianos and an aggregation of nonmelodic bars and surfaces. A year later he assigned with equally telling effect whole blocks of *The Story of the Soldier,* the diabolic finale most notably, to the battery alone. Some time after, Milhaud, the score of whose *Man and His Desire* and *Creation of the World* are full of the pulsatile effects of the Brazilian and Harlem jazz bands, wrote a charming little concerto for orchestra which originally gives the leading role to instruments of percussion. We have already

---

* *Choephoroi,* the second play of Aeschylus' Orestean trilogy.

spoken of the novel orchestra set up by Varèse in *Hyperprism*. The step from this point to the apparent prodigy of his piece for nonmelodic instruments alone is thus plainly a logical one, particularly so when one takes into account the motive for the whole ultramodern musical assault on the battery.

This motive rose from the feeling of the individual composers and that of our whole time, precisely as the motive for the incorporation of percussion instruments in the orchestra sprang from the romantic feelings of the late nineteenth-century and early twentieth-century composers. That the ultramoderns' intensive exploitation of the battery has also to an extent been externally conditioned, it would of course be foolish to deny. The romanticists had indicated the possibilities of percussion to their successors; in fact, they had laid the battery in the moderns' path. And the virtuosic exploitation of percussion in post-war jazz bands had further demonstrated the hitherto unsuspected potentialities of this component of the musical means. Material considerations, decidedly pressing since the world catastrophe, undoubtedly also helped influence the orientation toward the pulsatiles, since percussive means are economical of manpower, one player being sufficient to several instruments in the percussion orchestra. The forty-two pieces called for by Varèse's score for *Ionization*, for example, require only thirteen executants. Still, without an inner feeling not only adjustable to these external conditions, but able to adjust them to its own ends and in sympathy with its own idea, they would never have been fruitful, at least not in musical form. Authentic creativity is neither apish of the work of others nor impelled in any great way by external conditions and considerations but by feeling and spirit. The feeling actually determinative of the general assault on the battery was, to begin with, primitivistic. An aftercrop of late romantic "barbarism," born both of the divided culture-being's yearning for the unindividualized, will-less condition of unity with nature which the European associates with the state of pre-Christian barbarian or African life, and of the threatening eruption of raw forces which culture subordinates or sublimates, it engendered dreams and ideas and pictures of Scythian and Negro worlds that, for reason of the excessive, subhuman indeterminacy of the sounds of percussive instruments, naturally found expression through frenetic and monotonous rhythms of the pulsatiles. Another source of the feeling making for the predominance of the battery lay in the astringent quality of life itself, creating an unlyrical disposition in composers as in other artists, a natural aversion from the more excessively vibratory and humanly singing instruments toward the both more brutishly and more mechanistically expressive ones. Still another is to be found in what may be termed "skyscraper mysticism." This is a feeling of the unity of life through the forms and expressions of industrial civilization, its fierce lights, piercing noises, compact and synthetic textures: a feeling of its immense tension, dynamism, ferocity, and also its fabulous delicacy and precision, that impels artists to communicate it through the portions of their mediums most sympathetic to it, and through forms partly imitative of those which excite their intuitions.

Varèse in particular among composers would seem to be subject to this feeling: he is somewhat the mystic of the sounds of sirens, horns, gongs, and whistles afloat in the air of the great industrial centers, in the sense in which Picasso is that of the city landscape with its house-wall, billboard, newspaper textures; and the pre-war Stravinsky, of the machine and its rhythms. That the other feelings, the primitivistic, the unlyrical, are also his, is not to be doubted: the first of his important compositions, *Amériques*, has affiliations with the extremely primitivistic *Sacre;* and, excessively austere, his music as a whole is almost bare of cantilena-like passages. But, himself one of the surviving members of the Guillaume Apollinaire group moved almost as a whole by this skyscraper mysticism, Varèse has pretty consistently retained its feeling; and thus spontaneously become one of the most audacious exploiters of the pulsatile and friction instruments, and of the medium's possibilities for high and piercing and shrill and brute dynamic sonorities. In this, he has undoubtedly been influenced by still another intuition, his vision of the perspectives of modern science. Those perspectives have been comprehending mind-stuff in what hitherto had appeared the inanimate regions of life; events in the physical realm having come to show greater and greater resemblance to human expression and events in the psyche. The old antithesis between mind and matter has been proving more and more illusory; and Varèse, who was trained for engineering, would seem to have been standing before this new reality; finding it charged with emotion and generative of feelings of the relation between the forces known to physics and chemistry and those of the human psyche, and of ideas in the form of complexes and relations of the sounds and timbres of the instruments related to the whole realm of the semi-material. It may even be, as has been suggested, that he has in him something of the alchemist; that like the medieval scientists, he is moved by the desire to unveil god-nature and its divine or diabolic springs. Probably no chance cause is responsible for the affixion to his *Arcana* of an aphorism of Paracelsus of Hohenheim's.

In any case, his music gives us an overwhelming feeling of life as it exists in the industrial sites, and of the perspectives of recent science. Not that his art is in any way illustrative. His medium is independent, and if his expression is "metaphysical," like Wagner's and Scriabin's and Mahler's, and musically mythological, like theirs it addresses the senses, possibly with an unparalleled dynamism and aggressivity, but nonetheless beautifully and completely. Each of his pieces can be enjoyed sensuously for reason of its new, fabulously delicate and fabulously dynamic sonorities, its terrifically telescoped, concentrated, telegraphic form, its hard outlines, cubic bulks of brassy sound, powerful dissonances, subtle complex rhythmicality, golden screams; above all, for reason of its incredibly emotional tensity, that of the most characteristically modern life. He is thus the actual creator of the music the Futurists theoretically projected, but could not, for reason of their personal unmusicality, achieve. For what was theory in them, in him is feeling, and a musical one.

Take *Ionization,* the work for percussion alone. It is, as we have said, a complete piece of music: one is never conscious, during performances of it, of the limitation of the special medium the composer is exploiting. The performance creates, sustains, and finally releases a high nervous physical tension. The form which comprises the inordinate, delicate, overwhelming volumes of the piece is clear, apparently that of a three-part song, with distinct themes, developments, recapitulations. And still it is a myth: the representation of processes and the immanent creator. Subjected to it, one feels life wonderfully afresh in one of its apparently inhuman, excessively dynamic changes. By reason of their extreme hardness, extreme indeterminacy, and other points of dissemblance from the more humanly vibrating sounds of string and wind instruments, the tones of the forty-one percussion and friction pieces for which the composition is cast—triangles, Chinese blocks, rattles, snare drums, cymbals, lion roars, gongs, tom-toms, bells, piano (nonmelodic, playing only tone clusters), and the rest—in themselves somehow suggest the life of the inanimate universe. The illusion, if illusion it is, of an analogy between the subject of the music and events or processes in the physiochemical fields, is reinforced by the volumes of the extremely simplified, extremely skeletonized form, which, explosive, curiously timed and interrupted, and curiously related and responsive to one another, further suggest incandescent manifestations of material entities in stellar space. And the terrific conciseness of the style, telegraphically succinct in its themes, rapid in its mutation and developments, overleaping connective steps, and nervously alive with dialectically generated new ideas; and the acute high timbres, the abrupt detonations, and tremendous volumes of sound which figure almost incessantly, quite specifically suggest the spirit of some intensely dynamic process of the sort imperceptible to the senses but not to the penetrating organs of science: say the famous one by which gas is transformed into a conductor of electricity, with its separation of neutral molecules into ions by the impact of the swiftly mobilized ions originally present in the gas subjected to the electrostatic field, and its mobilization and generation of further ions by the newly formed particles. Thus one felt oneself identified anew vis-à-vis the cosmos of the physicists, amid and still upon the surface of some new ocean of heaving, bursting, strangely sensitive matter, and filled with power and preparedness by this new experience of the intense way and orderliness of things.

As for the process of the elevation and coronation of the battery as the king of the orchestra, leading to its autonomy, that may well have attained its term in *Ionization*. In music, we know how not only fashions but feelings change, and even if the skyscraper mysticism of Varèse should persist, as undoubtedly it will in himself, it may never again lead him to write for percussion and friction instruments alone. His very latest piece, *Equatorial,* is cast for an ensemble not wholly percussive in character, and the other composers who have recently taken to producing pieces for the battery alone have no claim on our consideration. But even if *Ionization* should prove a unicorn it would still maintain its place in the ranks of music. It is a little work of genius, born of the evolving life of music and its means, and the spirit of an individual and an epoch, a credit to its mother and its father. And it is both an individual and an epoch that are being denied in the stupid, extreme, entirely undeserved neglect—the most stupid, extreme, and entirely undeserved of all that are being inflicted by the musical world upon any living composer—that is still the part of the brilliant composer of *Ionization,* of *Hyperprism* and *Intégrales* and *Arcana* and all the rest of his powerful music.

Carl Ruggles

WE MUST . . . go on to a consideration of the work of Carl Ruggles. And this consolation is possible: that no matter how much space would be at our disposal, it would still be with a word on Ruggles' compositions that the discussion of the unavoidable subject of American eclecticism would come to an end. For Ruggles' music is a borderline phenomenon; and as such the link between the works we have just been examining and those which, both integral and intense, stand on the free ground beyond.

In fact, it is difficult to say which camp his music favors more. Ruggles' harmonic schemes are of the greatest distinction. This quality, neither rich nor magnificent, and nonetheless exquisitely refined, and new to harmonic writing, ineluctably associates itself with early American furniture and Hartley's color, Portsmouth doorways and Hawthorne's prose. His instrumental timbre is equally this Cape Cod American's own, particularly when confined to instruments of a single family; trumpets in the middle section of *Men and Angels;* strings in *Portals,* and in the middle section of *Men and Mountains.* The feeling of all Ruggles' more recent, rounder compositions is intensely local. The melancholy and smothered passion of the eloquently weaving violin music in "Lilacs," middle section of *Men and Mountains,* is as characteristic of the New England countryside as anything by Robinson or Frost. So, too, is the harshness of certain of Ruggles' brazen sonorities; and in instances his acrid trumpets and trombones preach and dogmatize ministerially at imaginary congregations.

At the same time, there is a noticeable tenuity and inarticulacy in his frequently ejaculative, but always sincere creations. The music labors, slightly. The line at best is only competent, built as it is of short repeated phrases effortfully varied and intensified. The check of preconceptions is equally obtrusive: Ruggles like Schoenberg has a tendency to construct his works on formulas. He will tell you that he never doubles a note in his harmony, nor repeats a note nor its octave in the melody nor in the inner parts, until the passage of from seven to nine different notes has taken place. Now, while it is not to be doubted that certain extraordinary pages of music exhibit this heterogeneity of elements, mere heterogeneity of elements does not constitute music; and the attempt to force it on material involves a violation as destructive as any flowing from other preconceptions. The strained quality sometimes apparent in

Ruggles' scores, and the unusual slowness with which he produces, are quite attributable to it.

It is this feeling of a slightly impeded impulse, that, together with the vaguely Tristanesque or Schoenbergian cast which Ruggles' music frequently wears, makes it straddle the line dividing the more eclectic American music from the more original. This position on the fence is signified by the ease, never the best of conditions, with which one places Ruggles in the ultrareligious camp of musicians. Ruggles is all elevation, seriousness, apocalypse. Music for him is an expression of the depths, an explosion, a scattering of the seeds of revelation. To *Men and Mountains* he prefixes a quotation from Blake, "Great things are done when men and mountains meet"; and over the symphonic ensemble, *Portals,* there stand Whitman's lines:

> What are they of the known
> But to ascend and enter the Unknown?

Hear Lawrence Gilman:*

> Mr. Ruggles . . . is a natural mystic, a rhapsodist, a composer who sees visions and dreams fantastic dreams. The wild, gigantic, tortured symbols of Blake's imagination, his riotous and untrammelled excursions in the world behind the heavens, are all of a piece with Mr. Ruggles' thinking. There is a touch of the apocalyptic, the fabulous, about his fantasies. He is the first unicorn to enter American music. He is the master of a strange, torrential and perturbing discourse.

But here, again, we must be wary. While Ruggles is to be placed in an already well-defined category, it must be confessed that he manages to move about in it restlessly enough. This idiom, alternately naïve and childlike, and violent and prophetic, is never either derivative or imitative. Warm and vibrant, embodying the characteristic "romantic" surge and as-

---

* Lawrence Gilman (1878–1939), music critic for the *North American Review* (1915–1923) and the New York *Herald Tribune* (1923–1939).

piration, it remains robust and reserved. The aching violin music of *Portals* may come thrust out by a Tristanesque storm of feeling, and rise in steep tumultuous waves; and proceed with great warmth of accent and vibrancy of sound. The polyphony may have a tapestry-like richness, the harmonies a singularity and mysteriousness, the thrilling sequence of single notes left to vibrate and die away in the coda possess mystic seductiveness. Nevertheless, muscularity, and freedom from languor place Ruggles' work apart from its kin; and we feel that with but one more degree of purity, this music would indeed be indisputably individual; and that if there are any American compositions actually more autochthonous than that of this Cape Cod Yankee, a force from the soil like a charge must have sent them into the world.

Bibliography

AUTHOR

Musical Portraits: Interpretations of Twenty Modern Composers. New York, Harcourt, Brace & Howe, 1920. Reprinted by Books for Libraries, Inc., in 1968.

Musical Chronicle (1917–23). New York, Harcourt, Brace & Co., 1923.

Port of New York: Essays on Fourteen American Moderns. New York, Harcourt, Brace & Co., 1924. Reprinted by the University of Illinois Press, with an Introduction by Sherman Paul, in 1961, and in paperback by Illini Books, in 1967.

Men Seen. New York, Dial Press, 1925. Reprinted by Books for Libraries, Inc., in 1967.

Modern Tendencies in Music. The Caxton Music Series, Vol. 18. New York, The Caxton Institute, Inc., 1927.

By Way of Art. New York, Coward–McCann, Inc., 1928. Reprinted by Books for Libraries, Inc., in 1968.

Boy in the Sun (novel). New York, Macaulay Co., 1928.

An Hour with American Music. Philadelphia, J. B. Lippincott Co., 1929.

Van Gogh (pamphlet). Pasadena, Enjoy Your Museum, 1934.

Discoveries of a Music Critic. New York, Harcourt, Brace & Co., 1936.

EDITOR AND TRANSLATOR

The American Caravan: A Yearbook of American Literature. Vol. I (1927), Vol. II (1928), Vol. III (1929), Vol. IV (1931), New York, Macaulay Co. Vol. V (1936), New York, W. W. Norton. Van Wyck Brooks was Rosenfeld's coeditor for Vol. I, and Alfred Kreymborg and Lewis Mumford were coeditors for Vols. II–V.

America and Alfred Stieglitz: A Collective Portrait. New York, Doubleday Doran, 1934. Coedited by Rosenfeld, Waldo Frank, Lewis Mumford, Dorothy Norman, and Harold Rugg.

Bédier, Joseph, *Romance of Tristan and Iseult*. New York, Pantheon Books, 1946. Translated by Hilaire Belloc, with four chapters translated by Rosenfeld.

Schumann, Robert, *On Music and Musicians*. New York, Pantheon Books, 1946. Edited by Konrad Wolff, translated by Rosenfeld.

Sherwood Anderson Reader. Boston, Houghton Mifflin Co., 1947. Selected and edited by Rosenfeld.

FOR A COMPLETE LIST of articles by Paul Rosenfeld and articles about him through 1947, see *Paul Rosenfeld, Voyager in the Arts*, Jerome Mellquist and Lucie Wiese, eds., New York, Creative Age Press Inc., 1948. For articles about Paul Rosenfeld from 1947 to the present, consult the annual bibliographies in *PMLA*.

Index